Alston W. Purvis

Dutch Graphic Design, 1918-1945

VNR Van Nostrand Reinhold
New York

Library of Congress Catalog Card Number 92–3878
ISBN 0–442–00444–3

Printed in the United States of America.
Designed by Alston W. Purvis

Van Nostrand Reinhold
115 Fifth Avenue
New York, New York 10003

Chapman and Hall
2–6 Boundary Row
London, SE1 8HN, England

Thomas Nelson Australia
102 Dodds Street
South Melbourne 3205
Victoria, Australia

Nelson Canada
1120 Birchmount Road
Scarborough, Ontario MIK 5G4, Canada

16 15 14 13 12 11 10 9 8 7 6 5 4 3 2 1

Library of Congress Cataloging-in-Publication Data

Purvis, Alston W., 1943–
Dutch graphic design : 1918–1945 / Alston W. Purvis.
p.   cm.
Includes bibliographical references and index.
ISBN 0–442–00444–3
1. Printing—Netherlands—History—20th century. 2. Graphic
arts—Netherlands—History—20th century. 3. Book design—
Netherlands—History—20th century.   I. Title.
Z161.P87   1992
686.2′0942—dc20   92–3878
                                                   CIP

Contents

Preface

In 1971, I was invited by Joop Beljon, at that time Director of the Koninklijke Academie van Beeldende Kunsten (Royal Academy of Fine Arts) at The Hague, to teach graphic design there for one term. I ultimately stayed for eleven years, and to a large extent this book is the result of a long and enduring love affair with The Netherlands.

In spite of growing interest, only marginal attention has been given to the history of Dutch graphic design in this century. Although there have been numerous articles, treatises, and monographs, there has yet to be a comprehensive survey, in Dutch or in English. This book serves such a purpose, covering not only the avant garde, but the monumental achievements of the Dutch traditional designers as well. What developed in The Netherlands between the end of the first and second world wars constituted no less than a graphic design phenomenon, both in quality and complexity. No single volume could even begin to record all the accomplishments that took place during this twenty-seven year span. However, it is my hope that this volume will provide a clear overview while at the same time dispelling some of the myths surrounding this extraordinary epoch in our graphic design heritage.

For titles and expressions I have, whenever possible, used the original Dutch, followed by English translations. Because translations may in some degree differ, reference to the original Dutch will permit those who wish to conduct further research to find the original sources.

The project involved extensive research in numerous collections and libraries, both in Europe and in the United States. Especially helpful were the memorable hours spent with Wilma and Max Schuhmacher discussing all aspects of the book, particularly the traditional designers. Sharing their abundant knowledge, as well as allowing me to use and photograph their extensive collection, was invaluable. I am deeply indebted to Wilma Schuhmacher for her patient advice, which proved to be an inspiration throughout: Not only did it help to produce this book, but it also brought a deep and lasting friendship. The prodigious research assistance of Ditte van der Meulen at the Antiquariaat Schuhmacher was also an indispensable ingredient.

I would like to thank my wife Roxane Olson Purvis for her patience in enduring this project and especially for her help in editing and proofreading the text as well as cataloguing the illustrations.

I would like to express my deepest gratitude to Jan van Loenen Martinet not only for continually offering his unique knowledge on H. N. Werkman, but also for his unparalleled kindness in making available information and illustrations from his comprehensive Werkman archives.

The tireless, generous, and astute editorial counsel of James M. Storey proved to be a guiding beacon from the beginning to the end of the project, and for this I thank him immensely.

Interviews with Dick Dooijes, Reinold Kuipers, J. J. Beljon, Huib van Krimpen, Pieter Brattinga, Gerard Unger, and my former colleague from the Royal Academy of Fine Arts, Gerard de Vries, all served to enrich my knowledge of this period. The enthusiastic support of Amanda Miller, my editor at Van Nostrand Reinhold, was a vital factor in bringing this project to a successful conclusion.

In addition, I would like to express my gratitude to the following people:

Anne-Marie Rutten   Mevrouw M. Elffers
Mrs. R. N. Landreth   Pieter van Voorst van Beest
Marianne Baas   Henny Cahn
Hanneke A. Schuitema   Dr. Robert Polak
Mevrouw Y. Brusse   W. Michael Sheehe
Bernice Jackson   Michael Lance
Russell Miller   Jos de Bruin
Geoffry Fried   Ernst H. von Metzsch
Almaar Seinen   Kevin Callahan

Alston W. Purvis
Boston, Massachusetts

Chapter 1
Prologue

To present an entire epoch in a few pages is a hazardous endeavor. There are always countless factors to consider—historical, social, economic, cultural, religious, geographical, and technological. The twentieth century graphic design renaissance that took place in The Netherlands did not follow miraculously from the debris of World War I; the seeds had been planted far earlier and arose from many yet related sources. The renaissance too did not develop in isolation or autonomously, but was closely related to other events and movements outside The Netherlands: Aspects of Dadaism, Futurism, and Constructivism influenced even reclusive figures such as the printer-painter-designer H. N. Werkman.

Beginning and ending with specific dates tends to force one into artificial parameters, yet the 1918–1945 period in The Netherlands, from the end of one world war until the end of the other, was an intensely rich and diverse time that encompassed the origins of much of our present graphic design vernacular and legacy. Certainly modern Dutch typography did not begin precisely in 1918 nor did it cease in 1945, although the end of World War I brought with it a fresh supply of new ideas, and with the close of World War II another generation took the helm.

The Dutch Landscape and People

The Netherlands has always exerted a cultural, historical, and mercantile influence far out of proportion to its size, and had the Dutch language been more widely spoken the nation's dominance would have been even greater. By the sixteenth century The Netherlands had become one of the most important artistic, industrial, and trading centers in Europe. During the seventeenth century it experienced what amounted to a cultural and commercial renaissance. What had previously been swampland turned out, because of its central location, to be geographically ideal for prosperous commerce by a maritime power. By sea The Netherlands was within easy reach of the British Isles, Russia, the Scandinavian countries, and Africa, and its colonial empire in Indonesia provided a wealth of trading opportunities. Being situated at the mouth of the Rhine, which touches six European countries, was also an advantage. Rivers and canals offered easy access to the markets of Central Europe, including the German Ruhr region.

The influence of The Netherlands has been especially strong in graphic design. What are the fundamental characteristics that make Dutch graphic design unique? How does it differ from graphic design produced in other parts of Europe? There is no single answer to these questions.

Geographic conditions had an effect upon the Dutch vision, and there is a distinct link between the landscape of The Netherlands and the origins of modern Dutch graphic design. Designers have not intentionally replicated the landscape, yet its particular characteristics had an unmistakable effect upon their intellectual and artistic perspectives. Indeed, Mondrian wrote in a 1937 article:

> [A]ll that the non-figurative artist receives from the outside is not only useful, but indispensable, because it arouses in him the desire to create that, which he only vaguely feels and which he could never represent in a true manner without the contact with visible reality and with the life which surrounds him. It is precisely from this visible reality that he draws the objectivity which he needs in opposition to his personal subjectivity. It is precisely from this visible reality that he draws the means of expression and, as regards the surrounding life, it is precisely this which has made his art non-figurative.[1]

The landscape of The Netherlands is quite different from that of the rest of Europe. Viewed from an airplane, it resembles the rectangular units of an Amish quilt. The straight highways, canals, and railroads seem to divide the countryside like the black lines in a painting by Mondrian or Van Doesburg. The flat horizon is broken intermittently by the verticality of a few church steeples,

1-1. Piet Mondrian, *Windmill at Sunset*, oil, circa 1907, 75 × 132 cm. Collection, Gallery Van Voorst van Beest, The Hague. © Estate of Piet Mondrian/VAGA, New York, 1991.

windmills, electrical towers and trees (Fig 1–1). When the surface of the land does display some undulation, a hill is called a mountain; the highest one, in Limburg, is 1000 feet. The landscape is the most synthetic and orderly countryside in all of Europe, and to a large extent natural forms have been removed, supplanted, and reorganized by man's creations.

Following the—abstract—laws of nature and the precepts of economy, the Dutch engineers and dyke-builders had already imparted a rigidly mathematical character to their countryside. They had, in common with the town planners of the modern metropolis, straightened the curves of the incidental streams and rivers into rectilinear canals, they had connected the cities by straight roads, often running parallel with the canals and, in the 19th century, the railroads had added another mathematical element to this accomplished construction.[2]

There is a feeling of tranquil serenity between the expansiveness of the sky and the horizontal fields below. The color of the sky is forever changing from blues and grays to the violet red so accurately depicted in Vermeer's *View of Delft*. Water is omnipresent, and the canals and dikes are lined by regular rows of trees uniformly bowed by a relentless wind from the North Sea. On the other hand, the monotony of the horizon and the harshness of the weather are broken by lush green vistas and vast fields of flowers. Today The Netherlands is the largest exporter of flowers and bulbs in the world.

For centuries the Dutch have had to grapple not only with larger and quite often belligerent Teutonic neighbors but also against frequently unpredictable and inclement weather and constant vulnerability to the capriciousness of the North Sea. Water is inevitably interlaced with the Dutch way of life. Twenty-seven percent of the land is below sea level, and from as early as the twelfth century, this generated a perpetual need to sustain an intricate network of dikes, bridges, aqueducts, dams, windmills, and canals. The Dutch became quite adept at draining ponds and lakes to create new polders. Even now, there are further reclamation projects on the drawing board.

To a large extent, the very existence of the Dutch depended on their mastery of natural forces, and for this reason perfection, exactness, computation, order, and planning for the future have all become a part of the Dutch consciousness.[3] On a less positive side, this has also resulted in an unyielding and sometimes exasperating recalcitrance. But their success in defying their neighbors' belligerence, the unpredictable weather, and the North Sea has only fortified their conviction that struggle, diligence, and confidence can conquer all. It has also helped to produce a unique sense of national unity, self-assurance, tolerance, and pride.

By their own admission, the Dutch are a diverse and complex people. Their fortitude and integrity in times of adversity are ex-

emplified by the motto of the House of Orange, "Je maintiendrai" (I shall maintain).[4] The Dutch are innovative, tolerant, and receptive to new ideas, while at the same time tenacious in their beliefs. The uniqueness of the Dutch language has allowed the people to absorb foreign ideas while at the same time providing their own special national identity. As evidenced by the unusually large number of active political parties (22, at a recent count), the Dutch are sharply reproachful both of themselves and others, and governments are often comprised of incongruous coalitions. A Dutchman delights in an energetic debate and, seldom reticent, will usually defend his values with reason, spirit, persistence, and intellect. Indeed, he is not averse to giving his opponent a stern and sometimes didactic admonishment.

The harshness of the damp climate helped to engender a love of domestic life, which is embodied in the word *gezellig*, generally translated as "cozy," but in reality a combination of several English words, including "contented" and "intimate." The Dutch also have an innate appreciation for the diminutive and for small things (a decided advantage for anyone working with type).

The Netherlands is the most thickly populated country in Europe; more than 15 million people live in an area roughly half the size of the state of South Carolina. There are few places in The Netherlands where a man-made structure cannot be seen, and land is utilized to the greatest extent possible. The Dutch do not seem to have a great desire for space; this need is filled by the vastness of the sky.

Religious traditions have undoubtedly had an important influence in shaping the Dutch national consciousness. This was to a large extent a result of the *gezelligheid* (intimacy) of the home. Study and memorization of the Bible was a standard way of life and resulted in a unique and contemplative form of Calvinism. The parents of a household were spiritual as well as material supporters for the family.[5] Many of the important figures of twentieth-century Dutch art were raised in devout religious settings. The father of Piet Mondrian (1872–1944) was director of a Protestant school, and Bart van der Leck (1876–1958) was an ardent Calvinist until the early part of the century. Vincent van Gogh (1853–1890) and Willem Sandberg (1897–1984) also grew up in such households.[6] The intrinsic Calvinist temperament of these Dutch artists made them disparage insincerity, excessive show, and superficiality, and also made them strive for integrity, spiritual purity, and a clarity of means and expression in design. Self-restraint and orderliness are ingrained in the Dutch temperament, and cleanliness is so much a part of their nature that the word *schoon* expresses both "clean" and "beautiful."[7]

An obsession for perfection helps complete the sketch of the Dutch identity. The Dutch are averse to improvisation, to the non-

essential and the arbitrary, and they have a distinct proclivity for simple logic and basic common sense. They are constantly seeking an unambiguous and unpretentious visual language.[8] The current design grid is ideal for this part of their temperament, and with a few notable exceptions, Dutch graphic designers have always pursued a firm rationale and theoretical basis.[9] In the words of Spinoza, their "ethics became clear in their rectilinear rules of conduct."

Naturally, many of these characteristics are seen in other peoples as well, and as always with generalities, there are the ever-present exceptions. However, taken as a whole they begin to summarize the cultural distinctiveness of The Netherlands. The Dutch historian Johan Huizinga described this as the *Nederlands geestesmerk* (the spiritual imprint of The Netherlands).[10] The art historian H. L. C. Jaffé refers to this phenomenon in the introduction to his definitive book on De Stijl, one of the most important indigenous Dutch art movements of this century.

These characteristics do not belong to any given historical period; whereas one century may stress this aspect, another period will accentuate that. "Nederlands geestesmerk" has been moulded by the country's shape and essence, by its social pattern and religious trends. It is made visible and audible and thus brought to greater consciousness by its painters, poets and philosophers. . . . No doubt the contemporary attitude, in other countries and all of Western Europe, greatly influenced De Stijl, but there are too many facts which are inherently Dutch to make us believe that Dutch traditions, that "Nederlands Geestemerk" may be neglected when investigating the specific conditions which account for the birth and the growth of De Stijl.[11]

The Modern Dutch Typographic Tradition

Decadence and the Seeds of Renewal

A brief historical survey of developments leading up to the 1918–1945 epoch is necessary to understand the extraordinary work done in this period.

By the second half of the nineteenth century, most European typography, including that in The Netherlands, had become to a large extent a visual clutter. Scientific inventions brought drastic changes in printing techniques that had been only slightly modified since Gutenberg's achievements in the fifteenth century. As handwork was taken over by machines, the printing business began to become a big industry, and the demand for more and more printing could only be met by more and better machinery. Craftsmen gradually became less important; a single foreman and a few younger and less costly assistants could now, with machinery, equal or exceed hand production. Paper, which had previously

been made primarily from rags, was replaced by a variety made from wood pulp, straw, and grass, thus freeing the printing industry from its dependence on the more expensive cotton and linen. Inking pads were replaced by large rollers. Once Ottmar Mergenthaler's Simplex Linotype Model I typesetter came into use in 1890 and the Limited Font Monotype in 1898, type was set more and more by machine.[12]

A more fundamental cause for the bad typography of the period was the disappearance of sensitivity for design, color, or materials (Fig. 1-2).[13] Printers appeared to be trying to outdo one another by embellishing pages with countless sorts and sizes of the most outlandish typefaces available (Fig. 1-3). Except for a vapid imitation of classicism, any sense of page composition was lost; materials were usually inferior, choice of typefaces indifferent, and the binding was either innocuous or garishly overdone. Basic legibility became such an acute problem that in 1866 Dutch medical authorities delivered an official written remonstration to the government.[14]

M. R. Radermacher Schorer in his *Bijdrage tot de Geschiedenis van de Renaissance der Nederlandse Boekdrukkunst* (Contribution to the History of the Dutch Printing Arts) wrote a somber evaluation in 1951: "When we compare the 19th century book to the Incunabula the type is pallid and without character, often damaged and badly printed, the arrangement is confusing, the color faded, the

1-2. Anonymous, *Harddraverij* (Trotting Race), poster, 1869. 60 × 43.5 cm. Collection, Antiquariaat Schuhmacher, Amsterdam.

paper is of bad quality, the spine is covered with gold stamping without beautiful ornaments. . . . and thicker paper is used to make the book look larger than it actually is."[15]

However, even at this point, a search for a new course had already begun in The Netherlands. One of the first efforts to find a new path began in the second half of the nineteenth century in the studios of Dr. Petrus Josephus Hubertus Cuypers (1827–1921), architect of the French-inspired Rijksmuseum and the Central Station in Amsterdam and restorer of the cathedral at Mainz.[16] He emphasized a return to traditional skills, historical principles, and a search for the essentials of design. His students diligently studied calligraphy, using as their models printing and manuscripts from the Renaissance and Middle Ages. Rejecting the artificiality of the second half of the nineteenth century, Cuypers paralleled William Morris (1834–1896) except that Cuypers did not reject the Industrial Revolution and even encouraged the production of work for mechanical reproduction.[17] Both Morris and Cuypers, although anachronistic in approach, helped build essential bridges between a time of lost standards and a new beginning, preparing the way for the new typography. Even though Cuypers idealized the Middle Ages and advocated a revival of the excesses of Gothic ornamentation and medievalism, his insistence upon excellence and solidity was a glimmer of inspiration and hope for the new generation.[18] Also, we must not forget the typographical environment in which Cuypers was working; he provided the necessary push for a revival of craft during lackluster times. The architects Karel Petrus Cornelis de Bazel (1869–1923) and Johannes Ludovicus Matthieu Lauweriks (1864–1932), both students of Cuypers, persevered in his mission by maintaining a similar workshop for architecture and the decorative arts and continuing to pursue craftsmanship and fundamental principles of design.[19]

In spite of bleak predictions by those apprehensive about the effect of the new technology on the quality of printing, by the end of the nineteenth century industry was finally in a position at least to make printed material a more inexpensive and influential commodity. Although the new rotary presses entailed costly initial investments that caused entrepreneurs to avoid them in the beginning, it quickly became clear that they would pay for themselves in the long run. Offset printing was just over the horizon, and bookbinding had to some extent already been mechanized. The use of photographs as illustrations had opened up an entirely new field, especially after Meisenbach's development of the photo-screen technique in 1882.[20]

All the technical components seemed to be in place, but there was still something missing. The design arts remained without any sense of direction, and a benign indifference on the part of both publishers and readers also adversely affected the quality of reading material. From the point of view of communication, expe-

1-3. FIO (pseudonym), *De Kleine Pretmaker, Voordrachten en comische scenes voor jongens en meisjes* (The Little Pleasuremaker, Recitations and Comical Scenes for Boys and Girls), title page, 1885. 17.5 × 11 cm. Collection, Antiquariaat Schuhmacher, Amsterdam.

dience was the principal consideration; between 1890 and 1900 books that were prototypes of bad taste were eagerly bought by the public. Many people read only newspapers, and by any standard their design was appalling.[21] A small movement again to make typography an art did begin to take shape during the last decade of the century. In general, this impetus came not from publishers or printers, but from painters, sculptors, and architects who believed that the next century would witness a revival of unity in the arts like that during the Italian Renaissance.[22]

One of the first major proponents of this movement was the leading and most controversial architect and city planner in The Netherlands at the time, Hendrik Petrus Berlage (1856–1934). Beginning as a typical eclectic of the time, he became an avid proponent of this philosophy of artistic unity, and his revolutionary Exchange Building in Amsterdam (especially the interior), completed in 1903, exemplifies these principles. In unequivocal terms he advocated honesty in construction and the use of materials, and his work embraced the graphic arts as well as furniture design and city planning.[23] Berlage became acquainted with the work of Frank Lloyd Wright (1869–1959) after a trip to the United States in 1911. Captivated by Wright's technical and artistic innovations and work in the field of vernacular architecture, Berlage soon became one of Wright's principal champions in Europe. Wright's influence is notably evident in Berlage's design of the Gemeentemuseum (Municipal Museum) at The Hague.

Even though it was not his field, Berlage exerted a significant influence on the development of Dutch graphic design. In 1893, Berlage designed a poster advertising a "new short route" between the Hook of Holland and Harwich on the east coast of England. The composition is packed with an extensive medley of motifs, and the glut of ornament almost succeeds in camouflaging the text. On the other hand, his poster for the Noord Hollandsche Tramwegmij (North Holland Tram Company), designed to announce the opening of the Amsterdam–Purmerend–Alkmaar line in 1895, is more open and moves a step toward simplicity (Fig. 1-4). Although both posters clearly break out of the Art Nouveau style, they still display "Victorian overkill," the propensity to squeeze as much into a space as possible; moderation seems to have been equated with tedium. Nothing was left bare, as if it would have been a waste of paper. Berlage was, however, moving in a new direction, and his basic premise, published in his article *Gedanken über Stil in der Baukunst* (Thoughts over Style in Architecture; Leipzig, 1905), maintained that decoration must always be secondary to structure.

Berend Modderman, manager of the Amsterdam printing firm Ipenbuur en Van Seldam, founded in 1806, became its owner in 1895. He sought the assistance of artists, whom he, in contrast to many of his colleagues, considered and treated as peers rather

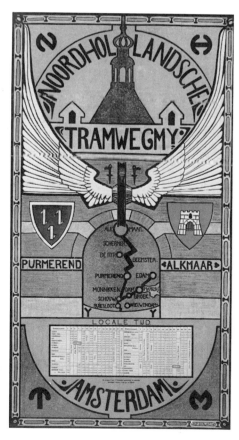

1-4. H. P. Berlage, *Noordhollandsche Tramwegmij* (North Holland Tram Company), poster, 1893, 102 × 58 cm.

than lackeys.[24] His collaboration was especially successful with the brothers Antonius (Antoon) H. J. (1872–1960) and Theodorus (Theo) M. A. A. Molkenboer (1871–1920). Theo Molkenboer's 1897 poster for the Amsterdam bookbinder Elias P. van Bommel was another manifestation of change (Fig. 1-5). Here, the diligent artisan at work suggests both reliability and craftsmanship. Originally produced as a woodcut, the flat, simple, severe composition contrasts sharply with the Berlage posters designed only a few years earlier. Although the work is rudimentary and less polished in the orthodox sense, it is notable for the absence of superfluous detail. The letters are a distortion of an existing face, stretched and contorted to reach the end of the page. The poster is still filled from top to bottom, but it shows a Calvinistic rigidity that will be a recurring component of Dutch graphic design.

Modderman's friendship and compatibility with his brother-in-law, the author and typographer Jan Willem Enschedé, resulted in two

1-5. Theodorus M. A. A. Molkenboer, *Elias P. van Bommel, Boekbinder* (Elias P. van Bommel, Bookbinder), poster, 1897, 85 × 61 cm. Collection, Bernice Jackson, Concord, Massachusetts.

publications. The first, titled *De Boekletter in Nederland* (Text Type in The Netherlands), appeared in 1902, and the second, *Mededelingen over boekkunst* (Information on the Art of the Book), in 1904. These books were unusual because they emphasized the integrity of the typeface rather than decoration. Since there were no schools even teaching the printing trade until 1907, these texts were especially significant. In 1907, a third in the series titled *Logica in boekdruk* (Logic in Book Printing) was published by Enschedé. The traditional book designer S. H. de Roos later referred to it as the "catechism of the modern book printer."[25]

The new generation was in dire need of specific precepts to which it could refer, and in 1898 the author Jan Kalf delivered an important lecture called "The Book" at a meeting of the Architectura en Amicitia in Amsterdam which was subsequently published in their magazine *Architectura*. He stressed a respect for traditions in typography, harmony of form and content, unbiased acceptance of the intrinsic possibilities of machinery, an emphasis on functionalism and a repudiation of unnecessary decoration, insistence on the suitability of materials, a sense of proportion, a concern for legibility, the use of single well-designed typefaces, the necessity for proper letter and word spacing, and good printing and bookbinding. This talk drew a sharp contrast between true typography and mere embellishment and, for the first time, put forth unequivocal guidelines for designers.[26]

Early Dutch Poster Designers

Poster design as an art form had a late beginning in The Netherlands. Because so few of the earlier examples have survived, it is difficult to assess them as part of a whole body of work.[27] They were seldom saved because they were considered to have no artistic merit; most that still exist are the usual depressing agglomeration of typefaces and type sizes. Surviving photographs, however,indicate that posters did not play a significant role in The Netherlands at the time.[28] At the turn of the century, Dutch cities lacked the wide and grandiose boulevards of Vienna, Munich, Berlin, and Paris that were so appropriate for the presentation of large images meant to be seen from a distance and to lure onlookers into reading the message.[29] The center of Amsterdam, with its canals and narrow streets, was quite different from the Paris created by Baron Hausmann. Public buildings were usually included among houses, and there was a distinct, almost deliberate, absence of opulence. Dutch pedestrians tended to inspect wares in store windows, and posters were meant to be seen from close up. Detail was dominant, and posters were intended to be read. The Dutch were astute shoppers who liked to get their money's worth. Customers preferred sound reasoning to visual solicitations and were more inclined to be swayed by argument and plain common sense rather than enticement and sales pressure.[30]

In his introduction to *A History of the Dutch Poster,* Dr. H. L. C. Jaffé suggests that "this whole pattern of social behavior was also directly influenced by the old Calvinist heritage—originating in the Old Testament—of sticking to the text, to the scriptures."[31]

Jan Ros (1875–1952) was a painter who taught at the Royal Academy of Fine Arts at The Hague, and his very colorful 1895 poster for Blooker's Cacao was one of the initial serious attempts at Dutch poster art. In a very correct setting, an elegantly attired lady is shown being served by another lady from a steaming pot of cocoa. On the left a column is made from the leaves and beans of the cacao tree, topped off by the Amsterdam coat of arms. In the patterns created by the plant forms and the steam from the pot there are distinct overtones of Art Nouveau.

Art Nouveau represented a new creative freedom and broke with the previous excessive ornamentation. With a few exceptions, it was called Nieuwe Kunst in The Netherlands, Art Nouveau in France, Belgium, and England, and Jugendstil in Germany, Austria, and the rest of Europe. The name Jugendstil was based on the title of a new magazine, *Jugend,* first published in Munich in 1896. Although there were distinct differences between the two, Art Nouveau and Jugendstil were essentially members of the same family. It was not just an art movement; it was a social movement as well, representing the lifestyle of a new, affluent, and broad-minded bourgeoisie that emerged as a potent force around 1900.[32] Art Nouveau was inspired by stained glass, medieval manuscripts, and a return to forms from nature, as well as the decorative arts of India, Syria, Egypt, Persia, Japan, and in The Netherlands, Indonesia. A characteristic image is one of heavy contours derived from flower stems and vines that have the function of binding the composition together. This new decorative movement was principally exploited in architecture, industrial design, and typography and was displayed in such diverse forms as posters, doors, lamps, and books.

One of the most important Dutch books in this style was *Sonnetten en Verzen in Terzinen Geschreven* (Sonnets and Verses Written in Terzarima, 1896) by Henriëtte van der Schalk (1869–1952) (later Henriëtte Roland Holst–van der Schalk). It was designed by her future husband R. N. Roland Holst (1868–1938), the wall painter, poster designer, decorator, and director of the Rijksacademie in Amsterdam. A favorite typeface was Eckmann Schrift, produced around 1900 by the Klingspor Type Foundry. Designed by Otto Eckmann, a painter by profession, this face had a great influence on Art Nouveau typography.

Jan Toorop's (1858–1928) famous poster for Delftsche Slaolie (Delft Salad Oil) was a supreme example of the Art Nouveau style (Fig. 1-6) as practiced in The Netherlands. Probably printed in 1895, this was one of the first Dutch posters on a par with those

1-6. Jan Toorop, *Delftsche Slaolie* (Delft Salad Oil), poster, 1895, 100 × 70 cm. Collection, Bernice Jackson, Concord, Massachusetts.

produced in other European countries around the same time. Two female figures resembling goddesses and dressed in elegant gowns conjure up some kind of enchanted salad with delicate fingers. The salad oil being advertised seems irrelevant in the torrent of sinuous, elaborate, intertwined lines. Twenty-three floating peanuts encompassed by a vine in the upper left are turned into what resembles a formal garden, and the standing goddess gazes at them (and the NOF company logo, a coat of arms) with consummate reverence. Text and illustration work in harmony, but the dictum of the time remained *horror vacui*, the fear of open space, and every niche is filled with decoration.[33]

An 1898 poster by J. A. Zon (1872–1932) for the Nederlandsche Gist & Spiritus-Fabriek (Dutch Yeast and Methylated Spirits Factory) presented their *Spiritus Gloeilicht* (alcohol lightbulb) with all the splendor of an Olympic torch (Fig. 1-7). Zon's poster for Dobbelmann Frères Savon Modern (Dobbelmann Brothers Modern Soap) is far more polished and for this reason suggests that it came later (Fig. 1-8). The fragrance of the product is clearly implied by two daydreaming women engulfed in a profusion of flowers. Another poster by Zon for the Levensverzekering-

1-7. Jacob Abraham (Jacques) Zon, *Spiritus Gloeilicht, Nederlandsche Gist & Spiritus-Fabriek* (Alcohol Light Bulb, Dutch Yeast & Methylated Spirits Factory), poster, 1898, 99 × 64.5 cm.

1-8

1-9

1-8. Jacob Abraham (Jacques) Zon, *Dobbelman Frères Savon Modern, Nimègue (Hollande)* (Dobbelman Brothers Modern Soap, Nijmegen [Holland]), poster, circa 1898, 72×42 cm. Collection, Bernice Jackson, Concord, Massachusetts.

1-9. Jacob Abraham (Jacques) Zon, *Levensverzekering-Maatschappij "Neerlandia"* (Life Insurance Company "Neerlandia"), poster, circa 1898. 110×80 cm. Collection, Bernice Jackson, Concord, Massachusetts.

Maatschappij Neerlandia (Neerlandia Life Insurance Company), produced around 1900, reached a new level of saccharine Victorian melodrama (Fig. 1-9). The insured, a mother embracing a child, is depicted being rowed across a choppy sea by a sturdy, steely-eyed Dutchman. At the stern, an angel provides guidance as a threatening lightning bolt cleaves the sky. Zon's posters were clearly influenced by the work of the Czech-born Parisian Alphonse Mucha (1860–1939), but Zon missed most of the poetic quality in Mucha's work, and grasped only the style. As with most Dutch posters of this period, Zon's designs bore only a tangential connection to the matter at hand.

There was another current comprised of progressive artists such as R. N. Roland Holst, J. J. C. Lebeau (1878–1945), J. Thorn Prikker (1868–1932), C. A. Lion Cachet (1864–1945), Louis Raemaekers (1885–1956), and Jan Sluyters (1881–1957). Designers like W. A. van Konijnenburg (1868–1943) and J. C. Braakensiek (1858–1950) were interesting in themselves, but still very

much entrenched in the nineteenth century. Unpolished as it might be, Lion Cachet's 1897 poster for the cigar purveyor W. G. Boele is exceptional for its simplicity in a time when this was not usually the case (Fig. 1-10). It consists of the silhouette of a man in a cap apparently relighting the stub of a cigar, framed by two vertical smoldering cigars. It is even more unusual since Lion Cachet's previous work was generally in the Art Nouveau mode.

Johann Georg van Caspel (1870–1928) began as a portrait painter and was eventually commissioned to do murals for private houses and public buildings. One of these was done for an artists' pub near the Damrak in Amsterdam. The decoration was noticed by C. J. Schuver, director of the Koninklijke Stoomsteendrukkerij Amand (later Senefelder), who subsequently invited Van Caspel to work for his company. The association lasted seven years, and during this time Van Caspel designed posters, book covers, catalog covers, a calendar, and advertisements. His career in the graphic arts was short-lived, though: in 1903 he retreated to the painters' village of Laren, where he painted portraits and still-lifes and worked as an architect.[34]

1-10. C. A. Lion Cachet, *Boele Cigars*, poster, 1897, 74 × 57 cm.

Van Caspel's 1896 poster for Hinde bicycles was widely noticed as soon as it was issued and was reproduced in the December 1, 1897 issue of the English magazine *The Stationer, Printer and Fancy Trades Register* (Fig. 1-11). In an article titled "Dutch posters and show cards" J. Geo. van Caspel is described as a young artist, who "was casually discovered by Mr. Schuver, of Amand's Printing Company who saw his decorative work in a new café in Amsterdam. Mr. Schuver went to see him and persuaded him to try his hand at poster work, though: curiously enough the artist did not consider himself capable of doing much in this respect. However, he went to work, and after some time the Hinde poster, the first one he did, was printed . . . and was much talked of when it made

1-11. Johann Georg van Caspel, *Hinde-Rijwielen* (Hinde Bicycles), poster, circa 1896, 77 × 108 cm.

its appearance on the hoardings in Amsterdam and other places, the new style of art poster being at that time a great novelty on the Dutch walls and hoardings."[35] In the poster, a trimly dressed girl is depicted blithely cycling through an idealized and bucolic Dutch landscape, informing the viewer that cycling is altogether pleasant, safe, reliable, and proper.

The poster the Steendrukkerij v/h Amand (Lithographic Printers v/h Amand) produced in the same year was quite different. The solidity of the message is augmented by black borders that divide the page into three distinct sections—one in the middle for the image and two at the top and bottom for the text. In the foreground a dependable-looking craftsman rolls ink on a traditional lithographic stone, while in the background a colleague inspects a poster that has recently been printed on a large modern press, implying that the company is both traditional and innovative (Fig. 1-12).

Unlike most of his other posters, Van Caspel's 1897 poster for the Nederlandsche Gasgloeilicht Maatschappij (Dutch Gaslight Company) is completely symmetrical and very much imbedded in the nineteenth century (Fig. 1-13). A woman with wings, resembling an extra in a Wagnerian opera, holds a gaslight aloft, much like

1-12. Johann Georg van Caspel, *Steendrukkerij v/h Amand* (Lithographic Printers v/h Amand), poster, 1896, 107 × 75 cm.

1-13. Johann Georg van Caspel, *Nederlandsche Gasgloeilicht Maatschappij* (Dutch Incandescent Light Co.), poster, 1897, 73 × 50 cm.

the woman in Zon's 1898 poster for the Nederlandsche Gist & Spiritus-Fabriek. (It is likely that Zon saw Van Caspel's earlier piece.) The image of the lady reading on the 1900 poster for *Boon's geillustreerd magazijn* (Boon's Illustrated Magazine) is repeated in miniature on the cover of the magazine. This in turn is repeated again in an even smaller size, like the Russian egg toy in which each egg contains a smaller replica of itself.

Although they show the contemporary inclination to fill up space, Van Caspel's posters move a step further toward simplification. His 1899 poster for Ivens and Co. Foto-Artikelen (Ivens Photographic Equipment Company) is a good example (Fig. 1-14). He always used models and designed everything in oil, but his posters are by no means simply reproductions of paintings. In this example, the combination of type and illustration is well-conceived, with the colors reduced to flat areas.[36]

In 1905, the use of a painting by the Amsterdam artist George Hendrik Breitner in an advertisement for Delftsche Slaolie precipitated an interesting and heated argument. The painting was meticulously reproduced through lithography and surrounded by an imitation frame containing the typography. The subject of the painting, two draft horses at a building site, obviously had nothing to do with the product itself. The objective was simply to suggest an association between the quality of the painting as a work of art and the quality of the product. This kind of promotion is now

1-14. Johann Georg van Caspel, *Ivans & Co. Foto-Artikelen* (Ivans Photographic Equipment Company), poster, 1899, 64 × 98 cm. Collection, Bernice Jackson, Concord, Massachusetts.

quite common, cigarette advertisements being a prime example, but then it produced a major outcry. Roland Holst led the offensive:

Where he [the client] had every reason to expect a good poster which, through its meaningful and beautiful design, would attract attention everywhere to his product, what he gets is a poster which has nothing to do with his product, that has no more connection with it than the white flanks of bulky cart horses under a grey sky have with the quality of a well known brand of salad oil. And in the press this is hailed as a highly artistic conception."

He went on to castigate it further by saying that skilled lithographers had been compelled to copy a painting even down to the brush strokes. They had been treated as "executants . . . of designs, which since they were made by people lacking the essential knowledge of the craft, result in unbearable stupidity and insane complexity, where true insight would have insured simplicity, beauty and an honest job of work."[37]

The actual intention was to provide, as museum posters do today, something that one could hang in one's hall or office. The restraint of the composition, with a picture framed by text above and below, represented a definite shift from Victorian and Jugendstil overstatement. But the controversy was never resolved and remained a major point of contention well into the 1930s.

After 1905 there were fewer Dutch commercial posters, and the ones that were produced were for the most part mediocre. The posters of greatest interest were those produced for the theater and for exhibitions. The theater posters by Roland Holst are noteworthy (Fig. 1-15). They were always in line with his strict socialist principles, and he drew them himself on lithographic stones. Since he was concerned mainly with socialism and the theater, his message was aimed at a very selective group. That narrow audience enabled him to develop a very specialized and personal visual language and his own mystic and symbolic style.[38]

The graphic designer and painter Jacob (Jac.) Jongert (1883–1942) was a student of Roland Holst at the Rijksacademie in Amsterdam and later worked as his assistant. Although Jongert's work would change radically over the years, his earlier posters clearly showed the touch of his mentor. One example is a 1920 poster for Apricot Brandy drawn directly on the lithographic stone in the manner of Roland Holst (Fig. 1-16). Jongert's best-known client was the Van Nelle food company, for which he did the corporate image. Although his later posters, in contrast to the earlier ones, were more functional and radically different in approach, Jongert never fully dissociated himself from the shadow of his very authoritarian teacher, Roland Holst, whose gospel it was that the artist's life and work must first serve as a model for society. He emphasized personal virtue, craftsmanship, and above all, an

1-15. R. N. Roland Holst, *Electra*, poster, 1920, 99 × 68.5 cm. Collection, Bernice Jackson, Concord Massachusetts.

1-17. Louis Raemaekers, *Tegen de tariefwet, vlieg niet in 't web* (Against the tariff law, don't fly into the web), poster, 1913, 100 × 76 cm. Collection, Bernice Jackson, Concord, Massachusetts.

1-16. Jacob (Jac.) Jongert, *Apricot Brandy*, poster, 1920, 100 × 76 cm. Collection, Bernice Jackson, Concord, Massachusetts.

awareness of one's responsibility toward the community, like Morris and the arts and crafts movement in England. In following Roland Holst's principle of responsibility to society, Jongert considered graphic design an excellent tool for assisting the less privileged classes.[39]

Another notable exception to the mediocrity of the post-1905 work was in the political sector. Outstanding examples are the posters of Albert Hahn (1877–1918), a political cartoonist by profession, who designed for the theater as well as the Social Democratic Workers Party and affiliated labor unions. In contrast to those of Roland Holst, his posters were simple in concept, with definitive lines and bold colors.

One especially eccentric piece is the poster by Louis Raemaekers (1869–1956) titled *Tegen de tariefwet, vlieg niet in 't web* (Against the tariff law, don't fly into the web, 1913) (Fig. 1-17). Tariff, the villain, is represented by an immense spider clutching a sack representing *voedsel* (food), while further possible victims, *gereedschap*

(tools) and *kleeding* (clothes), await a similar fate. The text is set in a sans serif type, and the images are enclosed in a two-section grid of heavy lines over which the legs of the spider are beginning to cross. Raemaekers was mainly known for his charged journalistic political illustrations and in this poster left little doubt as to the political importance of the message.

The painter Jan Sluyters (1881–1957), although an excellent poster designer, was far out of the Dutch mainstream and more in the French tradition of Toulouse-Lautrec. With its intense colors, broad gestures, and free drawing style, his vigorous and exuberant 1919 poster for the *Artisten Winterfeest* (Artists Winter Festival) displays many of the qualities of Fauvism (Fig. 1-18).

1-18. J. C. B. Sluyters, *Artisten Winterfeest* (Artists Winter Festival), poster, 1919, 122×77 cm.

The work of the political cartoonist, painter, and book illustrator Piet van der Hem (1885–1961) was more refined than that of Sluyters and stressed a simple balance between illustration and text. His elegant poster for Spyker Autos was printed before 1914, the year the company went out of business. Most of his posters were done for the theater, and many contained portraits of the leading actors of his day. A refined draftsman, he often made use of exaggerated facial expressions, reflecting his background as a political cartoonist. J. W. (Willy) Sluiter (1873–1949) was another painter who made posters in a mode similar to that of Van der Hem. Like Van der Hem, Sluiter was a political cartoonist and made use of caricature in his drawing. His posters are characterized by heavy contours and a vibrant use of color. Sluiter created some of the liveliest posters of his day. His 1914 poster *Naar Keulen via Kesteren Nijmegen* (To Cologne via Kesteren and Nijmegen) is typical of his penchant for underscoring the lightheartedness of a situation.

The painter and designer Bart van der Leck (1876–1958) was one of the original members of the De Stijl movement. Although still bound in symmetry, his remarkable 1914 poster for the Batavier Shipping Line (Fig. 1-19) represents another significant step toward visual orderliness, and the geometrical segmentation of the format can be seen as a forerunner to De Stijl. The composition is divided by heavy black lines that reflects his work as a designer of stained glass windows. The figures suggest those in Egyptian painting, where the body is shown in a frontal view and the head in profile. The lettering appears to be hand drawn. With the exception of the sky, the poster is filled to the brim. The passengers seem to be enclosed in watertight compartments, perhaps reminding the viewer that this will be a safe crossing to London. Lion Cachet's 1917 poster for the Utrecht Jaarbeurs (Utrecht Trade Fair) displays some of the same features, such as the use of a silhouette. Some of the shapes resemble the undulating smoke in his poster for the cigar merchant W. G. Boele.

1-19. Bart van der Leck, *Batavia Line, Wm. H. Müller & Co.*, poster, 1914, 116 × 56 cm. © Estate of Bart van der Leck/VAGA, New York, 1991.

Most of the poster designers remained outside other movements and continued in their own particular directions well into the next two decades. Others who emerged near the end of World War I were the painter, printmaker, and craftsman P. A. H. Hofman (1885–1965), the architect Sybold van Ravensteijn (1889–1983), the painter Leo Gestel (1881–1941), Albert P. Hahn, Jr. (1894–1953), H. M. Luns (1881–1942), and virtual unknowns such as Willy Klijn.

Transition

The Netherlands had remained neutral during World War I but by no means avoided its effects. However, life there in 1917, at least compared with that in most of Europe, was still economically and culturally stable. There were, to be sure, endless debates, a kind of verbal trench warfare, concerning the place of advertising within society. In 1917, the Stedelijk Museum in Amsterdam held an exhibition of advertising art, and this occasioned a lively exchange between two socialists, Roland Holst and the political cartoonist Hahn, regarding the role of the artist in advertising. Roland Holst was against artists who, in his opinion, prostituted themselves for commerce. He maintained that an advertisement could be either straight information or a "shout," and since truth did not have to be overstated, the "shout" was both undesirable, unnecessary, and the equivalent of visual histrionics. Hahn took the opposite position. He maintained that advertising was a true popular "street" art and affected people who would never think of going to a museum or gallery. He found the "shout" quite appropriate and thought an artist could successfully use this approach as well. This distinction is clear when one compares two of their posters from the same period. Roland Holst's 1920 poster for Raden Arbeid (Labor Councils), with its quiet symmetry, almost whispers the message. Hahn's 1918 poster Stem Rood (Vote Red) has the impact of a visual sledgehammer.

The dispute reduced itself to these two extremes, "shout or information," with no hiatus in sight. Proponents defended their perspective and prejudices, and sometimes where one or the other stood became quite confusing and irrelevant. Sadly, this issue has never been totally resolved in The Netherlands.

In a Europe destroyed by war, these were some of the heated artistic topics in The Netherlands. The security of the atmosphere there permitted discussion of issues that, in a more troubled society, might have seemed frivolous. By the end of 1917, though, there were already clear signals that a renaissance in graphic design had begun and that forces were in position for a new beginning. The end of World War I would serve as the catalyst to set this change in motion.

The armistice ending World War I was signed on November 11, 1918, bringing to a close the most devastating conflict in history. With all of Europe in turmoil, there was a yearning for a fresh beginning. New political, social, and artistic movements were abundant. As early as 1909 and 1910, Futurist manifestos violently attacked conventional typography. The Italian Filippo Marinetti acted as the group's theologian and spokesman. In 1910, just fourteen months after the first Italian manifesto, a group of painters and poets in Russia, led by David and Vladimir Burliek, published *Sadok Sudei* (A Trap for Judges), which is considered to be the first publication of the Russian Futurists. Another indication of change is Stéphane Mallarmé's 1914 poem *Un Coup de dés jamais n'abolira le hasard* (One Roll of the Dice Will Never Abolish Chance), begun as early as 1897 and one of the earliest examples of text enhanced by typography. In 1916 Dada had been established in Zurich by Tristan Tzara, Hans Arp, Hugo Ball, Hans Richter, and others. Apollinaire's 1918 series of poems *Calligrammes: Poèmes de la paix et de la guerre, 1913–1916* (Calligrammes: Poems of Peace and War, 1913–1916) is another instance of experimental typography where type plays an evocative role. On March 20, 1919, Walter Gropius officially opened the Staatliches Bauhaus in Weimar, a successor to the Grand Ducal School of Applied Arts. In its later and more outlandish stages, the Art Nouveau style was like an uncontrolled plague of burgeoning wisteria vines bedecking any available space and had effectively burned itself out with the First World War. By 1918 it had largely digressed into a meaningless conglomeration of printer's ornaments as its last extension, Art Deco, brought it to an end.

Before 1930, there were no graphic design schools as we know them today; with a few exceptions, all members of the vanguard worked in other professions as well: they were trained as painters, architects, industrial designers, or printers. Graphic design was only one of many applied arts and was still not even considered an independent profession. After 1930, however, changes began taking place as industry started using modern designers. The V.A.N.K., the Vereniging voor Ambachts-Nijverheidskunst (Association for Crafts and Industrial Design) became an increasingly important force. Since its inception in 1904, the V.A.N.K. had exerted considerable influence. A neutral arena where progressive as well as traditional designers could always count on finding a sympathetic audience, it was the first organization for practitioners in a broad range of professions ranging from graphic design to architecture. Essentially, the V.A.N.K. had three objectives: to support issues relating to the various professions; to promote the development and enrichment of arts and crafts within the industrial sector; and to keep the public informed about their own activities. Exhibitions were frequent, and members also participated actively in industrial fairs.[40] Services for members were both progressive and extensive; the V.A.N.K. acted as an advice and

information bureau, promoted participation in international exhibitions and trade fairs, obtained assignments, and established pricing guidelines. Its magazine *New Arts* encouraged cooperation between artists and craftsmen, and from 1919 until 1931 the V.A.N.K. published a yearbook that provided a review of members' work and articles on various affiliated professions. It was disbanded by the Nazi occupiers of The Netherlands in 1942.

Especially after 1918, Dutch typography was distinguished by two different factions serving diverse functions. The first—and traditional—approach is defined in the title of an essay by the typographic historian Beatrice Warde (wife of the American typographer and type designer Fredric Warde and writing under the pseudonym Paul Beaujon): "Printing Should Be Invisible" and subordinate to the writer; content is supreme, and clarity and legibility are the preeminent objectives. The designer's purpose is to accommodate and support the writer, and to emphasize subtlety; slight differences in spacing, size, placement, and choice of typeface are the critical factors.[41] The second approach is quite different: Type itself has an independent and autonomous function, emphasizing the expressive, associative, and plastic possibilities within the forms of letters themselves.[42] This dichotomy would prove to be one of the principal polarizing factors separating the Constructivists and traditional designers.

Although there were other important contributors, each faction was dominated by a handful of preeminent figures. The traditional side was led by S. H. de Roos (1877–1962) and Jan van Krimpen (1892–1958). The avant garde approach was essentially dominated by four diverse yet related forces: De Stijl, presided over by Theo van Doesburg (1883–1931); the *Wendingen* style of the architect H. Th. Wijdeveld (1885–1987); the Constructivism of Piet Zwart (1885–1977) and Paul Schuitema (1897–1973), and the inexplicable individualism of H. N. Werkman.

Chapter 2
De Stijl and Theo van Doesburg

Beginnings of De Stijl

De Stijl was one of many intense and iconoclastic reactions to the catastrophe and tragedy of World War I. All kinds of emotion and sentiment were proscribed, as these were associated with values such as patriotism and militarism, discarded ideals of a discredited past. In this way De Stijl was an attempt to prevent another, similar tragedy. This approach was expressed in De Stijl's first manifesto, published in 1918:

There is an old and a new awareness of time. The old is based on the individual. The new is based on the universal. The struggle of the individual against the universal is manifesting itself in the World War as well as in contemporary art. . . . The war is destroying the old world with its contents; the dominance of the individual in every sector.[1]

This line of thought is continued in the fourth volume of *De Stijl* (1921):

For Europe there is no longer any way out. Centralization and property, spiritual and material individualism was the foundation of the old Europe. In that it has caged itself. It is falling to pieces. We observe this calmly. We would not want to help even if we could. We do not want to extend the life of this old prostitute.[2]

The highly diverse De Stijl contributors proclaimed it their utopian ambition to cleanse and free art from nonessential and invidious features such as subject matter, illusion, ornamentation, ambiguity, and especially subjectivity.[3] They repudiated what they considered to be the sentimental, overly decorative and decadent art of the nineteenth century. For the future, they wanted to clear the way for a new hyper-rational art form for industrial society, a "collective impersonal style . . . destined, they felt, for adoption by architects and designers of the machine age."[4]

The adherents of De Stijl constituted no "lost generation," however; they embraced the values of an industrial culture. Earlier perceptions of beauty that depended on craftsmanship now had to be reformulated to adjust to the new necessities of a fresh age. There would be an alliance between the artistic and industrial sectors, taking into account the technological advances of the twentieth century.

It is the endeavor of this small magazine to make a contribution toward the development of a new consciousness of beauty. It desires to make modern man receptive to what is new in the plastic arts. It desires, as opposed to anarchy and confusion,—the "modern baroque," to establish a mature style based on pure relationship of the spirit of the age and expressive means. It desires to combine in itself contemporary ideas on the new plasticity, which, although fundamentally the same, developed independently from one another.[5]

There would be a "realization of a universal law and a universal spirit . . . a new spiritual equilibrium, a new reality was to arise, according to the universal principles which the painters of 'De Stijl' had rendered completely visible for the first time in history." It would also "serve to solve various actual problems of our present time."[6]

Any assessment of De Stijl would be inconceivable without a thorough examination of the work of Theo van Doesburg.[7] He was born in Utrecht as Christiaan Emil Marie Küpper. His father, Wilhelm Küpper, was a photographer from Bonn who returned to his native Germany when Van Doesburg was still a child. After his mother married for the second time when he was eleven, he assumed the name of his stepfather, Doesburg, adding the "Van" himself at a later date.[8] This was an early and subtle sign of his penchant for using pseudonyms. At first, Van Doesburg appeared destined for a theatrical career, but this was soon superseded by painting. When he had his first exhibition in 1908 in The Hague, he was working in an impressionistic style, but this changed radically over the next two years. In addition to painting, he wrote art criticism in 1912 for an avant garde newspaper, the *Eenheid* (Unity).

In 1917 Van Doesburg launched the De Stijl movement together with the architect J. J. P. Oud (1890–1963); the writer, poet, and music connoisseur Anthony Kok; and the painters Vilmos Huszár (1884–1960) and Piet Mondrian (1872–1944). The name De Stijl (The Style) can probably be traced to Van Doesburg's 1916 lecture "The Aesthetic Principle of Modern Art" in which he mentioned the realization of a new style brought about through a union of painting and architecture.[9] Stijl also means a vertical part of a cross connection in carpentry. Volume 1, Number 1 of their official journal *De Stijl* (they had seriously considered calling it "The Straight Line") appeared in October 1917, and one year later they published their first manifesto.[10] By that time the group had been joined by the architects Jan Wils (1891–1972) and Robert van 't Hoff (1887–1937), the sculptor Georges Vantongerloo (1886–1965) and the painter Bart van der Leck. Later the group would include the furniture designer and architect Gerrit Rietveld (1888–1964), the painters and graphic designers Vordemberge-Gildewart (1899–1962) and Cesar Domela Nieuwenhuis (b. 1900), the interior designer Truus Schröder-Schräder (1889–1985), and the film producer Hans Richter (1888–1976).

For Van Doesburg, life itself was a creative marathon. He was an inventive, eclectic, mercurial, and unyielding artist who worked in many media with passionate energy and was continually active as a lecturer, writer, painter, architect, poet, sculptor, furniture and industrial designer, and typographer. His own eclecticism reflected De Stijl's ambition to encompass all sectors of life and the multidimensional nature of the movement itself. In 1917 he began designing posters, advertisements, books, and other printed matter. In addition to serving as editor of *De Stijl*, Van Doesburg was responsible for the layout, where he was able to apply his theories to typography, although not always successfully.[11]

The first three volumes of *De Stijl* are fairly austere and prosaic, with the overall design probably delegated to the printer. Only the covers and a few advertisements provided any idea of what would follow (Figs. 2-1 to 2-3). Later, after being completely redesigned by Van Doesburg and Mondrian at the end of 1920, *De Stijl* would reflect the influence of Van Doesburg's collaboration with the Rus-

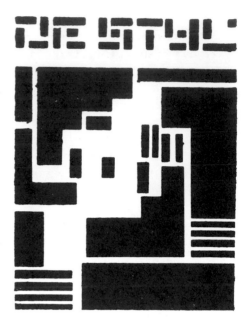

2-1. Vilmos Huszár, De Stijl Logo, 1918. Collection, Antiquariaat Schuhmacher, Amsterdam.

2-2. Theo van Doesburg, *De Stijl*, vol. 1, no. 1, page 1, 1917, 26.2 × 24.4 cm. Collection, Antiquariaat Schuhmacher, Amsterdam.

2-3. Theo van Doesburg, *De Stijl*, vol. 2, title page, 1918–19, 26.2 × 24.4 cm. Collection, Antiquariaat Schuhmacher, Amsterdam.

2-2

2-3

sian Constructivist El Lissitsky (1890–1941) and the Hanover-based Dadaist Kurt Schwitters (1887–1948). Then, heavily influenced by Constructivism, Dada, and Futurism, texts were rent asunder by an abundant use of rules, arrows, and upper- and lowercase letters. From then on, pages in *De Stijl* varied between conventional layouts and enigmatic and opaque compositions that require the reader to seek out the message. As Van Doesburg's ideas evolved, the logo was replaced in the fourth volume by a different and more dynamic cover. Of the two typographic functions described in the Prologue, *De Stijl* clearly served the autonomous, associative, and expressive purpose.

The design of the original *De Stijl* logo for the first three volumes has sometimes been erroneously attributed to Van Doesburg, but because the abstract part of the composition, designed by Huszár, and the letters are of the same dimension, it is clear that Huszár designed both. In fact, the letters in the logo were so consciously related to the abstract woodcut design that they became, in effect, barely legible elements rather than utilitarian letters. The style of the letters also has a direct stylistic relationship with Huszár's paintings from the same period. Huszár was influenced on the one hand by Van Doesburg and on the other by Van der Leck, who contributed an article for the first issue of *De Stijl* titled "The Place of Modern Painting in Architecture."

The basis for the fragmented letters on the cover of *De Stijl* is often found in the designs of Van der Leck (Figs. 2-4 to 2-6). An accomplished stained glass technician, in 1914–15 he designed a large window for the firm Wm. Müller & Company at The Hague. This led to other assignments for the firm, notably his Batavier Line poster of 1916. The poster for his Utrecht exhibition in 1919 and the advertising material for the furniture store and manufacturer Metz & Company in Amsterdam are examples of how his work in typography reflects what he was doing in his paintings. He continued to use his De Stijl-inspired alphabet, which appears again in a 1941 bibliophile edition of one of Andersen's fairy tales.[12]

In their correspondence, Mondrian and Van Doesburg questioned whether or not Van der Leck was actually suited for De Stijl, and apparently Van der Leck had similar doubts himself. Always somewhat aloof, Van der Leck refused to sign the De Stijl manifesto and withdrew from the group in March 1918, only a few months after its founding. His work was always pictorially anchored; total abstraction was never his intent or interest.

Like its founder Van Doesburg, the De Stijl movement was polemical in nature, embraced many disciplines, and was unusually receptive to new ideas. Ideally, its purpose was to bring about a universal bond between art and life, and the source of its mission toward spiritual purity and restraint could be found in Dutch Cal-

2-4. Bart van der Leck, *Tentoonstelling* (Art Exhibition), poster, 1919, 116 × 56 cm. © Estate of Bart van der Leck/VAGA, New York, 1991.

2-5. Bart van der Leck, *Metz & Co.* Collection, Antiquariaat Schuhmacher, Amsterdam. © Estate of Bart van der Leck/ VAGA, New York, 1991.

2-6. Bart van der Leck, *Het Vlas,* title page, 1941. Collection, W. Michael Sheehe, New York. © Estate of Bart van der Leck/VAGA, New York, 1991.

vinism. It was not only intended to effect a revolution in painting and architecture, but to change the very fabric of society itself. Van Doesburg wrote in the spring of 1921:

Painting is not intended to produce propaganda for any singular emotional or thought sentiment, such as religion, socialism, theosophy, etc. Neither is its aim to simulate. Painting—the art in general—implies that a single fundamental idea embraces all sectors of feeling: unity, that is to attain a harmony of forms with nothing more than the means which characterizes it: color.[13]

De Stijl was influenced both by rational and theosophical methodology.[14] "It therefore attempts to render visible and subject to contemplation something very close to the platonic idea. In its striving after abstraction, after the liberation of the arts from all accidentals, De Stijl constantly aims at the visible expression of the universal principle which its members consider the rendering of exact and equilibrated relations."[15] According to Mondrian, natural form is not universal, since natural forms are always individually defined. Thus, the new design must be totally abstract. Although De Stijl was to a large extent a logical consequence of Cubism, the Cubists Pablo Picasso and Georges Braque never sought pure abstraction as an objective and never fully distanced themselves from nature. Also, it was never their aim to bring about a utopian existence.

Although the rules were often violated, De Stijl was visually based upon functional, usually asymmetrical, harmony and elementary rectangular forms and was restricted to black and white, shades of gray, and the primary colors. By 1924 Van Doesburg began to include the diagonal in his paintings as well, and much to the aggravation of Mondrian he argued that this made room for a more active approach. Manifestos were profuse during these years, and this shift eventually resulted in yet another one, "Elementarism."

By the early 1920s *De Stijl* had become more and more a magazine where artists of various persuasions could air their beliefs (Fig. 2-7). Dada was represented by Raoul Hausmann and Hans Arp, Merz by Schwitters, abstract film by Hans Richter and Vicking Eggeling, Constructivism by Lissitsky and Laszlo Moholy-Nagy, Futurism by Gino Severini and Filippo Marinetti. This extensive cast increased even more the disparity between Van Doesburg and De Stijl fundamentalists such as Mondrian. Except for his role in the new design of *De Stijl,* Mondrian's work never involved typography, but his influence was nevertheless strongly felt in graphic design. While Van Doesburg was willing to open doors to new means of expression, for Mondrian painting was an end in itself. In 1924 Mondrian abruptly left De Stijl in protest for a number of reasons, the principal one being his objections to "Elementarism" and what he considered to be Van Doesburg's intolerable inconsistencies. Another cause for the rift was Mondrian's apparent sympathy for the expressive architectural style of Wijdeveld and the Amsterdam School, an anathema for Van Doesburg.[16]

For Van Doesburg, it was important to have a typeface that corresponded with De Stijl principles. His own display alphabet, based

2-7. Theo van Doesburg, *De Stijl,* vol. 5, no. 5, cover, 1922, 21.7 × 27 cm. Collection, Antiquariaat Schuhmacher, Amsterdam.

on the square, was confined to capital letters formed solely out of right angles, with vertical and horizontal slabs of the same thickness (Fig. 2-8). These could be distorted vertically or horizontally at will. To force a text longer than a single line into a particular rectangle, the letters would be compressed in one line and expanded in another, and through reducing or contracting them he was able to squeeze them into the desired format.[17] Esthetics played no role whatsoever, and because he had constantly to redraw the letters, he often produced some very eccentric forms. Obviously legibility did not receive a high priority either, and the premise that a first objective of typography is the conveyance of information is a marginal consideration. Laszlo Moholy-Nagy clearly had Van Doesburg in mind when he wrote that "clarity is the first prerequisite of all typography. For the sake of legibility

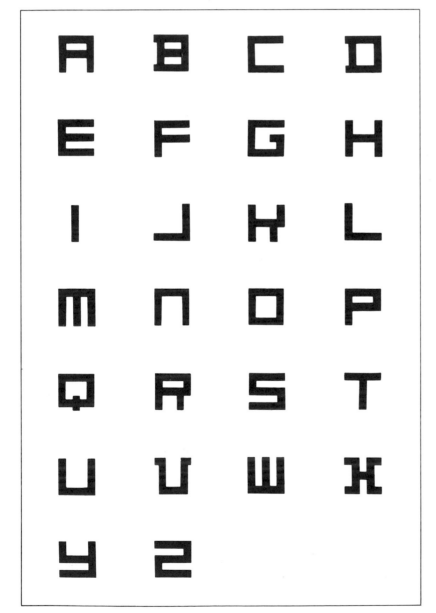

2-8. Theo van Doesburg, 1919, Alphabet design.

the message must never suffer from a priori aesthetics. The letter types must never be forced into a pre-planned form—for instance, into a square."[18] An example is Van Doesburg's cover for his published lecture *Klassiek Barok Modern* which he gave in Antwerp in 1920 (Fig. 2-9).

Two of the most prominent architect members of De Stijl were Gerrit Rietveld and Jacobus Johannes Pieter (Ko) Oud. Rietveld was the son of an Utrecht furniture maker, a situation that led to his education in this field. He produced his first De Stijl furniture in 1919, and the prototype for his famous Lean Chair was finished in 1918. This was originally made in natural wood and four years later painted in the primary colors we know today. Rietveld is mainly known for the 1924 Rietveld-Schöder house. Berlage despised it and accused Rietveld of destroying what he had achieved. Oud was a social activist and for all practical purposes the official architect of Rotterdam. He was concerned with public housing and applied the repetition principle in standardizing urban architecture. In 1925 he designed the Café De Unie in Rotterdam, a building that could be described as a De Stijl layout in the third dimension. The façade is a careful asymmetrical arrangement of flat and typographic elements and a direct architectural translation of De Stijl principles. He aimed to have the façade of the Café De Unie (Fig. 2-10), situated between two traditional buildings, break the "serious character" of the street. The original structure was destroyed during the bombing of Rotterdam in 1940 and rebuilt in 1985 close to its original site.

The Dada Influence

Van Doesburg's writings in *De Stijl* made it clear that he had an early empathy for Dadaism, but he initially approached it with reticence and somewhat after the fact.[19] The Dada movement was essentially a nihilistic and anarchistic protest against tradition and artistic dogma in general, and the Dadaists had no interest in new esthetic theories to replace what they had so vehemently rejected. They seized upon any and every available medium to forward their principles, and found collage and montage to be especially susceptible.[20] The actual term Dada was included for the first time in a short article titled "Rondblik" (Look Around) in volume 3, number 4 of *De Stijl* published in February 1920. Van Doesburg's first Dada article appeared on May 8, 1920, in *De Nieuwe Amsterdammer*, a weekly publication to which he regularly contributed. He wrote that one would only be deceiving oneself by attempting to find in conventional terms a logical meaning for each word in Dada writing. "Dada doesn't want that. Then what does Dada want? It wants nothing. But 'nothing' in a positive sense."[21] Or the "absence of any value becomes in itself a value."[22]

2-9. Theo van Doesburg, *Klassiek, Barok, Modern,* cover, 1920, 22.5 × 14.8 cm. Collection, Antiquariaat Schuhmacher, Amsterdam.

2-10. J. J. P. Oud, *Café De Unie*, Rotterdam. Designed 1925. Destroyed during the bombing of 1940 and reconstructed close to the original site in 1985.

In Volume 3, Number 6 of *De Stijl,* Van Doesburg published in collaboration with Mondrian and Kok a manifesto on literature in Dutch, French, and German titled *Manifest II van 'De Stijl' 1920— De Literatuur* (Manifesto II of 'De Stijl' 1920—Literature). It stated that they wanted to give "a new meaning and new power of expression to words." In the next number, Van Doesburg published an equivocal series of poems titled *X-Beelden, Letter-klank beelden* (X-Beelden, Letter-sound Images) (Figs. 2-11 to 2-15) by the arcane writer I. K. Bonset. A footnote indicated that these *X-Beelden* were part of a series of *Kubistische Verzen* (Cubist Verses) written between 1913 and 1919. With these poems Van Doesburg attempted to give sound a typographic form, and the meanings of the texts were amplified through type arrangements and variations in type sizes to emphasize individual words, reminiscent of the *Calligrammes: Poèmes de la paix et de la guerre, 1913–1916* of Apollinaire. The *X-Beelden* were far different from any previous Dutch poetry and contain most of the characteristics of Dada typography—numerous typefaces in all sizes, lines going in all directions, and enormous contrasts.

2-11. Theo van Doesburg, *De Stijl,* vol. 4, no. 11, November 1921, *X-Beelden, Letter-klank beelden* (X-Beelden, Letter-sound images) by I. K. Bonset, page 161, 21.7 × 27 cm. Collection, Antiquariaat Schuhmacher, Amsterdam.

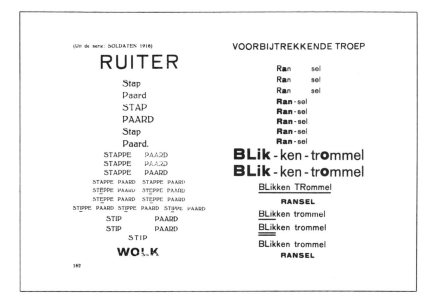

2-12. Theo van Doesburg, *De Stijl*, vol. 4, no. 11, November 1921, *X-Beelden, Letter-klank beelden* (X-Beelden, Letter-sound images) by I. K. Bonset, page 162, 21.7 × 27 cm. Collection, Antiquariaat Schuhmacher, Amsterdam.

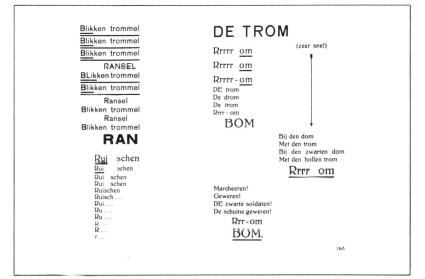

2-13. Theo van Doesburg, *De Stijl*, vol. 4, no. 11, November 1921, *X-Beelden, Letter-klank beelden* (X-Beelden, Letter-sound images) by I. K. Bonset, page 163, 21.7 × 27 cm. Collection, Antiquariaat Schuhmacher, Amsterdam.

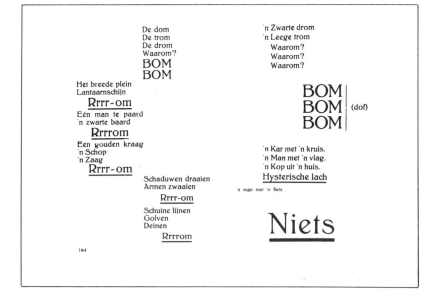

2-14. Theo van Doesburg, *De Stijl*, vol. 4, no. 11, November 1921, *X-Beelden, Letter-klank beelden* (X-Beelden, Letter-sound images) by I. K. Bonset, page 164, 21.7 × 27 cm. Collection, Antiquariaat Schuhmacher, Amsterdam.

2-15. Theo van Doesburg, *De Stijl*, vol. 8, no. 85/86, back page. Collection, Antiquariaat Schuhmacher, Amsterdam.

Van Doesburg clearly had a malevolent side and was never reticent about lecturing others. Apparently, envious over what the Flemish Paul van Ostaijen (1896–1928) was doing in a similar mode, he unfairly disparaged his work in a patronizing review in *De Stijl*. Although Van Ostaijen was born in Antwerp, he nevertheless merits a place in the development of Dutch graphic design. His best-known piece was *Bezette Stad* (Occupied City), published in 1921 (Figs. 2-16, 2-17). Van Ostaijen referred to the typographic interpretations of his poetry as "rhythmic typography," and in this tumultuous and visceral 153-page poem written in Dutch, he indicates time durations through typographic intervals and cadences: one is conducted through the series as a director leads a viewer through scenes in a film.[23] Oscar Jespers designed the cover and made the woodcuts, and together with René Victor "interpreted" the text from Van Ostaijen's manuscript and notations. The basic text is set in Caslon combined with other faces ranging in sizes from 10 to 48 points. It is important to note that Van Ostaijen was a poet and in no sense of the word a typographer, yet typographically *Bezette Stad* is decidedly a step above what Van Doesburg was trying to do in the same idiom.

regisseur aartsengel Michaël

aero's blokkade duikboten vreemde rassen

het begin van het einde

de borst is leeg

het kind werpt de fles weg

kindermeiden - huilen

De Laatste der MoHikanen

is de meest passende roman

alles beproefd

wij zijn aan 't einde van alle ismen isthmen

van alle katedralen

van alle profeten

van alle kateders

staan paf

met het enige pozitieve

dat wij 't verdommen nog een mik te doen

mik mec miché

N ihil in alle richtingen

ihil in alle geslachten

ihil in alle talen en

alle dialekten

NIHIL in alle lettertekens

draaiend nihil

nihil in Andreaskruis

NIHIL in crux suastica

Nihil in vagina

Zut katedralen bouwen en omverschieten

schuld bij anderen

natuurlik

citron nature

anderen maakt kinderen

de gelofte van zuiverheid kost niets

verdommen en

vertikken

statistiekers bisschoppen generaals genoegen gunnen

kinderen te tellen

Deo Gratias

amen

en kinderen die malheur of toeval daar zijn is enkel te leren

zich zelf te verdedigen

draaiend *nihil*

rechthoek nihil

driehoek **nihil**

piramide NIHIL

uw moraal the one plausible thing for us

to do

de treinen hebben het matte ritme

van

moeë

mensen

NIHIL

terug van \ Bapaume
Noyon
/ le Chemin des Dames

m k n o d t n ij
a e s l a e r

als voor een voedingskomiteit

(de mens leeft niet van brood alleen)

! HIER ! schöne junge mädchen

Eh là-bas Väterchen

par ici →

De politieman handhaaft de orde

elk op zijn beurt

Wie is de laatste

van 4

tot

4

ZEPPELIN

Dagbladen

**ZEPPELIN
LONDEN**

good bye Piccadilly
SQUARE
farewell Leicester

BEATA INSULA

In 1922 Van Doesburg published the first of four issues of the journal *Mécano,* again using the pseudonym Bonset, this time as the *gérant littéraire* (literary editor) and his own name Theo van Doesburg as the *mecanicien plastique* (plastic engineer) (Figs. 2-18, 2-19). This publication was largely Dada in its outlook and was produced to "poke fun at the solemnities of the Bauhaus."[24] It even satirized De Stijl and contained work by Schwitters, Max Ernst, Raoul Hausmann, Tristan Tzara, Hans Arp, and the Paris-based Dadaists Georges Ribemont-Dessaignes, Francis Picabia, and Paul Eluard. In a number of ways, though, the actual structure of *Mécano* gave away its underlying source, *De Stijl.* For example, each issue was identified through the use of a primary color (the

2-18

2-16. Paul van Ostayen, *Bezette Stad* (Occupied City), double-page spread, 1921, 22.3 × 27.8 cm. Collection, Antiquariaat Schuhmacher, Amsterdam.

2-17. Paul van Ostayen, *Bezette Stad* (Occupied City), double-page spread, 1921, 22.3 × 27.8 cm. Collection, Antiquariaat Schuhmacher, Amsterdam.

2-18. Theo van Doesburg, *Mécano,* cover, 1922, 16.3 × 12.9 cm. Collection, Antiquariaat Schuhmacher, Amsterdam.

four numbers are called yellow, blue, red, and white). Numbers 1, 2, and 3 are folded from a single sheet to form sixteen sections, eight on the front and eight on the back. The texts in the different sections are often set in contrasting directions, and when viewed unfolded, the pages work as individual units within a loose typographic coalition. Issue number 4 is cut into four sections and bound as an 8-page book.

Van Doesburg became acquainted with Kurt Schwitters in the summer of 1921 and immediately seized upon him as a kindred spirit. He published three of Schwitters' poems in *De Stijl,* and a "Sonata" in *Mécano 4/5.* In 1923 Schwitters came to The Netherlands and met the painters Van der Leck and Mondrian, the architects Oud, C. van Eesteren, Berlage, and Rietveld, and the designers Zwart and Schuitema. Schwitters published the initial issue of *Merz* in January 1923, the same month that he traveled to The Netherlands. In this issue he reciprocated by publishing Van Doesburg's "Letter-sound images." This first *Merz* number was devoted to Holland Dada, and its formal structure with bodies of text separated by slabs and lines was heavily influenced by *De Stijl* and *Mécano* (Figs. 2-20, 2-21). The playful typographic children's book *Die Scheuche* (The Scarecrow) appeared as a Merz publication in 1925 (Fig. 2-22). Although this was a joint effort by Schwitters, Käte Steinitz, and Van Doesburg, the typography was mainly by Van Doesburg. Some of the constructions are reminiscent of the figures built out of type in Werkman's second number of *The Next Call.*

Bonset was first mentioned by Van Doesburg in a 1918 letter to Tristan Tzara, and at that time he referred to Bonset as a "Dutch Dadaist." Bonset became, in effect, Van Doesburg's Dada alter ego, and he was not the only one. During a trip to Milan in 1922, Van Doesburg supposedly discovered a long manuscript by a deceased painter, Aldo Camini. This was apparently quite a treasure, containing an assortment of parodies, pseudo-scientific discourses, implausible philosophies, verbal frays, caustic art criticism, and poetic torrents.[25] All were published in *De Stijl.* Only after Van Doesburg's death was it openly revealed that Bonset, Camini, and Van Doesburg were one and the same person. Even some of Van Doesburg's closest associates were apparently unaware of the charade. Mondrian warned Van Doesburg against this strange Bonset whom he suspected of filching their ideas. Van Doesburg went so far as to publish a photograph of his wife Nelly with a mustache as one of Bonset. She later remarked that her husband had always relished playing the actor and could easily insert himself into any role.[26] Had he not earlier considered a career on the stage?

Contradiction and capriciousness were omnipresent components of Van Doesburg's makeup, and it remains, to some degree, an enigma why he never published his Dada leanings under his own name. Were his pseudonyms a private joke, or a convenient

2-19. Theo van Doesburg, *Mécano, Red issue, no. 3,* cover, 1922, 16.3 × 12.9 cm. Collection, Antiquariaat Schuhmacher, Amsterdam.

2-20. Kurt Schwitters, *Merz, Holland Dada,* cover, January 1923. Collection, Antiquariaat Schuhmacher, Amsterdam.

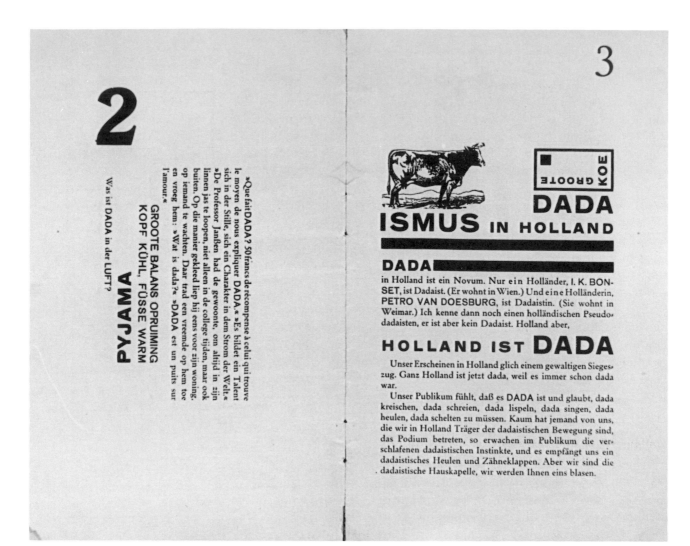

2-21. Kurt Schwitters, *Merz, Holland Dada,* double page spread, January 1923. Collection, Antiquariaat Schuhmacher, Amsterdam.

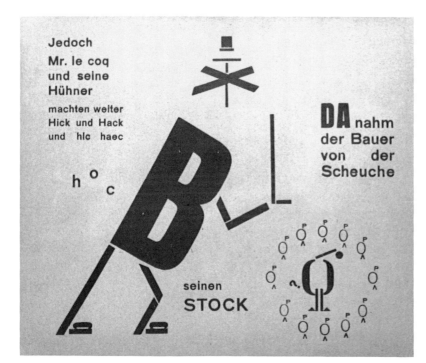

2-22. Theo van Doesburg, Kurt Schwitters, Käte Steinitz, *Die Scheuche* (The Scarecrow), *Merz 14/15,* page 7, 1925, 24.4×26.2 cm. Collection, Antiquariaat Schuhmacher, Amsterdam.

weapon for ventilating opinions that did not conform with those of De Stijl? It must have been a bit of both. Van Doesburg was able to increase his critical portfolio, with which he attacked any and everyone, including himself. An alias may have also provided him with freedom like the anonymity enjoyed at a masquerade ball. Resolute supporters of De Stijl could strongly disagree with Bonset's views but still tolerate them, since they were being expressed by an unknown outsider.[27] If this was indeed the case, it was a clever and witty tactic.

Van Doesburg is a primary example of F. Scott Fitzgerald's belief in the artist's ability to maintain two contradictory emotions: "The test of a first-rate intelligence is the ability to hold two opposed ideas in the mind at the same time, and still retain the ability to function."[28] Still, how Van Doesburg could actively and concurrently champion two contrary doctrines remains a paradox. He realized quite well that Dada was essentially an anarchistic protest movement very different from De Stijl, with its stringent rules. However, he was aware that Dada, like De Stijl, was also challenging established values in art and society, and in this way he could have felt an obvious affinity between the two.[29]

Van Doesburg and the Bauhaus

Shortly after the founding of De Stijl, the Staatliches Bauhaus was started in Germany. In April 1921, Walter Gropius invited Van Doesburg to spend a week at Weimar and see the Bauhaus first-hand. In Van Doesburg's opinion, he found it still tied to a postwar romantic mentality, and he especially objected to the teaching methods of the "Vorkurs" of Johann Itten, which all students were required to take. Itten emphasized expression in all aspects of the arts, the opposite of Van Doesburg's stance. Perhaps Van Doesburg was partially vindicated, for later the Bauhaus approach did change radically under the influence of Laszlo Moholy-Nagy, Joost Schmidt, and Joseph Albers. Expressionism was replaced by a Constructivist approach when Moholy-Nagy took over the teaching of the Vorkurs. In any event, Van Doesburg decided to extend his stay and offer his services to what he considered to be the still overly-conservative institute. This relationship between De Stijl and the Bauhaus was at best an odd alliance. The Bauhaus historian Bruno Adler supposedly remarked that Van Doesburg arrived there with "his gospel of redemption through the right angle."[30]

Although Van Doesburg undoubtedly would have liked to have been a part of the Bauhaus, he was never accepted as a peer by most of the members. He never forgave them for this affront and soon began conducting his own De Stijl courses in the studio of Peter Röhl, a Bauhaus student. It was also attended by several

Bauhaus faculty members. Eventually, Van Doesburg's audacity and the obviously sensitive situation fomented such vehement hostility on the part of other Bauhaus teachers and students that actual gunfire resulted and windows of Röhl's studio were broken by rocks.[31]

Among other criticisms, Gropius considered Van Doesburg's philosophy too inflexible. His fundamental objection, though, was Van Doesburg's total repudiation of individualism, which was in sharp contrast to the subjective approach of the Bauhaus. Van Doesburg's eventual exclusion by Gropius also had something to do with Van Doesburg's often uncompromising, condescending, and contentious manner. This was quite evident when he wrote to Kok in January 1921 about the Bauhaus period:

In Weimar, I have radically turned everything upside-down. This is the acclaimed academy with the most modern teachers! Each evening I have talked to the students and have spread the toxin of the new spirit. De Stijl will soon re-materialize in an even more radical shape. I have mountains of strength and now know that our ideas will prevail over everything and everybody.[32]

Van Doesburg left Weimar at the end of 1923 and continued, undiscouraged and unabated, to give De Stijl lectures in other German cities.[33] At that time Hanover was an active cultural center, and meetings there between Van Doesburg, Lissitsky, and Schwitters continued to generate ideas that were to have an enduring impact on graphic design. They all saw typography as a medium perfectly attuned to the new industrial epoch and recognized in the objectivity of advertising an opportunity once and for all to expunge the individuality of the graphic designer. In their eyes only the needs of the client, not those of the designer, were to be considered.

Van Doesburg and Constructivism

While attending the Düsseldorf Congress of Progressive Artists in May 1922, Van Doesburg, Lissitsky, and the Dada artist and filmmaker Hans Richter, produced a declaration for the international Constructivists. In October of that year, the Constructivists decided to hold a congress in Weimar with Van Doesburg presiding as official ringmaster. Among the guests were some Dadaists and Constructivists, including Schwitters, Richter, Lissitsky, Max Burchartz, Tristan Tzara, Hans Arp, and Laszlo Moholy-Nagy. It precipitated an amusing turmoil when the Constructivist participants discovered that Dadaists had been invited as well. The orthodox Constructivists always considered Dadaism to be a negative, detrimental, and outdated force when compared to their own approach, and having to work with Dadaists was a difficult pill to swallow. According to Moholy-Nagy, this episode generated an

outright rebellion against Van Doesburg by the Constructivists. Van Doesburg somehow managed to calm them down, but much to the consternation of Constructivists, the assembly gradually became a Dada event. So far, no one there was aware that Van Doesburg was already embracing both doctrines and surreptitiously producing Dada poems using the pseudonym Bonset.[34]

The October/November 1922 issue of *De Stijl,* volume 5, number 10/11, was devoted to a Dutch version of Lissitsky's Constructivist fairy tale, which had recently been published in Germany. The Dutch title was *El Lissitsky suprematisch worden van twee kwadraten in 6 honstrukties* (El Lissitsky becomes suprematic from two squares in

2-23. El Lissitsky, *El Lissitsky suprematisch worden van twee kwadraten in 6 konstrukties (El Lissitsky becomes suprematic from two squares in 6 constructions), De Stijl,* vol. 5, no. 10/11, 1922, 21×26 cm. Collection, Antiquariaat Schuhmacher, Amsterdam.

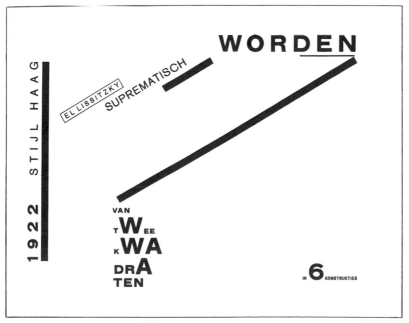

2-24. El Lissitsky, *El Lissitsky suprematisch worden van twee kwadraten in 6 konstrukties (El Lissitsky becomes suprematic from two squares in 6 constructions), De Stijl,* vol. 5, no. 10/11, 1922, 21×26 cm. Collection, Antiquariaat Schuhmacher, Amsterdam.

6 constructions) (Figs. 2-23, 2-24). Although it was a diluted version of the original Russian edition, it had a significant impact in The Netherlands and revealed the great potential for using words and abstract images in a rectangular page format.[35]

Lissitsky visited The Netherlands in 1923 and found an audience hungry for his revolutionary thoughts on typography. He gave lectures on the new Russian art, and became acquainted with Huszár, Zwart, and Oud, who happened to be a member of the Comité Voor Economische Opbouw van Rusland (Committee for the Economic Development of Russia). Lissitsky's influence was soon very evident, especially in the work of Zwart.

Vilmos Huszár

Huszár (1884–1960) was one of the founders and lesser known members of De Stijl and remained indirectly associated with the movement until 1922, when he returned to figurative painting. Huszár was born in Budapest as Vilmos Herz, but twenty years later his family assumed a more Hungarian-sounding name, Huszár. After leaving Hungary for good in 1904, he ended up in The Netherlands in 1909 and lived there for the rest of his life.

In addition to designing the woodblock logo and masthead for *De Stijl* in 1917, he was involved with its overall planning and decisively influenced its initial typographic approach. Huszár was far more important as a graphic designer than is generally credited; since so much of his work between 1916 and 1930 has disappeared, the full impact of his contribution is still difficult to evaluate. From 1918 until 1921 he had some heated altercations with the equally impetuous Van Doesburg, and during this time his work was banned in *De Stijl*. Huszár angrily cancelled his subscription to the magazine after his design was supplanted by that of Mondrian and Van Doesburg.

Like Van Doesburg, Huszár was a versatile artist who was active in painting as well as interior, furniture, fabric, and industrial design. During 1915–16 he was in close touch with Van der Leck, which led to his work in stained glass. Later he worked with Zwart, producing designs for the interior architectural firm Bruynzeel, and also with the architect Wils. Huszár had tried typography as early as 1906, but it was not until his 1917 collaboration with Van Doesburg on the magazine *De Stijl* that he began working seriously in this area.

Other early pieces are a 1919 cover for "Volkswoningbouw, Haagsche Kunstkring" (Public Housing, The Hague Art Circle) and a 1920 letterhead design for the same group (Fig. 2-25). These relate closely to his paintings of the same period, and as

2-25. Vilmos Huszár, *Volkswoningbouw, Haagsche Kunstkring,* (Public Housing, The Hague Art Circle), cover, 1919, 42 × 32 cm. Collection, Antiquariaat Schuhmacher, Amsterdam.

with the cover for *De Stijl*, he used an abstract rectangular composition and geometrical, constructed letters. The letter forms are made from vertical rectangles with indentations, quite similar to his 1922 bookplate design for Lena de Roos (Fig. 2-26).[36] But it was not until 1926 that his work in graphic design began to take on a more serious approach, and he began to devote more attention to the design of advertisements and other printed pieces. To a large extent this was a result of his contact with Lissitsky, Schwitters, and Zwart, but his own work in typography was quite different in its approach from theirs. It was not directly derived from printing elements such as letters and rules. Instead, he used flat pictorial designs, which he referred to as "visual advertising compositions."[37] Together with the text, they were intended to suggest symbolically the characteristics of the products.

Clearly influenced by Cubism, Huszár's 1926 poster for *Filmliga* (Fig. 2-27) was one of his conscious attempts to give background and foreground equal status in the composition through the use of overlapping forms. This was also a result of his ambition to bestow upon advertising an artistic value in addition to its functional

2-26. Vilmos Huszár, *Lena de Roos,* bookplate, 1922.

2-27

2-27. Vilmos Huszár, *Filmliga,* poster, 1926, 18 × 12.9 cm.

2-28. Vilmos Huszár, *Miss Blanche Cigarettes,* advertisement, 1926, 14 × 11.5 cm.

2-29. Vilmos Huszár, *Miss Blanche Virginia Cigarettes,* advertisement, 1926, 22.2 × 15.3 cm.

2-30. Vilmos Huszár, *Miss Blanche Egyptian Cigarettes,* advertisement, 1926, 19 × 13 cm.

use.[38] He expressed these ideas in various magazine articles, including one in 1927 for the international revue *i 10,* volume 1, number 5. In this article, *De Reclame als Beeldende Kunst* (Advertising as Fine Art), he remained somewhat vague as to when advertising could be considered art. However, in a 1929 piece two years later for *De Reclame, 8* (Advertising, 8) and *Bouwkundig Weekblad* (Architectural Weekly), he was more precise: Contemporary Constructivist advertising was dismissed as being "anti-art." "It is historic that, for example, opponents of the so-called De Stijl group of 1917, those who at the time were still working in a romantic mode, the 'Weiner-Sezession-Stil,' were the first ones to brazenly imitate us and now surpass us with 'hyper-rationalism.'" Zwart was clearly the target, and the article did not nurture their friendship.[39] In the latter article Huszár excluded typographic advertisements from fine arts entirely, targeting especially those which used printing elements exclusively, such as the NKF advertisements that Zwart began to produce in 1923.[40] Huszár's own earlier Bruynzeel pieces and many of his smaller designs after 1925 could themselves be categorized as typographic advertising, and cigarettes were represented solely through typographic elements in some of his 1926–27 advertisements for Miss Blanche (Figs. 2-28 to 2-30). However, he never completely removed himself from the pictorial: a typographic block, for example, would still indicate ashes.[41]

2-28

2-29

2-30

In Huszár's own work for The Vittoria Egyptian Cigarette Company he created new logos for the two brands of cigarettes made by the company: the design for Miss Blanche used a silhouette of a smoking figure in profile, and the design for Miss Blanche Virginia Cigarettes was a new rendering of an older pictorial image of a smoking woman wearing a hat. They were used both in color and black-and-white for stationery, cards, billboards, and advertising wagons. The company obviously wanted to saturate the public with its products, and Huszár accomplished this with much success.

In addition to his work for Bruynzeel, Huszár worked for the PTT (the Dutch Postal Telephone and Telegraph Service). Although he had disassociated himself from De Stijl by the end of 1922, he abandoned De Stijl completely in 1930, and all of his work in typography came to an end after 1931. The Bruynzeel account was taken over by Zwart.

The End of De Stijl

In 1929 Van Doesburg wrote an article in the German magazine *Die Form* that appeared to reverse some of his earlier convictions. He stated that the era of "dynamic," disorderly typography, infected by the advertising plague, had raped and muzzled the book and went on to champion a careful division of text and white space on the pages in a good "dynamic balance"—or, "Das buch ist kein Bild" (The book is not a picture).[42]

A longtime sufferer of asthma, Van Doesburg went to Davos in Switzerland for treatment and died of a heart attack there on March 7, 1931, at the age of 47. With the exception of the Van Doesburg commemorative publication in 1932, the unnumbered *Dernier numéro* issue, *De Stijl* ceased to appear after 1928 (vol. 8, no. 87–89). Bonset and Camini also quietly exited the scene and were never heard from again. With Van Doesburg's early death, De Stijl lost its motivating force.

A truly indigenous Dutch modern art movement, De Stijl exerted an international influence far beyond its thirteen-year existence. As a whole, it was perhaps the single most important Dutch contribution to the development of modern architecture, painting, and design in the twentieth century. While Van Doesburg's typography taken alone has little tangible to offer us now, De Stijl's principal influence in graphic design lay in the use of vertical and horizontal rectangles for the placement of text and images. We must remember that for Van Doesburg, typography was only another element to promote the philosophical objectives of De Stijl. Also, Van Doesburg was a painter at heart, and he thought in terms of color, forms, and patterns—far removed from a typogra-

pher, who begins with function and for whom minute parts are equally as important as the overall image.[43] Nevertheless, the consummate intensity of his new vision and the purifying influence of De Stijl were of vital importance. Dutch Constructivism is to a large extent a direct antecedent of De Stijl, and it is fair to say that without De Stijl, graphic design in The Netherlands, as we know it today, would be quite different.

Chapter 3
The Wendingen Style

H. T. Wijdeveld

In the years immediately following World War I, there occurred a wave of experimentation with geometrically constructed letters. One of its principal exponents was the architect Hendricus Theodorus Wijdeveld (1885–1987).[1] In 1918, a year after the founding of De Stijl, Wijdeveld introduced the magazine *Wendingen* (translated as "turns" or "changes of direction") (Figs. 3-1, 3-2). *Wendingen* was ostensibly a monthly publication devoted to architecture, construction, and ornamentation for the society Architecture en Amicitia in Amsterdam. Published in Dutch, German, and French editions, the actual content of *Wendingen* was far more extensive, and during its thirteen years of existence it reflected in text and images contemporary issues in all sectors of the visual arts. Beginning with the twenty-third issue, each number was devoted to a single topic in the field of art and architecture. In addition to being its founder, Wijdeveld was its designer and, until

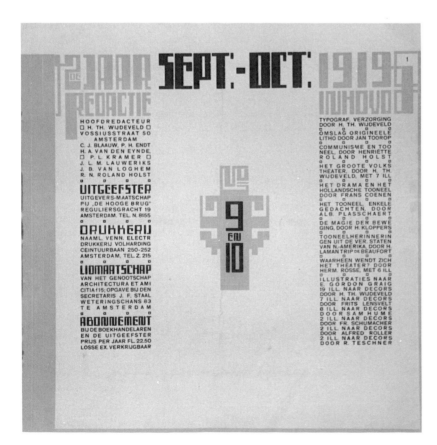

3-1. H. Th. Wijdeveld, *Wendingen XI*, no. 9 and 10, title page, 1919, 33 × 33 cm. Collection, Antiquariaat Schuhmacher, Amsterdam.

3-2. Staal A., *Wendingen XI,* no. 5, cover, 1930, 33×33 cm. Collection, Antiquariaat Schuhmacher, Amsterdam.

his resignation over policy issues in 1927, chief editor as well. The magazine's official address was always his own home. The strict vertical and horizontal asymmetrical framework that characterized the work appearing in *Wendingen* was soon referred to as the Amsterdam School, the Linear School, the New School, Amsterdam Expressionism, or the *Wendingen* and Wijdeveld styles, and *Wendingen* served as its semi-official journal.[2]

Born in 1885 at The Hague, Wijdeveld died in February 1987, having achieved the distinction of being the oldest living artist in The Netherlands.[3] He began his training at the age of 14 as a draftsman in the studio of Cuypers. His own work, however, moved in a completely different direction due to his acquaintance with two earlier collaborators of Cuypers, the architects Lauweriks and De Bazel, both of whom were involved with Architecture en Amicitia and played major roles in the Nieuw Kunst (New Art) movement around 1900.[4] Surely, Wijdeveld gained much of his inspiration for *Wendingen* from these mentors. Wijdeveld had even attempted in the beginning to get Lauweriks directly involved with the publication of *Wendingen.*[5] *Wendingen* is surprisingly close to Lauweriks' *Ring,* published ten years earlier, which can be seen as its logical precursor. Both utilized geometrical forms, sans serif letters, and Japanese paper.

Wendingen continued to deliver the gospel of decoration and eclecticism while *De Stijl* took another and more progressive direction (Figs. 3-3, 3-4). *Wendingen* was also different from *De Stijl* in that

3-3

its typography was indirectly related to its contents, but there is a similarity between the two in their inclination toward systematic organization.[6] In the fall of 1917 Wijdeveld went to Leiden to persuade Van Doesburg to become associated with *Wendingen,* then in preparation. Van Doesburg refused, and shortly after this meeting the first issue of *De Stijl* appeared, preempting *Wendingen* by three months. It is quite probable, especially given Van Doesburg's disposition toward self-promotion, that he accelerated the publication date of *De Stijl* in order to have it come out before its possible competitor, *Wendingen.*[7]

The format of *Wendingen* was a square, 33 × 33 centimeters. Rice paper was used throughout; letters were frequently set vertically like Chinese characters; and it was bound with raffia like a Japanese block book. All of this was a reflection of a growing fascination with Eastern art, which had begun with the world fairs in France and England during the previous century.[8] This interest was also a source of inspiration for Art Nouveau. Because of the

abundant use of ornaments, Wijdeveld's style has often been referred to as a natural corollary of Art Nouveau or Jugendstil—which, to a large extent, it was. Instead of using undulating lines and flourishes, Wijdeveld used solid, heavy borders, which were always constructed from right angles, consistent with one of the Art Nouveau approaches in The Netherlands. His elaborate compositions were built solely out of typographic elements, and for this reason Wijdeveld's designs have an austere character and an ingrained rigidity. The title pages of *Wendingen,* especially in the initial issues, are typographic reflections of the brick architecture of the Amsterdam School. Not only did he create his ornaments from the printer's composing material, such as lines and bars, but he used them to produce actual letters as a mason would use concrete blocks; entire words are created from these elements.[9] As with Van Doesburg, this style was often achieved at the expense of legibility. The Dutch type designer Gerard Unger referred to the Amsterdam School as "a ponderous and earthy derivation of Art Nouveau and Art Deco that found expression chiefly in rich and varied brick architecture."[10] The text was always set in a sans serif type, as this was in line with the general trend toward clarity. The sans serif was first used around 1830, but it was thought to be inappropriate as a text face due to the lack of serifs to connect words. To use in an art magazine what was considered a crude and ungainly face, suitable only for advertising, was a radical step.

Besides Wijdeveld himself, others who designed covers for *Wendingen* included Lauweriks (Fig. 3-5), Roland Holst, E. J. Kuipers, Lion Cachet, J. Sluijters, De Bazel, Toorop, Anton Kurvers (1889–1940), Jongert, Lissitzky, W. H. Gispen, Hahn, and Huszár. The covers for volume IV, number 11, designed by Lissitzky in 1922 (Fig. 3-6), and for the seven Frank Lloyd Wright issues, designed by Wijdeveld, Volume VII, Numbers 3–9, 1925–26, are among the more striking.

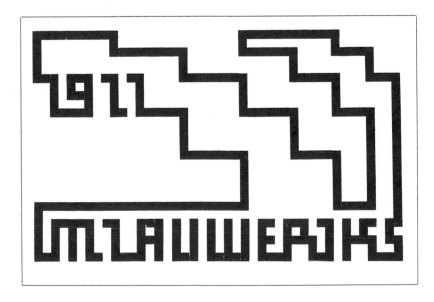

3-5. Lauweriks logo, 1911.

3-6. El Lissitsky, *Wendingen IV, no.11,* cover, 1921, 33 × 33 cm. Collection, Antiquariaat Schuhmacher, Amsterdam.

Huszár's 1929 cover for *Wendingen* was totally composed of typographic elements, and as a motif he interpreted the name of the magazine. The text is composed of letters alternately aligned at the top and bottom of a rectangular block on the top section of the page. Below, a square text block contains an abstract composition made from the same *Wendingen* letters set both vertically and horizontally, and the entire composition is repeated in simple block forms on the back. The cover subtly reflects the content of this particular *Wendingen* issue, which is devoted to the political murals of the Mexican painter Diego Rivera. The complimentary colors green and red resemble those of the Mexican national flag, and the patterns built up from geometric letters suggest friezes on Aztec architecture.

Wijdeveld's 1918–19 posters for the Stads Schouwburg (Municipal Theater) in Amsterdam are very different in approach from *Wendingen* (Figs. 3-7, 3-8). These are dominated by single, harsh, melodramatic theatrical images made from a woodcut. All are completely symmetrical, with an exclusive use of capital sans serif letters, often in a combination of styles. His dramatic 1922 poster for the *Internationale Theater Tentoonstelling* (Internationale Theater Exhibition) at the Stedelijk Museum is similar but more refined. In addition to *Wendingen*, Wijdeveld also designed books, bookplates, diplomas, alphabets, stationery, and other assorted printed material. His later poster designs, although few in number, display a freedom in design that the uniform *Wendingen* layouts lack. The

3-7. H. Th. Wijdeveld, *Hamlet,* poster, 1919, 91 × 35 cm.

1929 poster for an International Exhibition on Economics and History is especially noteworthy. Here Wijdeveld's architectural background comes to the forefront, and the asymmetrical organization suggests that of a solid modern building using the brick construction methods of the Amsterdam School. In contrast, the 1931 poster for the Stedelijk Museum Exhibition on Frank Lloyd Wright is completely symmetrical, although it too has a strong suggestion of architecture. Wijdeveld and Van Doesburg both took great liberty in stretching and condensing display letters in order to force the words to fit inside allotted spaces. The 1931 Wright poster is a prime example.

One of the finest examples of Wijdeveld's typography is J. W. Schotman's *Der Geesten Gemoeting,* a book having to do with Japanese fairy tales and Chinese legends. On the binding are Chinese arabesques translated into the Wijdeveld style. *Der Geesten Gemoeting* was printed in five separate sections, each with a different title page. Like *Wendingen,* it was bound in the traditional Japanese sewn style (Fig. 3-9).

Wijdeveld's singular style generated both imitators and avid opponents. Proponents of traditional typography such as De Roos found his creations outright blasphemy; others considered his work as it was conceived, a new beginning; many were captivated by what appeared to be its latent possibilities. Wijdeveld's style did produce a number of very serious followers, among them the Amsterdam graphic designer Fré Cohen (1903–1943) and the lithographer and decorative painter Kurvers (Fig. 3-10), but for the most part emulators drifted rapidly into superficiality.[11]

In *150 Years of Book Typography in The Netherlands,* G. W. Ovink referred to Wijdeveld as "Frank Lloyd Wright's paladin in The Netherlands who, in his magazine *Wendingen,* brought decoration *ad absurdum* and with his expensive, spectacular typographic constructions turned the heads of the élite. This unreadable, willful typography brought the whole printing art into discredit with the ordinary, reasonable public, so the reformers had reason to fear."[12] G. H. Pannekoek, Jr., in *De Herleving van de Nederlandsche Boekdrukkunst Sedert 1910* (The Revival of the Art of Dutch Printing from 1910) must have had, among others, Wijdeveld in mind when he wrote in 1925 that "today people all too often think—influenced by architects—that even though it is unreadable a letter must be constructed from pieces of lead."[13]

Even though *Wendingen* was inspired by the need for a radical new direction for design after the first world war, its actual physical structure did not support this purpose. In fact, the use of high-quality paper and tied string bindings had strong overtones of the arts and crafts era of the previous century. The first issues caused a sensation, and although *Wendingen* was considered the wave of the future by many, especially architects, its copious use of original

3-8. H. Th. Wijdeveld, *Kunst aan het Volk, Internationale Theater Tentoonstelling, Stedelijk Museum* (Art to the People, International Theater Exhibition, Stedelijk Museum), poster, 1918–19, 140 × 60 cm. Collection, Bernice Jackson, Concord, Massachusetts.

decoration at the expense of the functional contrasted sharply with the international trend toward sobriety and functionality. All in all, however, *Wendingen* was a unique publication and an exciting and daring undertaking for the period. The covers, which exhibit almost every style imaginable, fluctuate from the magnificent to the dull and the bizarre. On the other hand, with a few exceptions, the square pages follow an established format from the first until the last issue.

Although Wijdeveld was intensely occupied with typography during the 1920s, he always considered graphic design to be a marginal profession compared to architecture. The *Wendingen* style amply served his purposes and had a significant effect on Dutch architecture and applied arts. It was, though, irrevocably bound to its own particular period and so would not make a lasting contribution. Wijdeveld himself was the cultural powerhouse behind *Wendingen,* and without his direct involvement the style was doomed. The only designer of any significance who continued with the style was Fré Cohen.

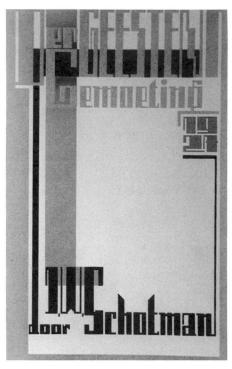

3-9. H. Th. Wijdeveld, *Der Geesten Gemoeting* by J. W. Schotman, title page, 1927, 91 × 35 cm. Collection, Antiquariaat Schuhmacher, Amsterdam.

3-10. A. Kurvers, *Tentoonstelling op het Gebied van Stedebouw* (City Planning Exhibition), poster, 1923, 100 × 79 cm.

Fré Cohen

Fré Cohen, although never a major innovator on the level of Wij-develd, nevertheless made a substantial contribution to the development of Dutch graphic design. Born in 1903 in Amsterdam, she was the oldest of three children in a Jewish diamond worker's family. After graduating from high school she did clerical work in an office, but her artistic skills were soon recognized, and she was asked to produce advertisements for the firm. She also became an active member of the AJC (Workers Youth Center) and designed many of their printed pieces as well as the pieces for other socialist organizations. This eventually led to her making drawings for the socialist book dealer and publisher N. V. Ontwikkeling, which

3-11. Fré Cohen, *Verslag No. 26,* (Report no. 26, Yearly Report of the Food Inspection Department of the City of Amsterdam), cover, 1928, 25.8 × 17.3 cm. Collection, Antiquariaat Schuhmacher, Amsterdam.

XXX

GEMEENTE
AMSTERDAM

SCHILDERIJEN
WANDSCHILDERINGEN
BEELDHOUWWERK
·SIERKUNST

TENTOONSTELLING
STEDELIJK MUSEUM
22 NOV.–7 DEC. 1930

3-12. Fré Cohen, *Gemeente Amsterdam*
(Municipality of Amsterdam), cover, 1929–
30, 18.3 × 17.5 cm. Collection, Antiquariaat
Schuhmacher, Amsterdam.

would later become the current Arbeiderspers. It soon became evident, however, that her education in this field was deficient. Many
of her book covers were difficult to execute because of her lack of
understanding of the technical aspects of production. It was then
that she decided to attend night classes at the Amsterdamse
Grafische School. The *Wendingen* style was very popular there,
and Fré Cohen felt its influence strongly.

In 1927, Cohen received a scholarship to attend the Institute for
Kunstnijverheidonderwijs (School for Applied Art) in Amsterdam,
which is now the Gerrit Rietveld Academie. After completing the
two and a half year course, she was the first student to receive a
prize for meritorious work. Among Cohen's first typographic
works were publications for the AJC, the youth organization of
the S.D.A.P. (Social Democratic Workers Party). Most of these were
strictly in the *Wendingen* style, characterized by heavy lines and
bold typefaces on dark paper and heavy ornaments created from
typographic linear material. Her professional connection with the
city of Amsterdam had begun even before she finished school,
and her first actual printed piece for the city printing office appeared in 1925. She began working for them full-time on September 1, 1929, and remained until 1932 when she was let go because
of stringent budget cuts. However, she continued to work for
them on a freelance basis until World War II.

3-13. Fré Cohen, *Overzicht der Muziek-geschiedenis* (Survey of Music History) by H. W. de Ronde, cover, circa 1930, 22 × 16 cm. Collection, Antiquariaat Schuhmacher, Amsterdam.

3-14. Fré Cohen, *Zomerfeesten Amsterdam, openlucht-uitvoeringen* (Amsterdam Summer Festivals, Open Air Performances), poster, 1934, 99 × 62 cm.

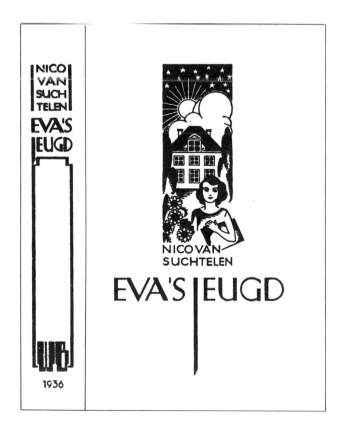

3-15. Fré Cohen, *Eva's Jeugd* (Eva's Youth) by Nico van Suchtelen, bookbinding, 1936, 19.5 × 12.5 cm. Collection, Alston W. Purvis, Boston, Massachusetts.

She also worked for a number of other municipal branches, including the energy company, the housing service, programs for the city theater, clean city campaigns, the Amsterdam summer festivals, the department of education, and the University of Amsterdam. Her work included posters, theater programs, books, annual reports, exhibitions, symbols, calendars, diplomas, brochures, checkbooks, and municipal reports and bookplates. Other clients included the publisher Querido in Amsterdam. Having seen the work of the Dutch Constructivists Schuitema and Zwart, she also experimented with photomontage in the 1930s.[14] One of the best examples of this side of her work is the cover for the Amsterdam municipal publication *La suppression des taudis et des quartiers insalubres à Amsterdam* (The elimination of the slums and unhealthy districts of Amsterdam) (Figs. 3-11 to 3-15).

Cohen's work for the AJC and the city of Amsterdam remained in the *Wendingen* style and had little to do with the concurrently developing functional typography. She did manage to skillfully tailor the *Wendingen* approach to accommodate government printing and remained a faithful devotee of the Wijdeveld style until her tragic death during the German occupation in 1943. This brought the *Wendingen* style to an end.

Chapter 4
Dutch Constructivism

Piet Zwart, Typotekt

During his long, influential, and prolific career, Piet Zwart worked in many spheres, often concurrently. These included graphic design, architecture, architectural criticism, furniture design, industrial design, painting, writing, photography, and design education. His association with the advanced design movements in other parts of Europe and his acquaintance with artists such as Schwitters, Berlage, Schuitema, Van Doesburg, Huszár, Rietveld, Wils, Kiljan, and Lissitsky all helped to crystallize his own convictions—and, if he would now permit us to say so, even his esthetic vision. Glimmers of the Bauhaus, De Stijl, Constructivism, Nieuwe Bouwen (New Construction), and Dada all surface in Zwart's oeuvre.[1]

Zwart was born in 1885 at Zaandijk in an industrial area north of Amsterdam, and had an extraordinarily productive and energetic life until his death in Wassenaar in 1977. Between 1902 and 1907 he studied at the Rijksschool for Kunstnijverheid (National School for Applied Arts), which was then based at the Rijksmuseum in Amsterdam. In those days the students' heroes were people such as Berlage, Lion Cachet, and other active pioneers in Dutch architecture and applied arts. At the Rijksschool Zwart took courses in architecture and drawing. He also learned a number of other crafts, such as copper embossing, weaving, batik, and woodworking. The last subject interested him the most; during his lifetime he made numerous articles for his own use, such as easels and weaving looms.[2]

After receiving his art school certificate and fulfilling the compulsory military service, he went to Leeuwarden in 1908, where he taught drawing and art history at the Industry and Household School for Girls. In 1913 he moved to Voorburg, a suburb of The Hague, to study architecture at the Technische Hoogschool (Institute of Technology) in nearby Delft. After a year his studies were interrupted when he was again called into military service due to the outbreak of World War I.

Until 1918, Zwart worked as a furniture and interior designer in a decorative manner influenced by Wijdeveld and the Amsterdam School. The only exceptions were some simple pieces of furniture that he made while teaching in Leeuwarden. It was then that he met Huszár and Wils, an independent architect in Voorburg who

had studied with Berlage. Both Wils and Huszár had been among the first members of De Stijl, but Wils left the group in 1919, feeling more and more removed from what he considered its obsession with theory. Zwart, Huszár, and Wils lived close to one another in Voorburg and often met at the Haagse Kunstkring (The Hague Art Circle) at exhibitions and lectures on modern art and music. Although Zwart's association with Huszár and Wils stimulated a dramatic change in his outlook, he never joined De Stijl and became indignant when anyone even suggested he had anything to do with the group. Both Zwart and the imperious Van Doesburg had very strong views, often diametrically opposed, and never really liked one another: on several occasions there were caustic verbal duels between the two. De Stijl, though, did have an impact on Zwart's development, and he felt an empathy for its purity, simplicity, use of primary colors, and sense of organization. But De Stijl's base was to him still too pictorial and not sufficiently committed to the new technology and construction methods.[3] Also, he strongly resisted what he considered to be its inflexible doctrines.

Zwart worked as a draftsman for Wils from 1919 until 1921. During this period the two engaged in endless dialogues on Berlage, De Stijl, Wijdeveld, and the "functional" approach of Frank Lloyd Wright. This was a different world for Zwart, whose schooling and mentality had been dominated by Art Nouveau and the arts and crafts movement.[4] One of his first known typographic works was a letterhead design for Wils, very much in the De Stijl manner and also showing strong overtones of the *Wendingen* style. Another was a bookplate design for E. G. de Roos (Fig. 4-1).

During his student days, Zwart had encountered the then prevalent, and sometimes innocent and quixotic, idealism and optimism. This led eventually to his reading Karl Marx and Friedrich Hegel and helped to crystallize his socialist philosophy on the responsibilities of the artist toward society. Later, he and many of his contemporaries believed that a new world order would arise out of the devastation of the Russian Revolution and World War I. They wanted to put the past behind them and to help create a new and better world. As with De Stijl, individualism, craft, and decoration were all part of a discredited world order. In the future, art would be based on technology, universality, abstraction, and functionalism. Many in the international avant garde believed in a social and artistic revolution through which art and daily life would become one.[5] Zwart wrote in 1919: "Our time has become characterized by an enthusiastic desire for change, born out of a growing discontent over social conditions, determined and guided by new means of production, new spiritual insights and new ideals."[6]

In 1921 Berlag hired Zwart as principal draftsman. It was an association that would last until the beginning of 1927. Although

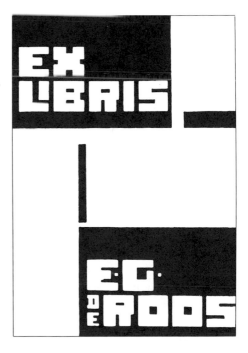

4-1. Piet Zwart, E. G. de Roos, bookplate, circa 1921, 6.5 × 4.5 cm. Collection, Antiquariaat Schuhmacher, Amsterdam. © Estate of Piet Zwart/VAGA, New York, 1991.

Zwart was given extensive freedom to develop in his own direction, Berlage was in charge. Zwart later wrote: "At that time the relationship of architect to co-worker was completely different from today. Assistants are now usually mentioned, at least if they are of any importance. In those days not, you were the humble employee, the architect was your employer and the relationship was quite fixed."[7] His first assignment for Berlage was to design a pressed-glass breakfast service for Hélène Kröller-Müller, whose collection formed the basis of the Kröller-Müller Museum at Otterlo. Other projects included plans for the new Gemeente Museum and the interior of the Christian Science Church at The Hague, complete with lecterns, church organ, lighting, stained glass windows, and signs. He also designed street furniture, street signs, and lampposts for the city.

At the age of 36 Zwart did his first typographic work for the Dutch representative of the importer Vickers House. The initial pieces suggest Huszár's approach in his 1917 cover for *De Stijl* and the bookplate design for Lena de Roos. The use of heavy horizontal and vertical bars recalls some of Zwart's earlier efforts with hand-drawn letters in the *Wendingen* style, and there is an overtone of engineering and solid construction. However, even in their formative stages Zwart's designs go much further than Huszár's and are far more playful and experimental (Figs. 4-2 to 4-5).[8] The trademarks XYLOS, LAGA, and IOCO are made into logotypes constructed within a square framework. These too are closely re-

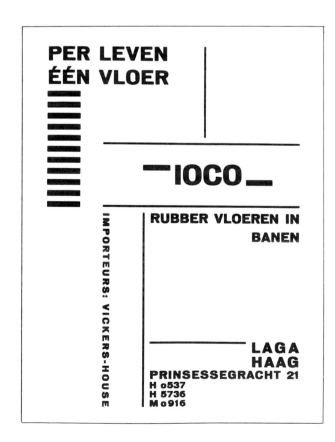

4-2. Piet Zwart, *IOCO Rubbervloeren in Banen* (Laga advertisement for rubber flooring), card, 1922, 11 × 15.5 cm. Collection, Antiquariaat Schuhmacher, Amsterdam. © Estate of Piet Zwart/VAGA, New York, 1991.

4-3. Piet Zwart, *Laga: Compagnie Den Haag, Vloeren* (Laga Company The Hague, Floors), envelope, 1923, 11 × 15.5 cm. Collection, Antiquariaat Schuhmacher, Amsterdam. © Estate of Piet Zwart/VAGA, New York, 1991.

4-4. Piet Zwart, *Laga: Compagnie, Haag, Vloeren* (Laga Company, The Hague, Floors), card, 1923, 15.3 × 10.7 cm. © Estate of Piet Zwart/VAGA, New York, 1991.

4-5. Piet Zwart, *Laga: Compagnie, Haag, Rubber Vloeren* (Laga Company, The Hague, Rubber Floors), Rubber bill statement, 1923, 12 × 30 cm. Collection, Antiquariaat Schuhmacher, Amsterdam. © Estate of Piet Zwart/VAGA, New York, 1991.

lated to the *Wendingen* style. Zwart's 1923 Vickers House metamorphic advertisement for "*zagen, boren en vijlen*" (saws, drills and files) clearly has its roots in *El Lissitsky suprematisch worden van twee kwadraten in 6 konstrukties* published by Van Doesburg in 1922 (Fig. 4-6). Like Lissitsky, Zwart made use of the visual pun, and a single *N* serves as the final letter of the first three words, *zagen, boeren en vijlen*. Then the design is shifted so that another *N* becomes the first letter of the word *Nu*. Finally, the *N* is transformed into an *H*, becoming the first letter of the words *Het* and *Haag*. The center diagonal stroke of the *H* is separated from the two verticals, and comes to a horizontal rest in the last stage. This design already shows hints of Zwart's phenomenal NKF advertisements, which began in 1923. The viewer is guided through the labyrinthine composition, an early example of Zwart's intent to include the time factor and structure information in a design. His strategy of directing the reader is now evident; he guides the reader through the text using letters and shapes as visual signals. In another advertisement for Vickers, no black is used at all; instead, he uses the complementary colors red and green. De Stijl is still very much present, but the overall design is much freer.

In 1923 Berlage introduced Zwart to his son-in-law, who was on the board of directors of the Nederlandsche Kabel Fabriek (Dutch Cable Factory). This began an extraordinary client–designer relationship that would continue until 1933. During these ten years, he produced no less than 275 advertisements for the *Tijdschrift voor Electrotechniek* (Magazine for Electro-technology) and the publication *Sterkstroom* (Strong Current). Essentially typographic, these advertisements constitute Zwart's major contribution to Dutch typography and form. Together with Werkman's *The Next Call* and Schuitema's work for the Berkel Scale and Meat-Packing Companies, it is the most original, venturesome, and provocative work by the avant garde in The Netherlands during this period. It is

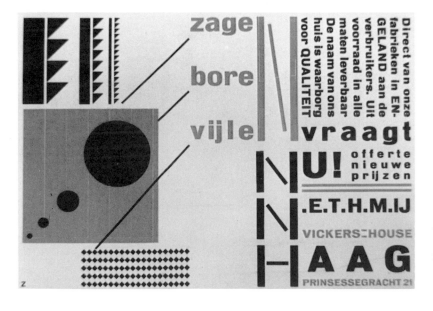

4-6. Piet Zwart, *zagen, boren, vijlen* (Vickers House advertisement for saws, drills and files), advertisement, 1923, 12×17 cm. © Estate of Piet Zwart/VAGA, New York, 1991.

the genesis of what would eventually change the face of Dutch graphic design.

Like most others during this period, Zwart was self-taught in typography, and although he had been designing printed pieces since the end of 1921, acquiring the Nederlandsche Kabel Fabriek as his main client made him realize just how little he actually knew about printing technology:

The first design that I made for the NKF was hand drawn. I was still not finished with it when the publication had already come out. At that time I realized that this was not a very good way to work and then plunged headfirst into typography. The nice thing about all of this was that I actually learned about it from an assistant in the small printing company where the monthly magazine in electro-technology was being produced. . . . After going through the bitter experience of that piece being too late, I made more sketches and then played typographic games with the assistant in the afternoon hours, how we could make this and that. . . . Actually, that's how I came to understand the typographic profession, I didn't know the terms, I didn't know the methods, I didn't even know the difference between capitals and lower case letters.[9]

Zwart's initial working methods were experimental: He would first make rough drafts and after ordering the typographic material would bring the original idea into focus, making, in a sense, typographic collages. The earliest advertisements are still very much in the Dada mode, with as many as five different typefaces on one page with a large bold letter, sometimes cut from linoleum, as the dominant component.[10] Later the advertisements become increasingly simpler, more open, and lighter, with an increased use of diagonals. There is greater use of white space, fewer typefaces, and more purely typographic elements. In 1929 NKF, which had previously been set in uppercase letters, was changed to lowercase. By 1924 the influence of Lissitsky on Zwart was evident, and some of the telephone cable advertisements of that year were again very close to pages from *El Lissitsky suprematisch worden van twee kwadraten in 6 konstrukties*.[11] The NKF assignment can be divided into four segments: the magazine advertisements (1923–1933); *Het Normalieënboekje* (Normalization Booklet) (1924–25) (Fig. 4-7); the 64-page catalog published in Dutch and English (1928–29); and the information booklet *Delft Kabels* (1933).[12] *Het Normalieënboekje*, one of Zwart's least known works, represents a turning point in his typography. One major difference is the use of an additional contrast, color, which was absent in the advertisements. However, color was included not as a decorative element, but more as a graphic cue.[13]

Zwart was imaginative, cogent, and decisive in his use of language, and in addition to being the designer of the NKF advertisements (Figs. 4-8 to 4-10), he acted as his own copywriter. A master of the visual pun, he amplified the intrinsic meanings of phrases and words by using basic typographic elements, and the text served as a catalyst for his creativity, with words and their interpretations

4-7. Piet Zwart, *? gaarne! Vraagt ons advies* (? Please ask our advice), N.K.F. Normalization booklet, 1924–25, 15.4 × 9.3 cm. © Estate of Piet Zwart/VAGA, New York, 1991.

4-8

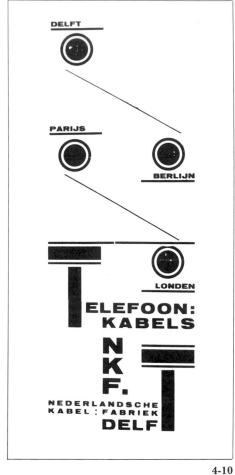

4-10

4-9. Piet Zwart, *Koper Kabel gevlochten voor spanleidingen* (Copper cable braided for tension control), NKF advertisement, 1924, 14×22 cm. © Estate of Piet Zwart/VAGA, New York, 1991.

4-8. Piet Zwart, *Telefoon Kabels* (Telephone Cables), NKF advertisement, circa 1924, 32×21.5 cm. © Estate of Piet Zwart/VAGA, New York, 1991.

4-10. Piet Zwart, *Telefoon Kabels* (Telephone Cables), NKF advertisement, 1924, 29×12 cm. © Estate of Piet Zwart/VAGA, New York, 1991.

merging into single entities, each reinforcing the other. Alliterations, ambiguities, similes, allusions, metaphors, hyperboles, reiterations, inferences, and contrasts of direction, positioning, axis, size, shape, and weight were all used to heighten the meaning and activate the page with a new and provocative energy.[14]

Anything extraneous was discarded, and only those parts that strengthened the meaning of the phrases were allowed.

Zwart referred to himself as *typotekt,* a combination of the words *typographer* and *architect.*[15] To a large extent this term did indeed express Zwart's conception of his profession—the architect building with stone, wood, and metal; the graphic designer building with typographic material and other visual elements: As the architect finds the right place for the windows, doors, and other parts of the building, the typographer assigns the positions of letters, words, lines, and images (Figs. 4-11 to 4-13). For Zwart, typography was also a question of ideology, and he wanted to free the reader from what he considered to be the monotonous typography of the past. Reading would now be a process that directly involved the reader. He felt that it would be possible through the new typography actually to change the way people read. Le Corbusier defined a house as a *machine à habiter,* and in the same sense Zwart's typography could be called a "machine for reading."[16]

Others such as the poets Mallarmé and Apollinaire in France, Van Ostaijen in Belgium, and Marinetti in Italy, had already accentuated words in their work through typography. Lissitsky had used this method in, for example, his poster *Beat the Whites with the Red Edge,* as had the Futurists and Dadaists. Zwart took the idea a step further by developing it into an unprecedented, transcendent, and feasible typographic method.

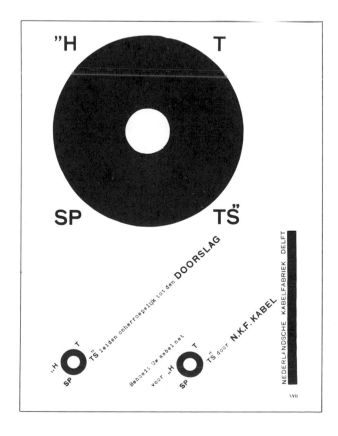

4-11. Piet Zwart, *Hot Spots*, NKF advertisement, 1925, 25 × 18 cm. © Estate of Piet Zwart/VAGA, New York, 1991.

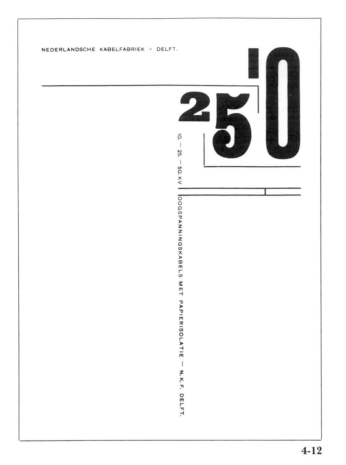

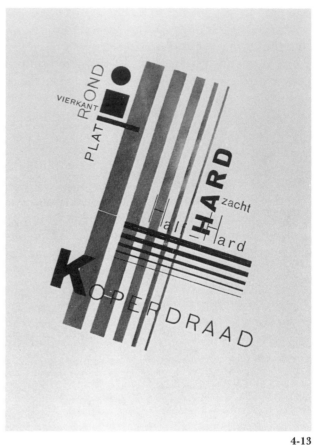

4-12

4-13

In 1923, when Zwart became acquainted with Schwitters and Lissitsky, the latter showed him the "photogram" process and his constructivist interpretation of Vladimir Mayakovsky's poem "For Reading Out Loud." In the photogram technique elements are placed on or above light-sensitive paper, which is then exposed to an enlarger light. Zwart included photograms in a *normalieënboekje* as early as 1924, but for the next several years they were used sparingly, for Zwart felt that their value in functional typography was limited.[17]

In 1925 Zwart produced for his own amusement a number of purely abstract compositions, which, like many of his advertisements, were composed on location at the printer. One, based on diagonals, clearly shows the Lissitsky influence. The use of color overprinting will later become a distinguishing ingredient in his work. These compositions reflect the same approach as the advertisements, but not being bound to texts, they move a step further into abstraction.

By 1925 Zwart's design statements, both verbal and visual, had become more succinct, substantive, clear, and decisive. Except for a few relapses, all superficialities and his earlier propensity to fill up the page disappeared, and the white spaces assumed an increasingly active role. The contrast in the size and weight of

4-12. Piet Zwart, *Hoogspanningskabels met papier isolatie* (High tension cables with paper insulation), advertisement, 1925, 25 × 18 cm. © Estate of Piet Zwart/VAGA, New York, 1991.

4-13. Piet Zwart, *Koperdraad, vierkant, rond, plat, hard, half-hard, zacht* (Copper wire, square, round, flat, hard, half-hard, soft), advertisement, 1925, 31 × 22 cm. Collection, Ex Libris, New York. © Estate of Piet Zwart/VAGA, New York, 1991.

letters gradually moved toward a spatial crescendo as Zwart pushed openness and voids to unexplored limits, and in spite of the infused humor and what Zwart referred to as "regulated dynamic tension," he succeeded in bringing about a phenomenal and provocative asymmetrical elegance. Any prior norms were now completely set aside, but even though the NKF designs do not adhere to any canons, self-imposed or otherwise, they do manifest a distinctive method (Figs. 4-14 to 4-17).

Later in 1938 Zwart referred to this as "functional" typography. Its purpose was "to establish the typographic look of our time, free, in so far as it is possible, from tradition; to activate typographic forms; to define the shape of new typographic problems, methods, techniques and discard the guild mentality."[18] Functional and constructive typography were basically one and the same. It was called *functional* because it discarded esthetic norms and was

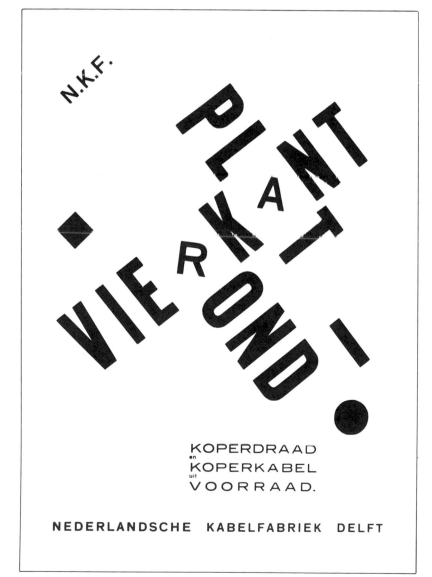

4-14. Piet Zwart, *Vierkant Plat Rond* (Square Flat Round), NKF advertisement, 1926, 25 × 18 cm. © Estate of Piet Zwart/VAGA, New York, 1991.

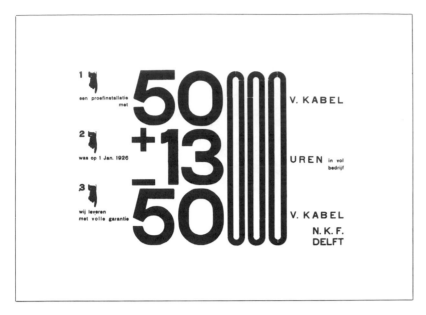

4-15. Piet Zwart, *1. een proefinstallatie met 50000 v. kabel 2. was op 1 Jan. 1926 + − 13000 uren in vol bedrijf 3. wij leveren met volle garantie 50000 v. kabel* (On Jan. 1 1926 a test installation with 50000 voltage cable was + − 13000 hours in complete operation. We deliver 50000 voltage cable with full guarantee.), NKF advertisement, 1926, 13.5×20 cm. © Estate of Piet Zwart/VAGA, New York, 1991.

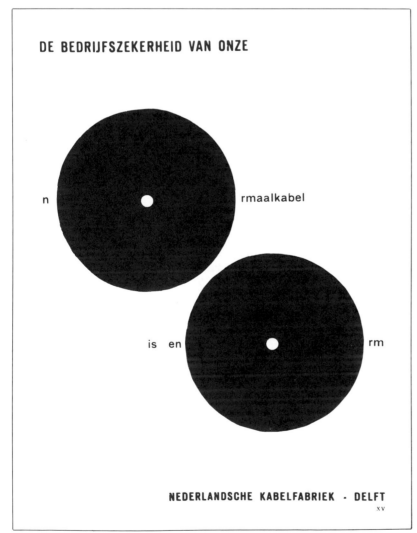

4-16

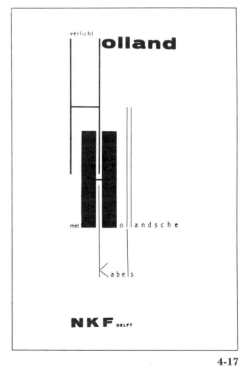

4-17

4-16. Piet Zwart, *De bedrijfszekerheid van onze Normaalkabel is een norm* (The dependability of our normal cable is a norm), NKF advertisement, 1926, 27×21 cm. © Estate of Piet Zwart/VAGA, New York, 1991.

4-17. Piet Zwart, *Verlicht Holland met Hollansche Kabels* (Light up Holland with Dutch Cables), NKF advertisement, 1926, 27×10 cm. © Estate of Piet Zwart/VAGA, New York, 1991.

based on purely utilitarian objectives; *constructive* because it had a rational structure and renounced subjectivity and relied on modern technology (Figs. 4-18 to 4-25).

As the printing of photographic reproductions became increasingly more feasible Zwart began to use them in his compositions, and by the summer of 1926 this "phototypography" also started to become part of his visual inventory. His first use of photographs was in the 1928–29 catalog for NKF in which he incorporated close-up cross-section photographs of electric cables. Products had never before been pesented with such clarity.[19] He achieved a dynamic balance between text, photograph, and white space on the page. Double-page spreads work as single compositions, and the catalog is distinguished by dramatic contrasts, asymmetry, and spaciousness.

The best examples of his use of photomontage are to be found in the 1933 Delft Kabels information booklet, the Brusse film monographs, and the postage stamp designs. As with any technical innovation, the use of photomontage and photograms was initially a topic of controversy, but eventually they were accepted as new mediums.

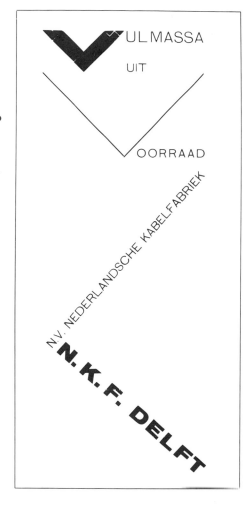

4-18. Piet Zwart, *Vulmassa uit Voorraad* (Large quantities from Stock) NKF advertisement, 1927, 27.5 × 10 cm. © Estate of Piet Zwart/ VAGA, New York, 1991.

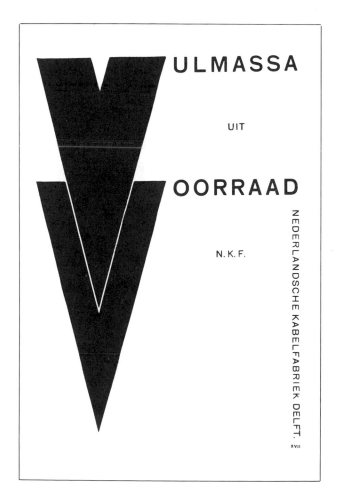

4-19. Piet Zwart, *Vulmassa uit Vooraad* (Large quantities from Stock) NKF advertisement, 1927, 30.5 × 21.5 cm. Collection, Ex Libris, New York. © Estate of Piet Zwart/VAGA, New York, 1991.

4-21

4-20

4-22

4-20. Piet Zwart, *Normaal Kabels* (Normal Cables), NKF advertisement, 1928, 27.5 × 11 cm. © Estate of Piet Zwart/VAGA, New York, 1991.

4-21. Piet Zwart, *n.k.f. Delft*, NKF advertisement, circa 1927, 22.8 × 30 cm. © Estate of Piet Zwart/VAGA, New York, 1991.

4-22. Piet Zwart, NKF catalog, cover, 1928, 29.7 × 21 cm. Collection, Ex Libris, New York. © Estate of Piet Zwart/VAGA, New York, 1991.

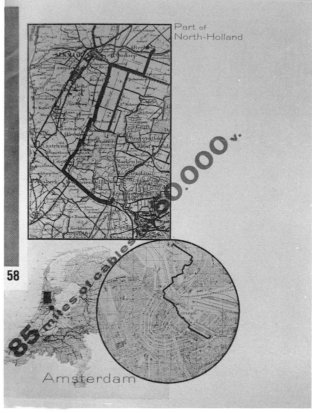

4-23. Piet Zwart, *Cable town,* page 55 from English NKF catalog, 1928–29, 29.7 × 21 cm. Collection, Antiquariaat Schuhmacher, Amsterdam. © Estate of Piet Zwart/VAGA, New York, 1991.

4-24. Piet Zwart, *85 miles of cable for 50,000 volts,* page from NKF catalog, 1928–29, 29.7 × 21 cm. Collection, Antiquariaat Schuhmacher, Amsterdam. © Estate of Piet Zwart/VAGA, New York, 1991.

4-25. Piet Zwart, *Koperdraad steeds uit voorraad leverbaar* (Copper wire still deliverable out of stocks), NKF advertisement, circa 1930, 27.5 × 10 cm. Collection, Ex Libris, New York. © Estate of Piet Zwart/VAGA, New York, 1991.

At first Zwart had to use the work of commercial photographers, but he soon became increasingly dissatisfied with the then-popular soft-focus approach, which was essentially an attempt to imitate painting. In 1928 he bought his own camera and very quickly learned the photographic technique. Within a year he was able to supply all of his own pictures. Zwart's work was characterized by sharp, fine-grained, close-up images and the use of angles and textures. He was also secretary of the Dutch contingent to FIFO, the 1929 international photography exhibition in Stuttgart where Zwart, Schuitema, and Kiljan were among the Dutch participants. After being exposed to the advanced work of photographers such as the American Edward Weston and the Russian Alexander Rodchenko, he lamented the rudimentary state of contemporary photography in The Netherlands.[20]

Zwart's designs fulfilled most of Jan Tschichold's criteria for *Elementare Typographie,* published in *Typographische Mittelungen* in 1925. Zwart's typography was functional, simple, and organized and restricted to basic typographic elements and photography. By 1930 he began to use mainly lowercase letters. The typefaces were unpretentious variations of sans serifs, nonessential decorative elements were excluded; color was used only for accent; and romantic "artistic" tendencies were rejected. With his 1925 card and envelope designs for the experimental theater group in The Hague, WijNu (We Now), Zwart briefly reverted to his Dada phase with a profuse use of assorted kinds and sizes of typefaces and symbols (Fig. 4-26).

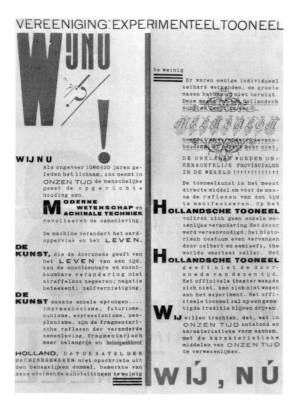

4-26. Piet Zwart, *Wij Nu Experimental Toneel* (We Now Experimental Theater), brochure, 1925, front, 29.2 × 21.2 cm. Collection, Antiquariaat Schuhmacher, Amsterdam. © Estate of Piet Zwart/VAGA, New York, 1991.

There was an active exchange of ideas between European graphic designers on the objectives and means of the new typography and phototypography. When Schwitters founded a group of "radical" designers in 1928, the Ring neue Werbegestalter, he invited Zwart to join the circle along with the Germany-based designers Jan Tschichold, Willi Baumeister, Cesar Domela Nieuwenhuis, Robert Michel, Walter Dexel, George Trump, Friedrich Vordemberge Gildewart, Max Burchartz, Hans Leistikow, Adolf Meyer, Werner Gräff, and Richter. It also included the Czecholslovakian Karel Teige and the Hungarian Moholy-Nagy. Schuitema joined in 1929, but, predictably, Van Doesburg declined. The principal objective of the Ring neuer Werbegestalter was to promote modern approaches in advertising design through exhibitions, articles, and lectures. Elementary design, functional design, and Constructivism all fitted in with their aims. Until 1930, the Ring neue Werbegestalter held exhibitions in many European cities, including Berlin, Hamburg, Hanover, Basel, and Rotterdam. Having at least partially accomplished its purpose of disseminating the new typography, it was dissolved in the spring of 1931.[21]

Not everyone was enthusiastic about the new functional typography, and in 1965 the Dutch design historian G. W. Ovink wrote about the mood of some of its detractors:

The evil did not bring on it's own destruction. Van Doesburg was followed by hotheads such as Piet Zwart and Paul Schuitema, who, without a good typographical education, plunged in and made crude and noisy things for Kabelfabriek and Van Berkel.[22]

In the 1929 V.A.N.K. yearbook, W. F. Gouwe, director of the Instituut voor Sier-en Nijverheidskunst (Institute of Decorative and Applied Arts) and secretary of the V.A.N.K., delivered a rebuttal to functionalism in favor of esthetics:

What principles guide the artist is a different question;—it is not so very important these days if artists in their functionalism feel so detached from "aesthetics," craftsmanship and applied art. . . . The balancing of proportions, the controlling and dividing of space, the handling of the power of color, have always been and still are activities for which the power comes from another source other than the intellect. And this power, this ability, is so much needed and sought after by industry, in everyday life, and not least by advertising, because it is active where the other, the intellect, is powerless, and it completes the process of formation."[23]

Another onslaught came from the interior designer Paul Bromburg in response to a 1929 V.A.N.K. lecture by Zwart:

Nowadays there is a new trend among artists to play the engineer. Everything has to look "machine produced," even if the machine has had nothing to do with the actual production. Everything has to look functional even in cases where there is no need for functionalism.[24]

Zwart had other clients in addition to the NKF. The most important was the PTT (the Dutch Post Office Telephone and Telegraph Service), which will be discussed in the next chapter. His monumental poster for the Internationale Tentoonstelling op

Filmgebied (International Film Exhibition) at The Hague again reflects his versatility as a designer. A central element is the logo ITF, which was also used on the front of the building during the exhibition. In black, red, and blue, its architectural structure shows Zwart at the height of his powers. The verticality of the red bars in the logo is repeated by a photogram made from a strip of film, also in red. In the lower center section of the composition, part of a face showing two eyes is framed in a white square. Seen as a unit, the white areas suggest an uppercase letter *F*.

Zwart's 1931 catalogue for The Hague printer Trio is one of his exceptional pieces. The page presenting their type collection is printed in black, red, blue, and yellow and is replete with over one hundred different typefaces ranging from large wooden display letters to text sizes. Even under this typographic cloudburst, he managed to realize a superb sense of unity and equilibrium. Every element, down to the smallest letter, is allocated its place.

Zwart's most important work for the publisher W. L. & J. Brusse of Rotterdam was a ten-part series of monographs on the film arts also produced in 1931 (Fig. 4-27). These rank among his finest work, and bring into focus many of the earlier experiments. Montage and multiple layers of ink are used throughout. Images are

4-27. Piet Zwart, *Serie Monografieën over Film-kunst, no. 7: Amerikaanse Filmkunst door Dr. J. F. Otten* (Series of Monographs on Film Arts, No. 7, American Film Arts) by Dr. J. F. Otten, cover, 1931, 22.5 × 18.5 cm. Published by W. L. and J. Brusse, Rotterdam. Collection Antiquariaat Schuhmacher, Amsterdam. © Estate of Piet Zwart/VAGA, New York, 1991.

distorted in the enlarger, as in issue number 9, where the face is elongated to counter the direction of the type. The play factor reigns, and all stops are pulled out with every conceivable contrast—size, color, direction, shape, and number as the images almost reach the realm of film itself. Another client from this period was the Rotterdam company Nijgh en Van Ditmar (Fig. 4-28). In this advertising booklet some of Zwart's now-familiar montage devices come to the forefront, especially the element of surprise and strong contrasts of size and direction. However, the use of capital letters on several of the pages was an unusual digression. Using his own text copy also gave him the opportunity to bring into being some of his ideas on advertising.[25]

Besides his own work, Zwart was committed to design education and felt that instead of teaching only painting, more attention should be devoted to advertising, modern reproduction methods, typography, photography, and film. In 1919, the same year that he began working for Wils, Zwart began teaching design and art history in the evening school at the Rotterdam Academy. Dick Elffers was one of his more prominent students. In 1931, Zwart presented a radical proposal to reorganize the course in "Decorators and Industrial Art." This was not well received by the board of directors, and Zwart was dismissed in 1933. A decade after the launching of *De Stijl* and eight years after the founding of the Bauhaus, design education in The Netherlands still seemed to be concerned with making attractive but useless ornamental objects. The most important influence was still the Amsterdam School, and only at the Academy of Fine Arts in Rotterdam was there any faint awareness of the developments that were taking place. The academy at The Hague unfortunately had not even reached this level, minimal as it was. In 1924 even the Applied Arts Department in the day school was discontinued. In the evening school, it

4-28. Piet Zwart, *Nijgh en Van Ditmar*, page from advertising booklet, 1931, 17.5 × 25 cm. © Estate of Piet Zwart/VAGA, New York, 1991.

was possible to study only lithography, artistic metalwork, decorative painting, and furniture design.[26]

Zwart was invited to come to the Bauhaus as a guest lecturer in 1929. He found the atmosphere depressing and students ready to leave, and in his opinion it had already become a part of history. He did, though, enjoy meeting some of the people there such as Albers. Zwart felt that

The greatest originality resulted from the tenacious search for restraint.... When students are given total license to create their own designs, the results are appalling. Rarely does one encounter an advertising exercise in which legibility has been given precedence. Triangles, squares and lines are arbitrarily used and simply to attract attention.... It is no small surprise that in all sectors of our discipline there is no advancement. The reason lies in the almost total dearth of proficient education.[27]

At the end of 1933 there was an abrupt change in Zwart's work as his attention turned more toward industrial and interior design. After a twelve-year period of ascendancy, he never again reached the heights of his earlier achievements in graphic design. Yet during that span, he earned his place among the modern masters of this medium.

Paul Schuitema, Visual Organizer

Paul Schuitema was born in the northern province of Groningen and from 1915 until 1920 studied drawing and painting at the Rotterdam Art Academy. From 1923 to 1925 he was the recipient of a Royal Grant for promising young artists, but even then he had already begun to entertain doubts as to a painter's role in the new society. By 1924 he was working as an advertising and industrial designer, the same year he was introduced to Zwart who, like Schuitema, was self-educated in typography.

Schuitema's first and most important clients were the P. van Berkel Meat Company, the Van Berkel Patent Scale and Cutting Machine Factory, and the printer C. Chevalier. He designed the trademark for Van Berkel, as well as booklets, brochures, advertisements, stationery, and exhibitions. Over the next five years his unprecedented designs for these Rotterdam companies would rank among the most innovative advertising typography in the history of graphic design, and in his hands what would have otherwise been pedestrian assignments were elevated to dynamic heights. From the very outset his approach was simple and to the point, and his emphasis on directness and clarity also made itself felt in his clients' product designs.

Schuitema's earliest work in typography was rudimentary and still displayed a glimmer of Wijdeveld and the Amsterdam School, but

over the next five years his development would be greatly influenced by Russian Constructivism and his contacts in the architectural association Opbouw (Construction) of which he, like Zwart, was a member (Figs. 4-29 to 4-31). Opbouw was founded in 1920 in Rotterdam by a group of functionally inclined architects, and the members included Oud, Mart Stam, and the city planner Cornelis van Eesteren (1897–1985). Another group of like-minded architects founded the association De Acht, (the Eight) and in 1928 they began publishing a joint periodical called *De Acht en Opbouw* (Fig. 4-32). Their first issue stated that *De Acht en Opbouw* was "concerned with the science of building rather than the art of building." For some time the members of Opbouw had been in touch with Schwitters, Lissitsky, the Bauhaus, and other figures and movements in the international art scene. Largely through them, Schuitema became aware of new developments taking place in The Netherlands and other parts of Europe. This awareness concerned not only typography, but also the Nieuwe Bouwen (New Construction) whose "form follows function" philosophy had a significant effect upon Schuitema.[28]

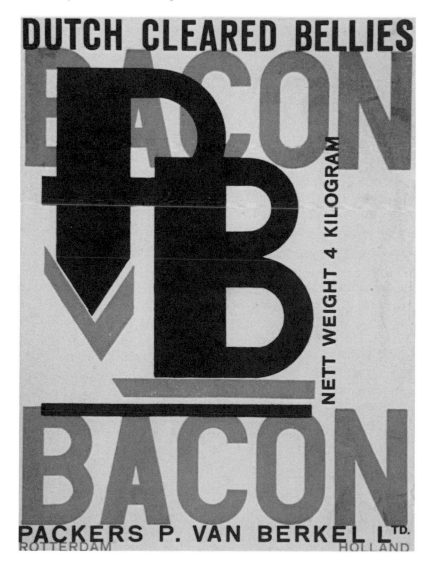

4-29. Paul Schuitema, *Dutch Cleared Bellies*, label, 1925, 19 × 14 cm. Collection, Schuitema, Wassenaar.

4-30. Paul Schuitema, *Onnauwkeurigheden zijn duur, constante betrouwbaarheid is goedkoop* (Inaccuracy is expensive, constant reliability is cheap), advertisement for Van Berkel Scales, 1927, 18.7×22.5 cm. Collection, Antiquariaat Schuhmacher, Amsterdam.

4-31. Paul Schuitema, *Toledo Berkel Snelwegers* (Toledo Berkel Speed Scales), advertisement, 1927, 19.9×14.1 cm. Collection, Antiquariaat Schuhmacher, Amsterdam.

Further changes in Schuitema's work were visible by 1927. Most vestiges of decoration had become history, and the pieces for Berkel now displayed a clearer and more functional, robust, and lucid use of typography. For him, design was now a question of unambiguous arrangement, planning, and control (Figs. 4-33 to 4-38). Dynamic effects were achieved through the use of light and bold letters and contrasts in type sizes, and there was often a subtle application of visual puns. The designs, no longer confined by the borders of the page, prompted a bountiful use of empty space. There was no "one-way traffic," and the reader was guided by graphic signals through the vertical, horizontal, and diagonal placement of text.[29] Through the free, asymmetrical, but rational grouping of words and the functional use of type, he created works of vibrant contrast, pushing designs to the very frontiers of instability. The type was narrowed to either sans serif or linear faces, and colors were also strictly limited and never blended. Red was the most important, followed by yellow and blue.

Antimilitarism and the social ideas for a changing society that originated in the renewal movements of the twenties did not escape Schuitema. He was never an active member of any particular political party, but like so many other artists of this period, he was associated with a number of leftist movements, such as the Internationale Antimilitaristische Vereeniging (International Anti-Militarism Association) and the Genootschap Nederland-Nieuw Rusland (Netherlands—New Russia Society).[30] His participation included producing covers and montages for the periodicals *De Wapens Neder* (Down with Weapons), *Nieuw Rusland* (New Russia), and *Links Richten* (Aim Left) (Fig. 4-39), and in August 1932 Schuitema took part in the World Congress against War. Former students from his teaching years at The Hague recall extended discussions on the duty of the graphic designer in the class struggle and his responsibility to the masses.[31] Schuitema's 1929 cover

4-32. Paul Schuitema, *De 8 en Opbouw 11*, cover, Schuitema, 1932, 28.7 × 22.1 cm. Collection, Schuitema, Wassenaar.

4-33. Paul Schuitema, *Snijdt witbrood, bruinbrood, roggebrood, koek, cake, snel, economisch, hygienisch* (The cutting machine cuts white bread as well as brown bread, rye bread, gingerbread, cake, quickly, economically, hygienically), advertisement, 1927, 8 × 17 cm. Collection, Schuitema, Wassenaar.

4-34. Paul Schuitema, Van Berkel's VP5 Snijmachine (Van Berkel's VP5 Cutting Machine), 1928, 19.5 × 23.5 cm. Collection, Schuitema, Wassenaar.

4-35. Paul Schuitema, Berkel Stand 3000, Utrechtsche Jaarbeurs Machine, circa 1928, 10.5 × 16 cm. Collection, Antiquariaat Schuhmacher, Amsterdam.

for the special number of *De Wapens Neder, 25 Jaar Oorlog aan Oorlog* (Down with Weapons, 25 Years of War against War), prominently displayed the defiant face of Ferdinand Domela Nieuwenhuis, a former Lutheran minister who became one of the most famous Dutch socialists of his day. His son was the painter and designer Domela Nieuwenhuis (Fig. 4-40).

Schuitema later wrote about these years in a 1961 article for the Swiss publication *Neue Grafik*:

The 1914–1918 war had shown us that everything, even the most beautiful expressions, were nonsense. Romance had gone under in mud and blood. Beauty, heroism, patriotism existed only for the sake of money and was dirty and untrue and full of false pathos. Art was the property of the rich. The socialist cry "art for the people" was also seen as sentimental

nonsense. It should not be the task and duty of society to grant commissions. The people should not wear secondhand clothing and become a new bourgeoisie.[32]

The Russian Revolution had in many ways served as a catalyst and an inspiration. Art for art's sake was no longer a valid goal, and the artist now had an irrefutable obligation toward society and the proletariat. The arts and crafts movement and Art Nouveau were repudiated as decadent and sentimental. New and dynamic technological means would be required to realized the new objectives. Schuitema continued in the same *Neue Grafik* article: "Mondrian rang the death knell for painting, this creation on the easel, a product of super-individualists. The era of painting was over. Neither should one make socialist paintings, since in our opinion this type of art could not exist."[33]

Although practical circumstances required Schuitema to accept the necessity of commercial advertising, he always emphasized that there were stringent guidelines as to how and when it could be ethically made and used. He again stressed the social responsibility of the artist:

When producing printed material one must begin with the principle that the function of advertising is to sell. It should tell the truth and portray to the public the benefits of the products. We acknowledged industrial products as necessary. It was the duty of the artist to give them a clearer and more functional form. Through our work in the workplaces and factories we wanted to give the people better and more beautiful things. At that time we had already contributed to industrial design, even though the term had not yet been coined. We intended to give products a new functional form.[34]

Typography should not misinterpret the text, but instead provide it with more possibilities for visual interpretation. Schuitema further contended that form must be determined not through preconceptions or individual desires, but through an objective assessment of the problem at hand, a natural consequence of purpose and means. "Order originates through making individual perceptions subordinate to the general issue. . . . The search for special forms for the sake of form is sheer nonsense."[35] Additional inspiration was found in the Bauhaus and in Russian Constructivism, where the quest for new forms was linked with the search for a new society.[36] Schuitema wanted to become directly involved with the products and the actual means of production. Manual labor and the tradition arts and crafts were out of tune with the times, and modern industrial methods were both desirable and necessary for a new society. For him, the new approach to advertising presented unlimited possibilities (Figs. 4-41 and 4-42).

Preceding Zwart, Schuitema pioneered the photograph as an important design element. Through the combination of photographs and type, he reduced the entire design to presenting essential information clearly, legibly, and quickly. This contrasted with con-

4-36. Paul Schuitema, *Groot en Duidelijk* (Large and Clear), advertisement for Van Berkel Scales, 15.5×22.5. Collection, Antiquariaat Schuhmacher, Amsterdam.

4-37. Paul Schuitema, *Berkel, het grootste weeginstrumenten concern ter wereld* (Berkel, the largest scale instrument concern in the world), double-page spread from catalog, 1927, 19.9×14 cm.

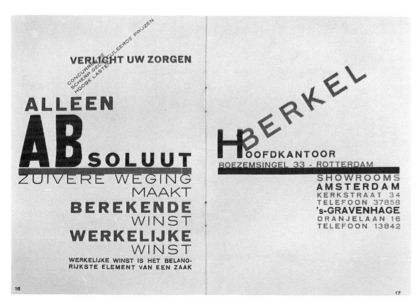

4-38. Paul Schuitema, *Verlicht uw zorgen, alleen absoluut zuivere weging maakt berekende winst werkelijk winst* (Lighten your worries, only absolute pure weighing makes calculated profits actual profits), double-page spread from catalog, 1927, 19.9×14 cm.

ventional advertising, which was distinguished by a want of meaningful facts and nebulous design utilizing arbitrary, eye-catching gimmicks, decorative material, and banal illustrations. Beginning in 1926, photography was used more and more; if something had to be drawn, it was abstracted and simplified. "No golden section, no drawing, since that would be like painting. When we did draw, it would be abstract or aiming at an objective, greatly simplified, direct and without ulterior, romantic motives."[37]

For Schuitema, photography was the natural medium for his advertisements. Like Zwart, in the beginning he relied mainly upon the Rotterdam photographer Jan Kamman. However, he soon became disenchanted by the styles of professional photographers and in 1927, like Zwart in 1928, he taught himself the technique. He concentrated on what he considered to be the intrinsic aspects of objects and went on to emphasize these essentials through color, size, type, and contrast of graphic elements. He felt that few words were necessary if the products were clearly represented.[38]

Schuitema considered the dissemination of information to be a fundamental basis for art, and photography one of the most important mediums for bringing this about. Using the pseudonym S. Palsma to avoid any problems with his commercial clients, he wrote an article for the short-lived magazine *Links Richten* titled "The Photograph as a Weapon in the Class Struggle" in which he discussed photography as a weapon for political agitation: "No romanticism, no art, but vividly suggestive propaganda; tactically geared to the class struggle, technically attuned to the trade. . . . The photograph reports, gives the situation as it is, does not lie, is not dependent upon a special explanation, can never be disputed."[39]

Schuitema felt that while the general public considered his work harsh, cold, and without emotion, unsophisticated people such as workers and farmers understood. "They had not been raised in an artistic cultural environment. They had never been bothered with these matters. They understood and grasped our work, not because they were cleverer, but because their whole life was occupied with work, with the goal of saving their bare lives and supporting their families." As Dick Dooijes so aptly observed, this resolute "anti-romantic" hero had a brief romantic lapse, one with Marxist overtones.[40]

On the basis of these principles, Schuitema, Zwart, and the designer and educator Gerard Kiljan introduced photographs as active design elements. In 1933, Schuitema and Kiljan consolidated their ideas on photography in an article titled "The Photograph as a Visual Element in Advertising":

4-39. Paul Schuitema, *Links Richten 1* (Aim Left), monthly periodical for Labor-Writers Collective, magazine cover, September 1932. Appeared Sept. 1932–Aug. 1933, 16.2×24, cm. Collection, Antiquariaat Schuhmacher, Amsterdam.

4-40. Paul Schuitema, *25 jaar oorlog aan den oorlog* (25 years of war against war), magazine cover, back and front, 1929, 29.6×23.8 cm; cover for the magazine *De Wapens Neder* (The Weapons Under). Collection, Antiquariaat Schuhmacher, Amsterdam.

Through the influence of pacesetters in the design field and through the phenomenon of technological development and the tremendous increase in the influence of photographic illustration in dailies and weeklies, the photograph and also montage have materialized in advertising design. . . . We maintain from the beginning, though, that we regard the photograph only as a plastic—or design element in the plastic organization of an advertising assignment.[41]

However, Schuitema did exhibit his photographs as independent images on numerous occasions, one being at a 1929 exhibition put on by the De Rotterdamsche Kring (The Rotterdam Circle).

Photographs also gave the page a suggestion of the third dimension. For Schuitema they were not just illustrations to accompany the texts, but instead vital design and expressive elements. No longer were they simply placed above, under, or beside the type as before; now they became an integral part of the entire statement.[42] Photomontage provided a means of merging incongruous elements and situations into single entities and the possibility to contrast large and small images. Since a montage was not bound to the rectangular format of the photograph, it was easier to connect the images with the less defined areas of text, allowing the image to become more plastic and effective. Often a movement suggested in a photograph was repeated in other parts of the de-

4-41. Paul Schuitema, *Berkel snijmachines en snelwegers zijn veel meer waard dan wat zij kosten, de baten zijn voor U* (Berkel cutting machines and quick scales are worth much more than what they cost, the benefits are yours), advertisement, 1927–28, 23 × 15.5 cm.

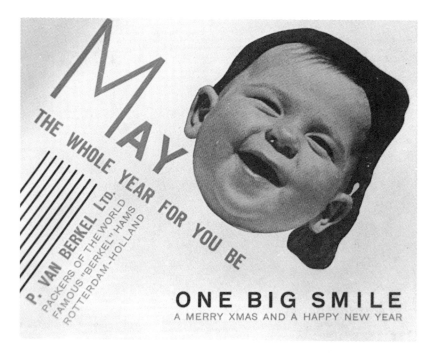

4-42. Paul Schuitema, *VBP Snijmachine Olie* (VBP Cutting Machine Oil), label, 1928, 16.2 × 38 cm.

4-43. Paul Schuitema, *One Big Smile*, card, 1928, 12.3 × 15.1 cm.

sign.[43] By using printing runs on top of one another, text and image became an even more integrated unit.

Schuitema's ingenious work in montage was clearly influenced by the Russian and German artists, and some of his pieces, the Van Berkel greeting cards in particular, recall the work of the Russian artist Alexander Rodchenko. The whimsical 1929 montage advertisement for Nutricia powdered milk shows the humorous face of Dick Elffers, then a student at the Rotterdam Academy, peering through the crowd (Figs. 4-43 to 4-47).

4-44

4-45

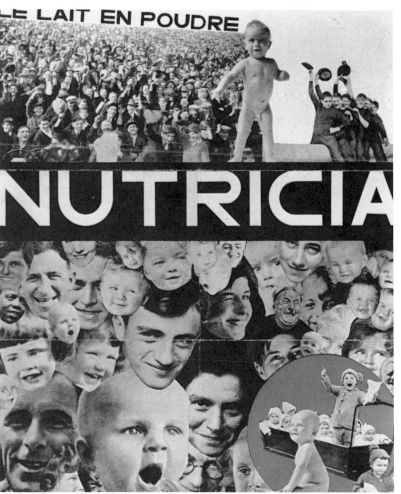

4-46

4-44. Paul Schuitema, A Merry Xmas and a Happy New Year, card, P. Van Berkel Ltd. Meat Packing, 1928, 14.8 × 12.1 cm.

4-45. Paul Schuitema, Back of Berkel advertising folder, advertisement, circa 1928, 28.5 × 21 cm.

4-46. Paul Schuitema, *Nutricia*, advertisement for milkpowder, 1929, 36.7 × 30 cm. Collection, Antiquariaat Schuhmacher, Amsterdam.

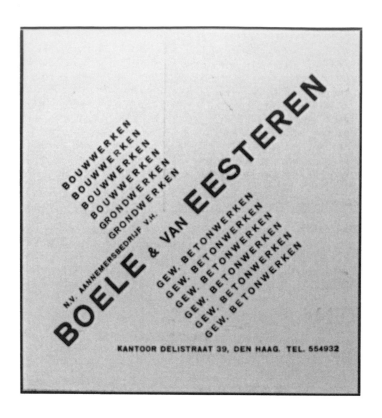

4-47. Paul Schuitema, *Boele & van Eesteren,* advertisement, 1928, 11.8 × 11 cm. Collection, Schuitema, Wassenaar.

In 1927, the progressive magazine *i 10* was founded by Arthur Müller Lehning, with Oud as its architecture editor and Moholy-Nagy the designer and editor for film and photography. Its purpose was to provide an international forum to promote the integration of art and society. During its two-year existence, its contributors included Huszár, Kandinsky, Mondrian, Roland Holst, Oud, Moholy-Nagy, Rietveld, Schwitters, Stam, Arp, and Schuitema (Figs. 4-48 to 4-50). The contributors included many De Stijl defectors as well as some of the current collaborators. As expected, Van Doesburg was irate and in *De Stijl* referred to the contents of *i 10* as leftovers from his trash can.

At the end of 1928, Schuitema published an article in *i 10* entitled "Advertising" in which he presented his convictions on the role of the contemporary designer. He wrote:

Yesterday was "artistic, decorative, symbolic, fantastic, anti-social, lyrical, passive, romantic, aesthetic, theoretical, craftsmanship-like," in other words "art." "Today" means: "real, direct, photographic, succinct, competitive, argumentive, active, actual, appropriate, practical, technical," in other words "reality."

Both postures were represented with designs, two of them his own. One of his first designs, a 1925 poster for Opbouw, represented "yesterday," and the poster for Nutricia met his standards

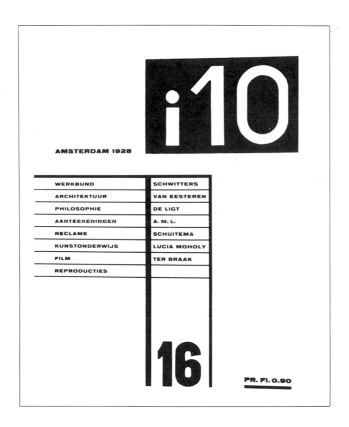

4-48. Moholy-Nagy, Laszlo, *i 10, International Review* no. 16, cover, editor and publisher, Arthur Müller Lehning, 1928, 29.5 × 20.5 cm. Collection, Antiquariaat Schuhmacher, Amsterdam.

4-49. Paul Schuitema, *i 10, International Review no. 17,* 1928, Schuitema's layout article on advertising, editor and publisher, Arthur Müller Lehning; 1928, 29.5 × 20.5 cm. Collection, Antiquariaat Schuhmacher, Amsterdam.

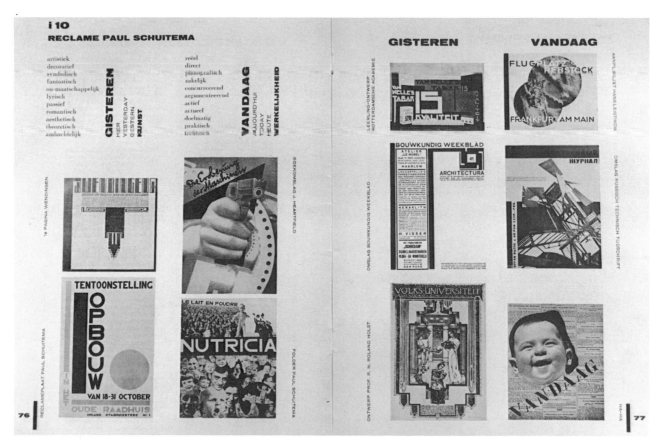

4-50. Paul Schuitema, *Politiek en Cultuur* (Politics and Culture), by Arthur Müller Lehning, book cover, 1931, 22 × 17 cm. Collection, Antiquariaat Schuhmacher, Amsterdam.

for "today" or "reality."[44] Even though Schuitema was influenced by Wijdeveld in the beginning, a title page from *Wendingen* as well as a poster by Roland Holst were relegated to the past. A montage book cover by John Heartfield, a placard for the city of Frankfurt by Hans Leistikow, and a cover for a Russian technical magazine signaled the future.

Schuitema's work for the two Van Berkel companies came to an end in 1930, and the large number of designs and exhibition stands for these companies displayed a definitive unity that can be viewed as one of the first total corporate design concepts in The Netherlands.[45] In the same year, he made a number of designs for the Rotterdam furniture and lamp manufacturer W. H. Gispen. Among them were catalogs, and at least two advertisements for *Wendingen*. Gispen knew Schuitema through Opbouw and admired his work, and as early as 1927 Schuitema was making photographs for the Gispen concern. He was an ideal choice,

since his products utilized the latest technology and the most advanced industrial design.

Since the early thirties he had been involved with the radical film group *Filmliga,* and designed covers for their magazine. Also, the collage design of the 1933 jacket for *Stad* by Ben Stroman is unique for this period. Some designs for the printer Chevalier and the publisher Brusse concluded his work for the Rotterdam companies (Figs. 4-51 to 4-54). Schuitema's interest in montage inevitably led him to filmmaking, and as with still photography, he learned the technique on his own, even developing and printing films himself. His first film was on the Rotterdam Maas Bridges, which he began in 1931, and later in the thirties he made two more documentaries, *De Hallen* on the Paris food market and *De Bouwhoek,* a district in the northern province of Friesland. Schuitema later wrote: "The meaning of film lay in its being a mass communication medium that directly stimulated the fantasy of the public and provided a propaganda tool of extraordinary power."[46] After moving to The Hague in 1935, one of his most successful uses of montage is seen in an advertising brochure for N.V. De Vries Robbé/N.V. Betondak in which he showed the com-

4-51. Paul Schuitema, *C. Chevalier,* blotting-paper advertisement, 1929, 23 × 11.1 cm. Collection, Antiquariaat Schuhmacher, Amsterdam.

4-52. Paul Schuitema, *Gonnermann en Co.,* 1905–1930, advertisement, 1930, 18.4 × 9.9 cm. Collection, Antiquariaat Schuhmacher, Amsterdam.

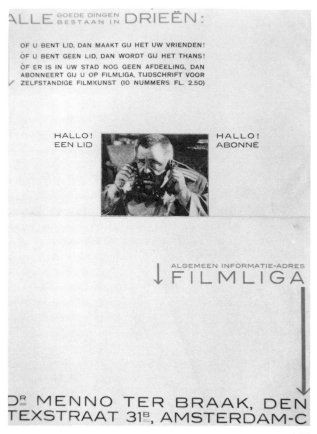

4-53

4-54

4-53. Paul Schuitema, *Filmliga*, brochure (unfolded), circa 1931, 48.8 × 31.9 cm. Collection, Antiquariaat Schuhmacher, Amsterdam.

4-54. Paul Schuitema, *Filmliga*, magazine cover, 1932, 30 × 21 cm. Collection, Antiquariaat Schuhmacher, Amsterdam.

pany's entire production process through this medium. Other clients included the construction company Boele en van Eesteren. This work brought his most characteristic period to a close (Fig. 4-55).

In the 1961 article for *Neue Grafik,* Schuitema elaborated on the objectives of Functionalism:

Each object, each letter, each form, each sound, each color should have a function. Also, the artist should have a functional role in society . . . a letter should support the function of reading, nothing else. It should have a clear and functional form, and not be elegant, not be feminine. It's beauty is in its function, and nothing mysterious should be sought behind or beyond it.[47]

This had been touched upon in the 1933 article by Schuitema and Kiljan titled "The Photograph as a Visual Element in Advertising." Here, however, the economical was emphasized as an organizational requirement:

This goes for the typeface as well, not because we consider this or that typeface more beautiful, squarer, rounder, straighter or more modern, but because we choose this or that typeface as the most appropriate for this objective . . . that is to say get the maximum result from a minimum of means, or in other words exploit every resource to the utmost. . . . the

4-55. Paul Schuitema, *Scheveningen*, booklet, double-page spread, possibly influenced Zwart's het boek van PTT 1936, 21 × 14.5 cm. Collection, Antiquariaat Schuhmacher, Amsterdam.

fact that well organized printing sometimes looks empty is not due to the aesthetic choice to have it white but a necessary result of the economical use of the medium. . . . beautiful and ugly are notions that today are impossible to rely on. These are situations over which exist so many differences of opinion that they certainly cannot be applied as norms. As a standard for something good we proffer objectivity, not aesthetics, which is a question of taste.[48]

Clarity through a minimum number of elements was the hard and fast rule. Any reference to mere esthetics was taboo, although it is clear in retrospect that esthetics did manage to slip through the net, albeit in a revolutionary form.

Schuitema always emphatically denied that he, along with Zwart and others, was attempting to establish a new design system:

Formalism was completely rejected by us. The new form should grow from itself and flow naturally from the matter at hand, resulting from the problems posed, the function and the material. The form was not conditioned in advance but resulted from an attitude toward life . . . it is a mistake to assume that the works stemming from this period are a new way of design. Today we are referred to as pioneers, but we never thought of ourselves as pioneers, even though we obviously wanted to make a pioneering effort to clarify things. We did not want to make new conquests but instead to confirm that the entire society was changing. . . . Evidently there were always snobs who believed that we had created a new, exclusive and sensational type of design. We are aware that misconceptions were to arise under the given circumstances. However, clients understood our work as a new expression which was both economical and pragmatic.[49]

Schuitema continued working until his death in 1973, although his innovative contribution to Dutch graphic design was over by the late thirties. A master of visual hierarchy in design, his greatest achievement lay in his concise structure of the total image. For

him design was always a question of arrangement, planning, and regulation. He was not making a whimsical comment when he referred to himself as a "visual organizer."

Schuitema and Zwart: Idealism and Practice

The foundations for much of Dutch graphic design produced after 1945 can be found in the work of Schuitema and Zwart, and reflection emphasizes both their similarities and differences. In both, the play element is always present. With Zwart, especially in the NKF advertisements, there is a definitive elegance and poetic tendency that is far removed from the more direct and unassuming approach of Schuitema.

A provocative question is how Schuitema, Zwart, and other innovative graphic designers sharing similar progressive political outlooks and radical convictions could, at the same time, produce their most important work for capitalist commercial interests. Both Schuitema and Zwart always maintained that they worked in the advertising sector for idealistic as well as material reasons. Not only were they attempting to discard the uniformity and boredom that characterized the typography of their time, but they also wanted to bring about a renewal of society and felt that artists could play an effective social role only through emerging from their elitist isolation. Paul Schuitema touched upon this issue in a 1928 talk for Arti et Industriae:

The Arts and Crafts as hand-work can only be sustained by a class of people who have enough money to pay the prices that these techniques demand; since this constitutes only a small segment of the present population, the arts and crafts are an absurdity and a personal hobby—in this way inhuman. . . . Individual labor has had its day and has done its part to clear the way for something else.[50]

The goal of an integration between art and society was also actively pursued by artists in the Soviet Union and the Bauhaus in Germany. Similar ideas were addressed in the De Stijl manifesto of 1918:

The artists of today, driven by a parallel consciousness throughout the entire world, on the intellectual terrain have participated in the war against the dominance of individualism, the arbitrary. Therefore, they sympathize with everything, be it intellectual or material, that strives for an international unity of life and culture.[51]

Schuitema and Zwart regarded modern production methods as necessary, even desirable, for a new society, but they also knew that technology alone was not enough to solve existing social problems. Although they designed advertisements for industrial clients, they were never blind to the fact that a radical change in society would be necessary to bring the actual products to the

masses, and they used their talents to serve this end well. Examples are Schuitema's covers for the magazines *Wapens Neder* and *Links Richten*.

Both Schuitema and Zwart were deeply influenced by their architectural colleagues in the Opbouw who, through modern technical means and materials, had been able to put their theories on contemporary achitecture into practice. In advertising, Zwart and Schuitema saw an opportunity to play a similar role while at the same time exposing a larger part of the public to their ideas. Schuitema and Zwart were not alone in the apparent discrepancy between practice and idealism. Many designers served with comparative ease both big business and their own personal political standards. Lissitsky's poster *Beat the Whites with the Red Wedge* was followed by his advertisements for the capitalist company Pelikan-Werke in Hanover. Another case is Domela Nieuwenhuis who, with no apparent pang of conscience, turned out anarchist book covers and brochures while at the same time producing advertising.[52]

The principal legacy of Schuitema and Zwart was confined mainly to advertising and had little effect on book design. As Dooijes observed, this was partially the result of an intrinsic conservatism in the book publishing sector. But it was also because existing book design, with a few noticeable lapses, had already proved to be very functional for more than four centuries.[53] This leads to a question regarding the realization of Functionalism itself: Was Functionalism actually reachable? *Functional* refers either to the way that something is formed or to the way that it is applied. Le Corbusier and some of his disciples have shown us that modern architecture can be functional both in its conception and its construction, but at times impossible to live in. Similarly, the point of departure in functional typography often overshadowed the concluding objective: Many designs were functionally formulated and functionally made but did not always realize the purposes for which they were intended.[54]

Chapter 5
The Traditional Designers

The Classical Vanguard

While Van Doesburg, Zwart, Schuitema, and others were approaching new typographic frontiers, another faction, albeit discrete, was searching for a new vitality with no less tenacity. This group was comprised of designers who remained totally committed to the classical style, and for them Dada, De Stijl, Constructivism, and the Wijdeveld style were the equivalent of personal affronts.

Leading this traditional vanguard were De Roos and the brilliant Van Krimpen who worked, respectively, for the N. V. Lettergieterij Amsterdam (Type Foundry Amsterdam) and Joh. Enschedé en Zonen at Haarlem. They were followed by J. F. van Royen and the two master printer-publishers from Maastricht, Charles Nypels (1895–1952) and A. A. M. Stols (1900–1973). Although there were clear professional connections and affinities among these protagonists, they were never in any sense a movement, partly because of the great contrast in their ages—which, in fact, separated them into two generations: De Roos (born 1877) and Van Royen (1878); Van Krimpen (1892), Nypels (1895), and Stols (1900). The fundamental reason, however, was their wide dissimilarity in quality and approach. They too wanted to foster a renaissance in Dutch typography, but most of them did not consider the Industrial Revolution a blessing. On the contrary, mass production was viewed as a necessary evil, cautiously tolerated, principally because of economic considerations. To them it meant only undistinguished paper, ugly typefaces, appalling halftones, and shoddy inking on cylinder presses.[1]

They sought to revive the printing arts through a return to exacting traditional standards. Their guidelines included symmetrical layouts, tranquil harmony and balance, careful margin proportions, proper letter and word spacing, single traditional typefaces in as few sizes as possible, exact letterpress printing, and in some cases, the use of decorative rules and borders. Extra decoration, though, was gradually phased out entirely, and in this respect their work displayed a Calvinist restraint when compared to the products of Art Nouveau. Above all, their view of a typographer was one who should first serve the text and stay in the background. In the eyes of the Constructivist vanguard, this approach produced little more than monotonous gray masses of type. At times it became all-out ideological warfare between the two camps, and only in rare instances was there ever any rapport.

Sjoerd H. de Roos

De Roos first received practical training in lithography and from 1895–1898 took a general course in art at the Rijksacademie in Amsterdam. Most signs indicated a career in painting. In 1900, Berlage, the silversmith W. Hoeker, and the interior designer J. van den Bosch founded Het Binnenhuis (The Interior) in Amsterdam, a progressive industrial and interior design firm that produced and exhibited well-made and well-designed industrial products. In addition to the founders, associates included De Bazel and Lauweriks. At the age of 23 De Roos was hired by Het Binnenhuis as an assistant draftsman, working principally as a furniture and fabric designer. At this early stage he became acutely aware of the dismal state of contemporary typography, and the revival of Dutch book design soon became his singular passion. De Roos designed his first stamped binding for the poet C. S. Adama van Scheltema's *Uit den Dool* in 1901, effectively beginning his career as what many consider to be the first Dutch typographic designer.[2]

To provide a better income, De Roos left Het Binnenhuis in 1903 and worked as a designer of labels for a tin can manufacturer. In the same year the Social-Democrat publisher A. B. Soep gave him an opportunity to design the book *Kunst en Maatschappij* (Art and Society), a translation of a collection of essays by William Morris (Figs. 5-1, 5-2). Legibility was a top priority, and in spite of many anachronistic leftovers from the previous century, this is considered by many to be one of the first well-designed and "modern" twentieth-century books in The Netherlands. It was, at least, a beginning of a new approach. Unlike Morris, De Roos did not attempt simply to imitate the incunabula. The book was set in the relatively new face designed by and named for the Swiss-French architect and typographic designer Eugène Grasset, an elegant typeface cast by the German foundry Genzsch & Heyse. This was the only book designed by De Roos in the Art Nouveau style, and although because of its simplicity and harmony it was unique for Dutch book design of that day, it was clearly very far removed from his ultimate objectives. Later his major influences would be Morris, Berlage, Daniel Berkeley Updike, Bruce Rogers, and the writings of J. W. Enschedé.

The design for *Kunst en Maatschappij* was noticed by Berend Modderman, director of Ipenbuur & Van Seldam, the Amsterdam printer that produced it. In 1907, he and J. W. Enschedé, librarian and publicist in the printing and book arts, commissioned De Roos to design the second *Drukkersjaarboek* (Printers Annual). De Roos drew the seven initial letters and produced the layout and the stamps for the binding. The result displayed an uncommon unity of elements for that period and was set in a new typeface, Nordische Antiqua, later called Genzsch Antiqua. This was a piv-

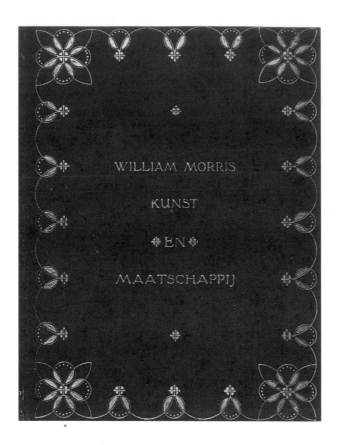

5-1. S. H. de Roos, *Kunst en Maatschappij* (Art and Society), book binding, 1903, 22 × 16 cm. Collection, Antiquariaat Schuhmacher, Amsterdam.

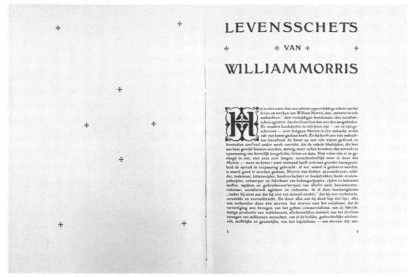

5-2. S. H. de Roos, *Kunst en Maatschappij* (Art and Society), title page, 1903, 22 × 16 cm. Collection, Antiquariaat Schuhmacher, Amsterdam.

otal point in De Roos' career and resulted in his being hired as artistic assistant at the Type Foundry Amsterdam (formerly N. Tetterode), a productive association that continued until 1941.[3]

It was De Roos' resolute conviction that the typeface was the foundation of sound book design and that ideally it should be practical and beautiful, clearly and easily readable and make possible the accurate and functional reproduction of the spoken language. The words formed from the letters should produce a tranquil and

easily flowing unit, while at the same time giving an esthetic appearance to the page. He felt that "legibility must not be impaired through beautiful form, and the beautiful form of a certain type must not be achieved at the expense of the total image."[4] In an article titled *American Book Art* for the 1908 Printers Annual, De Roos outlined his esthetic convictions:

The eye desires balance. The greater the refinement of the viewer, the more insistent his need for equilibrium, proportion and harmony. If these requirements are not met, a technically perfect design is not in a position to be called a thing of beauty.[5]

In De Roos' opinion no indigenous typeface in The Netherlands satisfied all these requisites. He felt that a true Dutch typeface was needed that would sum up their "entire historical and cultural tradition."[6] In January 1912, the Type Foundry Amsterdam issued De Roos' Hollandsche Mediaeval (Fig. 5-3), a "heavy and solid"[7] text face in ten sizes based on fifteenth-century Venetian types. This being the first typeface designed and produced in The Netherlands for over a century, it was received with great enthusiasm and for at least ten years was one of the most popular faces available. For the magazine *Onze Kunst* (Our Art), Van Royen wrote an enthusiastic review of the Hollandsche Mediaeval in 1913: "In circles where typography was never even considered 'the letter of De Roos' has become a familiar sound."[8] Stols, Van Krimpen, and Nypels all designed their first books with Hollandsche Mediaeval.

Ella Italic was designed in 1915; the lighter and more graceful Erasmus Mediaeval (Fig. 5-4) was released in 1923, followed by its semi-bold version Grotius (Fig. 5-5) in 1925, the sans serif Nobel in 1929, the Egmont series in 1932, the uncial face Simplex in 1937, and Libra (perhaps his worst) in 1938. In addition, De Roos designed the Zilvertype for Van Royen's press, De Zilverdistel in 1915, and in 1926, Meidoorn for his own ephemeral private press, De Heuvelpers (The Hill Press). De Roos' first type design, also for the Amsterdam Type Foundry, was actually a Javanese alphabet produced in 1909 for the State Printing Office to be used for publications in the Indonesian colonies.[9]

De Roos derived considerable status through his typeface designs. A prolific writer, between 1907 and 1942 he published 193 articles on type design and typography, emphasizing both instructive and historical facets. In the journal of the Type Foundry Amsterdam, he provided layout examples for other book designers to follow, as well as giving lectures and helping to organize typographic exhibitions. One such exhibition showing examples of good and bad typography was held at the Amsterdam Stedelijk Museum in 1913. This was mainly put together by Van Royen, with the text for the catalog written by De Roos.

For De Roos, the Wijdeveld style was tantamount to heresy. Wijdeveld's followers were outright enemies who were vitiating his field

DE SIERKUNST

EEN BLIK OP DE PROEVEN VAN de gieterij afkomstig, doet tevens zien, hoe ook hierover de inzichten van den ontwerper hebben gewaakt; een omstan- *digheid die afzonderlijk is te vermelden*

HET BLIJKT OOK UIT DEZE TEEKENINGEN de groote zorg, om het karakter der letters in de verschillende grootten toch telkens tot zijn recht te doen komen. De vormen van een kleine letter vergroot voldoen niet, evenmin, als die van een groote verkleind. Elk heeft zijn afzonderlijke eischen, waarmede de Roos *op gelukkige wijze steeds rekening heeft gehouden.*

ER IS WEL BEWEERD, DAT DE ROOS' LETTER EEN zakelijk, en daarmede een in het bijzonder hollandsch karakter zoude eigen zijn. Ik kan dat, vooral nu de verschillende corpsen en ook de cursief voltooid zijn, niet inzien Zij is gelukkig meer dan zakelijk en specifiek hollandsch, zij doet blijken van een vormgevoel van een lenigen, opgewekt-sierlijken aard en dit *gevoegd bij haar, zeker, niet hollandsch-vreemde maatvastheid*

5-3

LEUVEN GENT

IK ZEND U TWEE TREURSPELEN die ik vertaalde. Het was een heele waag van me. Overigens moet gij nu zelf maar oordeelen of ik het er goed afgebracht *heb. Niet alleen mijn, maar ook uw vrienden*

ERASMUS-MEDIÆVAL DOOPTEN WIJ DEZE letterserie. Wij meenden dat er naast de zoo algemeen geworden Hollandsche Mediæval behoefte is aan een letter, die lichter en siervoller zijnde, zich bovenal zou leenen om aan het fijne boek- en handelsdrukwerk meerdere distinctie te geven, en gebaseerd zou zijn op het vruchtdragende schrijfbeginsel. *Immers de door kunst*

ÉÉN DING VOORAL, ZEERGELEERDE MANUTIUS, HEB ik dikwijls bij mijzelven gewenscht, dat namelijk het voordeel, dat niet alleen uw boekdrukkunst en uw schitterende letters, maar ook uw geenszins alledaagsche aanleg en geleerdheid u brengen, even groot mocht zijn als de diensten die gij met een en ander bewezen hebt aan de studie van het Grieksch en Latijn. *Want wat de publieke opinie over u betreft, niemand twijfelt er aan*

5-4

5-3. S. H. de Roos, Hollandsche Mediaeval (1908) and Italic.

5-4. S. H. de Roos, Erasmus Mediaeval (1923) and Italic.

FRAGMENTEN

DIE HARMONIE VAN INHOUD en vorm werd onder den invloed van de wonderen der techniek maar al te zeer verwaarloosd. Voor ingenieurs en fabrieksarbeiders is de kunst een

DOCH NIET SLECHTS DE INHOUD DER brieven, maar ook de uiterlijke vorm, waarin zij thans hier verschijnen, verplaatst ons naar Grotius' eigen tijd, driehonderd jaar geleden, toen elk Hollandsch werkman een kunstenaar was, elk voorwerp van zijn hand, of het een tafel of schoolboek betrof, aan de hoogste eischen

NU DE INTERNATIONALE RECHTSORGANISATIE in Genève en in Den Haag een begin van verwezenlijking heeft gevonden, grijpt men allerwege weer naar Grotius' machtig boek, dat den grondslag vormt voor de wetenschap van het volkenrecht. Men wil daarbij zijne geheele totstandkoming volgen, zoekt verband met Grotius' vroegere geschriften, tracht de raadsels

Hugo de Groot was Humanist

5-5. S. H. de Roos, Grotius (1925) and Italic.

by a form of typographic disease. He had nothing positive to say about Zwart who, in his opinion, was yet another one of those architects who were tampering with typography. He contemptuously referred to him as "Piet Blok," alluding to Zwart's signature, a *P* next to a black square. On the other hand, Zwart considered De Roos' designs in general to be archaic throwbacks to the dark ages and his typefaces, Hollandsche Mediaeval especially, little more than modifications of earlier types. At least with regard to the latter, Piet "Blok" Zwart's judicious observation was not far off course. Hollandsche Mediaeval was very close in design to the Golden type of Morris and the Doves type of Emery Walker and T. J. Cobden-Sanderson.

In addition to book typography, De Roos designed hand-drawn letter compositions for posters, letterheads, labels, book jackets, bindings, title pages, and chapter openings. He worked for a number of clients, one of the most important being the progressive Rotterdam publisher W. L. and J. Brusse. Around 1912 De Roos was asked to give its publications a new appearance, and this resulted in a long and close friendship and a successful professional collaboration.[10]

The Brusse brothers, especially J. Brusse, had more contact with their designers than did other publishers, and since the company's beginning in 1903, they had produced an impressive array of books using disparate designers such as De Roos, Zwart, Schuitema, and Van Krimpen. In 1912, Brusse published *Een drietal lezingen in Amerika* (Three Lectures in America) by Berlage, the first book to be set in Hollandsche Mediaeval.[11] The diverse tastes of W. L. and J. Brusse are evident when one compares Zwart's design for the *Monografieën over Filmkunst* with that for the poet P. C. Boutens' translations of Aeschylus' *Smeekelingen* (Entreaties), published only a year apart. For *Smeekelingen* and the rest of Boutens' translation of books by Aeschylus and Plato, De Roos designed the binding and many of the initials, but it is uncertain whether or not he designed the complete books. However, De Roos was most likely the designer of Aeschylus' *Doodenoffer* (Sacrifice) and *Het Treurspel van Agamemnon* (The Tragedy of Agamemnon). It is certain that he designed *Eumenieden* and *Perzen* (The Persians) by Aeschylus as well as *Phaidros van Plato* (Phaidros by Plato). As with this translation series, De Roos would often provide an example, and J. Brusse would produce layouts along these lines.

Some of the best book designs by De Roos were done in the 1920s and 1930s. In addition to Boutens' translations from Aeschylus and Plato, he designed Dante Gabriël Rossetti's *Hand and Soul* (1929) for De Heuvelpers. De Roos designed the layout, the typeface Meidoorn, and the initial letters; in addition, he printed the book himself on a small press. Although he achieved a good classi-

cal balance of format, text, margin, and line length, his style was by no means purely conventional. Implicitness and clarity were his guidelines, and ornaments played a small role only in the beginning, later being excluded entirely.[12] De Roos' typeface *De Roos Romein* was published by the Type Foundry Amsterdam in 1947 on his seventieth birthday. His work in typography came to an end by the early 1950s.

Jan van Krimpen

Van Krimpen, born in Gouda, attended the Royal Academy of Fine Arts at The Hague, initially intending to become a calligrapher. He was related by marriage to the critic and poet Jan Greshoff, and through him, was introduced to literary circles. This connection helped to engender a deep and lasting love for literature, which was undoubtedly a factor that led him to typography. In the beginning he was heavily influenced by De Roos, and like De Roos, started out designing book bindings. However, he soon formed his own approach and direction and rapidly became by far the preeminent book designer of his generation in The Netherlands.

The first typographic design by Van Krimpen was probably the 1912 title page for Greshoff's *De Witte Mier* (The White Ant), a bibliophile magazine devoted to the printing arts that appeared in two separate series: volumes 1–2 (1912–1913); volumes 1–3 (1924–1926). The first book known to be designed by Van Krimpen was *Het Jaar der Dichters, Muzenalmanak voor 1915* (The Year of Poets, Muse Almanac for 1915) in 1914. Van Krimpen's own style began to crystallize with the design of *Sonnetten* (Sonnets) by Albert Besnard in 1917. This volume was the first of five books that would later be referred to as "pre-Palladium." Even though they did not bear that name, these five books would eventually be incorporated as part of the Palladium series itself. In 1920 the publication of *Deirdre en de zonen van Usnach* (Deirdre and the sons of Usnach) by A. Roland Holst inaugurated the actual 21-book Palladium series, which was dedicated to contemporary poets (Fig. 5-6).

The principal participants were Van Krimpen's brother-in-law Greshoff, the Flemish poet Jan van Nijlen, the Dutch poet J. C. Bloem, and Van Krimpen, who supplied the technical expertise. In 1922 they published a prospectus that stated the objectives of the press:

The goal pursued by Palladium is quite simple. Palladium wants to produce books in which the form is sound and which serve the text . . . what we mean by a sound book is one which is printed on good paper in a beautiful typeface and which, as much as possible, has all of the qualities which a good craftsman can provide through his labor. A good book is

one which does not offend the good taste of the reader and does not disturb the pure intellectual pleasure which the text provides him. Thus, it is not necessary—and even undesirable—that we produce a book with the aesthetic intentions that characterize the many deluxe editions.[13]

As evidenced by the design of *Deirdre en de zonen van Usnach,* the series did not, at least in the beginning, exactly meet such stringent standards. In this book the titles and initial letters, printed in red, are overly elegant, even extravagant in design.

The first five books that were later included in the Palladium series, the so-called pre-Palladium publications, were set in De Roos' Hollandsche Mediaeval. However, certain decorative details in this type gradually began to irritate Van Krimpen.[14] He considered it over-used, and in his 1920 article, "S. H. de Roos, Book Artist and Type Designer," he wrote that "a handsome book seems a bit strange printed in the same typeface in which a butcher sets his price-list."[15] In any event, in *Deirdre en de zonen van Usnach,* the first under the name Palladium, Hollandsche Mediaeval was replaced by the Dutch-based typeface, the omnipresent Caslon. Four of the most elegant Palladium numbers are Jan Veth's *De Zwerver spreekt en andere gedichten* (The Wanderer Speaks and Other Poems) (1920), Arthur van Schendel's *Safija* (1922), André Jolles' *Idylle* (1924), and one of Van Krimpen's majestic masterpieces, *Het zatte Hart* (The Drunken Heart) (1926) by Karel van de Woestijne, the latter book demonstrating his deft drawing and use of initial letters. Also, it is the only book in the series set in his own face, Lutetia (Figs. 5-7, 5-8, 5-9).

His collaboration on a 1923 commemorative stamp series for the PTT brought Van Krimpen into close contact with the printer of the series, Joh. Enschedé en Zonen in Haarlem. After approaching the head of the firm, Dr. Johannes Enschedé, with his ideas

5-6. Jan van Krimpen, *Deirdre & De Zonen van Usnach* (Deirdre & the Sons of Usnach) by A. Roland Holst, double-page spread, 1920, 23 × 17 cm. Palladium series. Set in Caslon. Collection, Antiquariaat Schuhmacher, Amsterdam.

on type design, he began at the age of thirty-one his prolific and mutually beneficial thirty-five-year association with the company, having acquired the position of art director. His duties included the supervision of the design and printing of books, the design of specimen sheets for types from the Enschedé archives, and the design of new typefaces aided by Enschedé's master punch cutter, P. H. Raedisch, a German who had received his training in Leipzig. Van Krimpen and Raedisch constituted an ideal blend of artistic perception and craftsmanship.

The elegant and unique Lutetia, his first typeface for the firm, was cut in 1923–24 and afterward went through two revisions (Fig. 5-10).[38] It was given the name Lutetia, the Latin name for Paris, because of its use in the publications for the 1925 International Exhibition of Decorative Arts in Paris. In 1926 Lutetia was given a favorable review by Stanley Morison in *The Fleuron V,* with the exception of a few critical remarks about the design (such as the slanted cross-bar of the lowercase *e*). Morison had special praise for the fact that Lutetia was not derivative of any previous typeface. With the design of this typeface Van Krimpen, at an early stage in his career, had firmly secured his reputation as a type designer.

In 1928, Porter Garnett, director of the School of Printing at the Carnegie Institute of Technology at Pittsburgh and its Laboratory Press, persuaded Van Krimpen to make some revisions in the design of a few of the Lutetia characters for the printing of a catalog for the Frick Museum in New York. Van Krimpen agreed, later saying they were changes he had wanted to make anyway. One, which must have pleased Morison, was the leveling of the crossbar in the lowercase *e*. Other changes included adjusting the proportions of some of the characters.

5-7. Jan van Krimpen, *De Zwerver spreekt en andere Gedichten* (The Wanderer Speaks and Other Poems) by Jan Veth, double-page spread, 1920, 25 × 16.5 cm. Palladium series. Set in Caslon. Collection, Antiquariaat Schuhmacher, Amsterdam.

5-8. Jan van Krimpen, *Safija* by Arthur van Schendel, double page spread, 1922, 18×13 cm. Palladium series. Set in Caslon. Collection, Antiquariaat Schuhmacher, Amsterdam.

5-9. Jan van Krimpen, *Sur un air de Paul-Jean Toulet, Chansons par Jean-Marc Bernard, Francis Éon en Henri Martineau,* double-page spread, 1927, 28×22.8 cm. Set in Lutitia. Collection, Antiquariaat Schuhmacher, Amsterdam.

The original version of Lutetia was followed by the Greek typeface Antigone (1927), Romaneé Roman (1928) (Fig. 5-11), a questionable companion for Christoffel van Dijck's seventeenth-century italic, and in spite of its technical flaws, the magnificent and elaborate chancery italic Cancelleresca Bastarda (1934–35). The incomplete Romulus family was issued in 1936, and Spectrum, Van Krimpen's finest and most widely used face, was designed between 1941 and 1945 for a Bible publication for the publisher Het Spectrum in Utrecht. In total, Van Krimpen produced 8 Romans, 7 italics, 3 majuscules, 4 sans serifs, and 3 Greek fonts.[16] Van Krimpen's last completed typeface was the Romanée Italic (1949), intended as a replacement for Van Dijck's seventeenth-century italic. Just before his death in 1958, he had begun a new typeface specifically designed for a phototypesetter.

For the unremitting Van Krimpen, no typography even existed other than that of the book, and all of his typefaces were designed

5-10. Jan van Krimpen, Lutetia Roman and Italic, 1923–24.

for this purpose. He viewed advertising as well as the people and professional jargon connected with it with evident disdain. Immensely secure in his beliefs, he never vacillated in defending what he considered to be the legitimate and sacrosanct principles of typography. In his eyes, the reader should never even be conscious of typographic design; the designer's single mission was to make reading as pleasurable as possible for the reader and never in any manner to come between the reader and the text. Van Krimpen clearly stipulated that the book designer was first and foremost one who served both author and reader. According to him, in book typography the words *beautiful* and *esthetics* simply did not exist, and among his favorite quotations was Eric Gill's statement that "beauty will look after herself."[17]

This was, of course, very close to the maxims of Morison and Warde. Van Krimpen aimed for an equilibrium between format, paper, typeface, and type size and at the same time vehemently denied that he ever intentionally tried to attain beauty. He advocated foolproof formulas, and, according to his ideals, what he accomplished did indeed come close to these objectives.[18] Fortunately, though, he usually broke away to some degree from his own rules, and each of his books has something subtly different to offer. Although he rejected decoration, his work is often characterized by flourishing initial letters, which give the pages a sublime quality. He attempted to attain his goals through the most fundamental means possible, and his almost total rejection of the superfluous to some extent even placed him in tune with the avant garde of his day. He took to heart Paul Valéry's words: *Le livre est un instrument á lire*. He did indeed make the book a beautiful instrument.[19]

5-11. Jan van Krimpen, Romanée Roman, 1928 and Open Capitals, 1929–30.

At least on the surface, both De Roos and Van Krimpen were type designers seeking similar goals. In a 1955 newspaper interview, De Roos affirmed that ". . . if the book looks beautiful, it is not yet beautiful. I am against experimentation with the book and the intrusion of the designer. I believe that too much of this is happening today. A problem in book design solved within the borders of tradition leaves ample latitude."[20]

When comparing the achievements of Van Krimpen and De Roos after 1920, there are some important differences. In 1925 De Roos, who began his career fifteen years earlier than Van Krimpen, was at the top of his creative powers, and in his innovative work still pursued serenity and beauty.[21] An egalitarian designer with socialist sentiments, De Roos longed for a better and more equitable world, and even though Van Krimpen was part of the same generation, the trauma and aftermath of World War I had much less effect upon his work. Van Krimpen was an intellectual with a distinctly patrician and urbane mentality. His typography was far more elegant, refined, and austere than that of De Roos, and his objective was to present the text so that it could be comfortably and quickly read by civilized people: his style was not directed toward the expression of feelings.[22] An unrelenting advocate of restraint, Van Krimpen refused to, in any way, affect or influence the reader's attitude, a principle evidenced by the Palladium series of books for which Van Krimpen even devised a standard system.

De Roos was more artistically inclined and did not share Van Krimpen's unequivocal veneration for the text, but in the final analysis Van Krimpen was by far the greater artist; his work, both in type and book design, reached a level of abstract beauty and re-

finement De Roos never attained. All in all, Van Krimpen's typography and type designs have a far less dated look than those of De Roos. Also, they were very influential outside The Netherlands, and this influence is still much in evidence.

Van Krimpen gradually became less of an admirer of De Roos and found his type designs to be "too round, too self-seeking and excessively decorated."[23] In 1930 he wrote for the English publication the *Fleuron* a pejorative essay that the editor, Stanley Morison, considered so overly critical of De Roos that he softened it somewhat by changing some of the wording. Referring to De Roos' typefaces, Van Krimpen wrote:

More and more, it seems to me, they have something too much: they have become drawings, and their details have become so minutely worked out that to my mind they no longer seem to be types which will satisfy the book printer. They certainly do not lack personality but theirs is a personality which seems to have been superimposed upon their essence. Their curves would have been better less rounded, their endless undulations charm one at first, but after a time become tiresome.[24]

In the same article he also attacked De Roos' book designs, which he considered to be regressing, and said that De Roos' use of hand-made paper, woodcut initials, and limited editions printed on the handpress were a waste of time. Later in a 1933 piece for *The Dolphin,* De Roos delivered a counterattack, referring to Van Krimpen's "sterile perfection."[25]

There was also another reason for the rancor between the two. From as far back as the 1850s, Type Foundry Amsterdam had been the bitter rival of Van Krimpen's employer Enschedé, and in 1856 the Enschedés even accused Nicolaas Tetterode, original owner of Type Foundry Amsterdam, of blatant thievery for having copied their Javanese typeface with the new electrotyping process. Despite some mutual respect, the fierce competition and harsh recriminations created a deep professional barrier between De Roos and Van Krimpen in the years before World War II.[26]

In 1948 Van Krimpen's design for the *Eerste Nederlandse Systematische Encyclopedie* (First Dutch Systematic Encyclopedia) was selected as one of the best designed books of the year in The Netherlands. Until his death in 1958 at the age of 66, the fiery Van Krimpen would continue to relentlessly oppose anything and everyone that, in his opinion, was deleterious to the craft of book typography.

Charles Nypels

The ties of Nypels to the printing profession in Maastricht began in 1786 when his great-great-grandfather Theodoor Nypels took

over what was left of the well-known French firm Roux et Du-four.[27] To learn the book design and production trade, Nypels began working in 1914 as a trainee in the proofprinting section at the Type Foundry Amsterdam. He became an apprentice to his mentor De Roos, who was employed as a designer by the same company, and it was through De Roos that Nypels received an early insight into quality printing. In 1917 he was officially hired by his family firm Leiter-Nypels, and in 1920 became a partner.

Working simultaneously as a publisher, printer, and designer, Nypels put his own stamp on his publications from the very beginning. The first books he designed, *Verzen en Fragmenten* (Verses and Fragments) by F. J. H. Lousbergh, and *Poésies* by Gérard de Nerval, were published in 1920 in Hollandsche Mediaeval, showing the indisputable influence of De Roos, to whom Nypels remained a faithful devotee throughout his career.[28] Nypels' work as a maker of books can be divided into three overlapping periods. The first spanned the years 1920 to 1932, when he worked in the Maastricht family company, where he also served as director for the last three years under his brother's supervision. This was a prolific interval, during which his book designs ranked among the best in The Netherlands.[29] In 1924, he published Pierre de Ronsard's *Les sonnets pour Hélène* in collaboration with the French publisher La Connaisance, the first of a long series of books in French.

Although launched in the European book design tradition beginning around 1500, Nypels had a fresh approach, evidenced by his title and text pages, his use of color and initial letters.[30] His finest example from this period is the 1927 Constantijn Huygens' *'t Voorhout ende 't Kostelick Mal* (The Voor-hout and the Delightful Comedy) (Figs. 5-12 and 5-13). De Roos' red and blue initial letters turn many of the pages into scintillating typographic symphonies of color. Published in four sections between 1929 and 1931, *Don Quichotte* shows Nypels at his elegant best, and the exceptional initials by De Roos added a finishing touch. However, this book was considered to be far too costly and eventually resulted in Nypels having to leave the firm.

Another aspect that distinguishes him from the other traditional innovators was his devotion to the illustrated book and his close collaboration with various well-known illustrators.[31] Although the quality of Nypels' work varies, it covers a very wide spectrum, and throughout his career he was able to work in various areas of book design. Of the traditional designers, he was the one who actively pursued originality and took the most chances. By breaking many of the traditional rules, his designs were sometimes visually enriched, but at other times fell short. As witnessed by his work, though, Nypels was in no way a typographic dilettante as he has often been unjustly labeled. In the 1933 article for *The Dolphin,* his mentor De Roos made his feelings about this clear:

He experiments with each new book in an effort to suit dress to content, and although the result is not always satisfying, what he achieves is invariably and entirely unique and pleasing to the eye, which, after all, is the object every book-producer has in view. The books he has issued vary greatly in style.[32]

Nypels too did not escape Van Krimpen's critical and uncompromising eye. The fact that Nypels had been an apprentice of De Roos was not auspicious; moreover, Nypels' flamboyant use of decorative elements condemned him, in Van Krimpen's view. In the 1930 *Fleuron* article, Van Krimpen wrote that a "book is really a book only when it has shaken itself free from the influence of the decorative artist."[33]

In 1930 Nypels produced his only book in collaboration with Paul Schuitema, one of the rare known occasions when the traditionalists and avant garde came together. This was *Balans,* a publication on Dutch art for which a photomontage by Schuitema was used for the cover. In 1925 he began an association with a group of young poets and their magazine and publishing house *De Gemeenschap* (The Community), and from 1927 until 1934 he designed many of their publications. Although his earlier work had a more bibliophile character, his work for *De Gemeenschap* was in general designed for the trade book market.[34]

Nypels' second period, overlapping the first, began in 1927 when he started his actual design and printing work for *De Gemeenschap.* This resulted in experiments that often drew him far out of the classical mold, and he began to play more freely with letters and text. Some of the more notable books included: *Songs of Kalua* by Albert Kuyle, 1927; *Hart zonder Land* (Heart without a Country) by

5-12. Charles Nypels, *Sonnets and Songs toward a Work to Be Called the House of Life* by Dante Gabriel Rossetti, 1927, 24.2 × 16.2 cm. Collection, Antiquariaat Schuhmacher, Amsterdam.

5-13. Charles Nypels, *'t Voorhout ende 't kostelijke Mal* by Constantijne Huygens, double page spread, 1927, 24.4 × 16 cm. Typeface Grotius and initials designed by De Roos. Collection, Antiquariaat Schuhmacher, Amsterdam.

5-12

5-13

Albert Helman, 1929; *Sine Nomine,* by Jan Engelman, 1930; *Het Wereldorgel* (The World Organ) by Anton van Duinkerken, 1931; *Porta Nigra* by H. Marsman, 1934. The relationship with *De Gemeenschap* began in Maastricht and intensified after he moved to Utrecht, where he continued his work for them while also working as a freelance designer for other publishers (Figs. 5-14, 5-15).

During the third period, from 1938 until 1948, he worked as typographic advisor to the publisher Het Spectrum (The Specter), which had acquired the book division of *De Gemeenschap*. Here he had an opportunity to exercise his formidable knowledge of printing and artistic talents in a more diverse manner, working with all kinds of publications, including pocketbooks.[35] Nypels brought his career to a triumphant culmination in 1948, when he won the State Prize for Typography with *De Heilige Schrift* (The Holy Script), designed for Het Spectrum. He died in January 1952 after a long stay in a sanatorium.[36]

A. A. M. (Sander) Stols

Like Nypels, Sander Stols was born into a Maastricht printing family. Visually he was the least exceptional of the second tier of the traditional designers, and his actual contribution to typographic design was nominal. The sheer amount of his production, though, was enormous, and even though the quality was often mixed, the best of his publications are superb, both in design and in technique.[37] In 1921 Stols was studying law in Amsterdam, but he and his younger brother Alphonse had already decided to continue in the family publishing tradition. They were both sharply critical of what the family firm Boosten & Stols had done in the past and were committed to introducing the highest possible design standards. It was very unusual for a printer to devote so much energy to producing fine printing, as it was simply not a viable commercial option. This made the ambitions of the Stols brothers and Nypels all the more commendable.[38]

5-14. Charles Nypels, *Sine Nomine* by Jan Engelman, cover, 1930, 25.5 × 19.7 cm. Publisher, De Gemeenschap, Utrecht. Collection, Antiquariaat Schuhmacher, Amsterdam.

5-15. Charles Nypels, *Het Wereldorgel* (The World Organ) by Anton van Duinkerken, title page, 1931, 14.5 × 22.5 cm. Collection, Antiquariaat Schuhmacher, Amsterdam.

Stols' doctrine was simplicity and maximum legibility, and his work was noted for its constrained classical typography, good taste, careful choice of texts, and craftsmanship. Stols admired, with some reservations, the fantasy of his friend the "mercurial bohemian" Nypels, who had advised him on his first publications.[39] Stols himself never once deviated from the traditional route. He preferred classical typefaces such as Garamond and Bembo, but on a number of occasions he used De Roos' Hollandsche Mediaeval, and even more often Erasmus Mediaeval.

The invective between Van Krimpen and De Roos surfaced again in the work of Nypels and Stols. While Nypels was a student and devoted disciple of De Roos, Stols revered Van Krimpen and used him as a designer for many of his publications. Stols became acquainted with Van Krimpen in 1923, when they were both living in The Hague. Their friendship and professional relationship caused a breach between Stols and Nypels, who simply did not like Van Krimpen.

Van Krimpen worked on a number of books for Stols' Halcyon Press, which was established in 1927. *The Sonnets* of John Milton (1929) (Fig. 5-16), set in the Italic typeface of Christoffel van Dyck, shows the unmistakable hand of Van Krimpen, both in the design and in the initial letters. Although Paul Valéry's *Le Retour de Hollande* (1926) (Fig. 5-17) was assumed to have been designed by Stols, both the typography and initial letters are clearly by Van Krimpen. *Strofen en andere Verzen uit de Nalatenschap van Andries de Hoghe* (Stanzas and other Verses from the Estate of Andries de Hoghe), 1932 (Fig. 5-18), written by Boutens, is set in Van Krimpen's Romanée and is a stately example of a book designed by Sander Stols with the initial letters by Alphonse. Valéry's *Existence du Symbolisme* (1939) (Fig. 5-19) again is a joint effort of the Stols brothers, with the initials by Alphonse. However, Alphonse Stols was essentially an unsuccessful imitator of Van Krimpen, and his initial letters seem somewhat commonplace when compared to those of the master.

Like Van Krimpen, Stols' view on the designer's role was clear and to the point:

Providing the form in which a book will be printed . . . the designer must never-the-less satisfy a number of requirements for the book, knowledge of its history and technology, artistry and taste, and insight as to production costs. In short all those factors which make it possible to make a written text into a printed book that satisfy the greatest demands of legibility.[40]

Stols continued his publishing business until 1951, at which time he was appointed typographic advisor for UNESCO in Ecuador, Guatemala, and Mexico. While in Mexico he lectured on the history of printing and from 1963 until 1965 served as a cultural attaché at the Dutch Embassy in Mexico City. He then moved to Spain, where he died in 1973.

Jean François van Royen

Van Royen was born in Arnhem in 1878 and died at the German concentration camp in Amersfoort in 1942. Although Van Royen was himself a book designer and private publisher, his principal contribution to graphic design in The Netherlands came through his position as general secretary of the Dutch PTT, and it would be impossible to evaluate his contribution outside this context. Though a few of his own book designs were commendable, they were limited in quantity, and he probably would not have been remembered beyond a small circle for this role alone. A born organizer and exemplary of a generation of idealists, Van Royen had an innate ability for leadership and an insatiable appetite for accomplishment. He saw everything and everyone in terms of his own esthetic and ethical principles and was a zealot in the best

5-16. Jan von Krimpen, *Le Retour de Hollande: Descartes & Rembrandt* by Paul Valéry, title page, 1926; set in Lutetia, 22.6 × 18 cm. Printed by Stols, design, initials and titles by Van Krimpen. Collection, Antiquariaat Schuhmacher, Amsterdam.

5-17. Jan van Krimpen, *The Sonnets of John Milton*, double-page spread, 1929, 25.7 × 17.8 cm. Published by Stols' Halcyon Press, initials and design by Van Krimpen, italic type by Christoffel van Dyck. Collection, Antiquariaat Schuhmacher, Amsterdam.

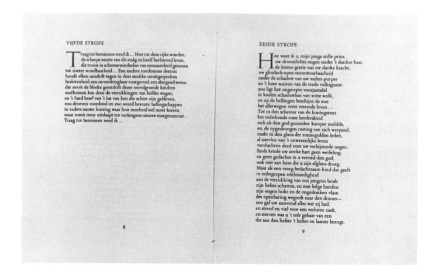

5-18. A. A. M. Stols, *Strofen en andere Verzen uit het Nalatenschap van Andries de Hoghe* (Stanzas and Other Verses from the Estate of Andries de Hoghe) (P. C. Boutens), double-page spread, 1932, 28.2 × 19.3 cm. Published by Stols' Halcyon Press, design by A. A. M. Stols, initials by Alph. Stols, set in Romanée by Van Krimpen. Collection, Antiquariaat Schuhmacher, Amsterdam.

5-19. A. A. M. Stols, *Existence du Symbolisme* by Paul Valéry, double-page spread, 1939, 28 × 19 cm. Initials by Alph. Stols, printing and design by A. A. M. Stols. Collection, Antiquariaat Schuhmacher, Amsterdam.

possible sense of the word.[41] His keen perception of art and remarkable organizational skills provided a unique combination. While working concurrently for the PTT and private publishing, Van Royen was also actively involved with the V.A.N.K. and the jury for selecting the year's best designed books.

Bibliophile Publications

After receiving his doctorate in law from the University of Leiden in 1903, Van Royen worked for a year with the publishing firm of Martinus Nijhoff at The Hague before assuming the minor position of clerical aide in the legal section of the PTT in 1904.

On Sinterklaus (Santa Claus) day, December 5, 1909, two young poets, Jan Greshoff and J. C. Bloem, decided to establish a private

press, De Zilverdistel (The Silver Thistle), at The Hague. Their objective was to show how literature (mainly Dutch) could be presented in well-designed publications. A few months later, in 1910, the poet (and later critic) P. N. van Eyck became associated with De Zilverdistel as well. In 1912 Van Royen joined Van Eyck, and very soon the publications took on a new character.

Two typefaces were specifically commissioned for De Zilverdistel. The first, De Roos' Zilvertype, was essentially an updated version of Hollandsche Mediaeval. The second, Disteltype, was designed by Lucien Pissarro, the son of the painter Camille Pissarro, and was basically a modern interpretation of the Carolingian Minuscule. In addition to designing typefaces for Van Royen, De Roos often gave Van Royen advice on typography. He also designed initials, and titles for De Zilverdistel. Much to the irritation of De Roos, Van Royen tried to work with him on the design of the Zilvertype and diligently followed the designs from conception to completion.[42]

The overlapping involvement of Greshoff, Bloem, Van Eyck, and Van Royen with De Zilverdistel was so transitory that it is impossible to separate the publications into any distinct periods. The first three books were completely designed and printed by Enschedé. In August/September 1912, Van Eyck, more and more interested in typography, asked Bloem, who had never been involved with this side of the publication, and Greshoff to dissociate themselves from De Zilverdistel. Apparently, he naively felt that he could actually turn it into a commercial enterprise. In 1912 Van Royen may have been involved with the fourth book, *Het Eigen Rijk* (The Private Kingdom) by Albert Vervey; although this was mainly designed by Van Eyck, it still bears many of the characteristics of an Enschedé publication. Greshoff, who had left De Zilverdistel in 1912, was nevertheless involved with the design of *Les Fleurs du Mal* in 1913.

Van Royen was self-taught in typography. He learned the craft of printing as an apprentice at the printer and typefoundry Enschedé in Haarlem. At first he printed everything on their handpress, one example being the 1913 *Lanseloet van Denemerken*. Beginning with De Zilverdistel catalogue in 1915, Van Royen began printing on his own handpress at home; he never went back to Enschedé.

Over Boekkunst en de Zilverdistel (Over Book Arts and The Silver Thistle), with a text by Van Royen and Van Eyck, was published in 1916 (Fig. 5-20). This is the first book set in the Zilvertype of De Roos. In the same year *Cheops,* designed by Van Royen, was printed in Zilvertype with the initial letters and titles also cut by De Roos following Van Royen's suggestions (Fig. 5-21).

Van Royen always had an exotic side to his nature, and his easily distinguishable titles, initials, and vignettes are far more extrava-

gant than those of Van Krimpen and De Roos. Van Krimpen had a low opinion of De Zilverdistel, and characteristically Dutch, he did not keep these views to himself. He considered its use of the handpress a form of snobbery. Although he himself used the Schoefferletter on a number of occasions, he later considered it to be an odd choice for *Lanseloet van Denemerken,* preferring instead more modern typefaces and contemporary printing methods. Typographically its publications held nothing for him, and ostensibly the only two books from the press he had anything at all positive to say about were designed by Van Eyck.[43]

Van Krimpen was in principle against interpreting texts through typography in any manner whatsoever, and his differences with Van Royen were in essence a symptom of his increasing offensive against any kind of decoration in book design. Referring to the last De Zilverdistel book, published in 1919, *Verzen uit de jaren 1880–1890* (Verses from the Years 1880–1890) by Willem Kloos, Van Krimpen said that it was too subjective by trying to express the literary meaning of the text through typography.[44]

In 1923, Van Royen changed the name of De Zilverdistel to De Kunera Pers (The Kunera Press), and it continued until his death in 1942. He never liked the name De Zilverdistel and wanted to give the press a name of his own choice. All of the books of De

5-20. J. F. van Royen, *Over Boekkunst en de Zilverdistel* (Over Book Art and the Zilverdistel) by P. N. van Eyck and J. F. van Royen, double-page spread, 1916, 19.5 × 14 cm; Published by De Zilverdistel, initials by De Roos on the instructions of Van Royen. This is the first book set in the Zilvertype of De Roos. Collection, University of Amsterdam.

Kunera Pers were produced without the participation of De Roos or Van Eyck. Van Royen designed the layouts, initials, and titles himself; the trademark was designed by Pissarro.

The first book published by De Kunera Pers in 1924 was *Oostersch, Verzen naar Perzische en Arabische Dichters* (Oriental, Verses after Persian and Arabian Poets), a collection of poems by J. H. Leopold based on Persian and Arabic models set in the Disteltype of Pissarro. The lavish title and initials by Van Royen reflect the calligraphic style of Pissarro's Carolingian-based typeface (Fig. 5-22). Four more books were issued by De Kunera Pers: *Oeuvres* by François Villon (1926) set in Disteltype; *Maneschijn* (Moonlight) by Arthur van Schendel (1927), set in De Roos' Zilvertype with initials and typography by Van Royen (1927) (Fig. 5-23); *La Tapisserie de Nôtre Dame* by Charles Péguy (1929), set in the Disteltype (Fig. 5-24); and *In den Keerkring* (In the Tropics) by Boutens (1942) also set in the Disteltype.

Van Royen and the Dutch PTT

One reason Van Royen produced so few books was the time and energy required by his work at the PTT. Van Royen's first years there were frustrating: Any new ideas were usually met with op-

5-21. J. F. van Royen, *Cheops* by J. H. Leopold, double-page spread, 1916, 24 × 17 cm; Published by De Zilverdistel, initials and titles by De Roos. Designed by Van Royen; set in the Zilvertype of De Roos. Collection, University of Amsterdam.

position from his conservative bureaucratic superiors. In 1914 Van Royen tried to persuade the interior minister to buy Hollandsche Mediaeval for the PTT, but the PTT bureaucrats were quite happy with the typefaces they had been using and besides, this change would only have cost more money. In 1920, however, Van Royen joined the PTT board of directors as secretary-general and from that point on assumed the task of reforming the dismal state of official design.

An indefatigable and steadfast proponent of good typography and totally committed to the betterment of official design, he took on the job with absolute dedication and, as a result, permanently transformed official design. Earlier in 1912, while still serving as a legal aide to the PTT, he had denounced the horrendous state of official printing in an article for the inaugural issue of *De Witte Mier*: "Three words suffice: government printing is ugly, ugly, ugly, thrice ugly in form, composition and paper, the three main elements which comprise the character of printing."[45]

Van Royen had two principal objectives at the PTT: to refine its design image and to provide better and clearer service for the users. He encouraged innovative design by giving assignments to fresh, original designers and always drew a line between his own traditional approach to typography and that of the PTT. Many

5-22. J. F. van Royen, *Oostersch, Verzen naar Perzische en Arabische Dichters* (Oriental, Verses after Persian and Arabian Poets) by J. H. Leopold, double-page spread, 1924, 23.5 × 16.5 cm. Published by the Kunera Pers, title, initials and design by Van Royen; set in the Disteltype of Lucien Pissarro. Collection, University of Amsterdam.

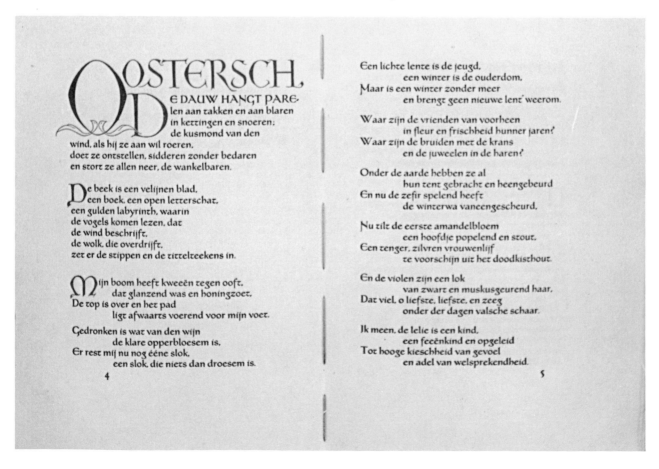

WY ZATEN DIEN EERSTEN AVOND NA, dat wij aan land waren gekomen tot laat in den tuin van mijn broeder, ik heb nog nimmer zulk een schoonen maanlichten avond weêr gezien, noch zulk een bekoorlijken tuin. Het was nog niet donker toen wij bedaard gaande bij de bank aankwamen waar Alfric zeide dat hij het liefst vertoeft, onder twee sierlijke seringenboomen; wij zetten ons daar neder en zwegen een wijle, want het vluchtige schemerlicht, dat steeds heim, lijker ontroeringen wekt waarvan de menschen niet gaarne spreken, maakte ons stil in 't gemoed. Vóór ons was een groot veld van witte violie, ren, dat zich uitstrekte tot de haag die den tuin scheidt van den weg; achter ons, naar rechts en naar links, groeiden velerlei bloemen, er waren de zeldzaamste in prachtige tierigheid, maar waar dien ganschen avond onze oogen voortdurend naar staren moesten was het veld van witte vio, lieren.

Toen wij een pooze gezeten hadden wezen wij elkander hoe licht het begon te worden, door het donkerst loover van daareven scheen een glans en koele rustigheid, en opziende ontwaarden wij

4

de maan, groot en klaar, boven het rank geboom, te in de verte. Het was met de stilte gedaan. Wij hoorden ginds in de straten de stemmen van men, schen en het gejubel van spelende kinderen, dat welluidend was als een keurig dansje. Eén van ons zeide iets over de zoetheid van 't oogenblik en weldra spraken wij te zamen, doch op zachten toon om ons vredig genot niet te storen.

Onze gedachten schenen gelijk van zin, wij spra, ken van het paradijs en van de heerlijkste oorden die denkbaar zijn. Dan verhaalde ik wat ik ge, hoord had omtrent den Grijsaard in het oosten & zijn zaligen hof op den berg; mijn vriend vertelde van een kluizenaar, die in een boom het blauwe vogeltje kweelen hoorde en zoo aandachtig luis, terde, dat hij verder en verder dwaalde van zijn kluis en het eindeloos kwinkeleeren volgde tot hij in den hemel kwam. Toen hief mijn broeder zijn hoofd en sprak op zijne beurt. Wij hadden hem in jaren niet gezien en waren verbaasd ge, weest hem zoo verouderd te vinden—nu vertel, de hij hoe dat gekomen was en in zijn stem klonk aandoening, die ons eerbiedig maakte in oplet, tend zwijgen, wij staarden met groote oogen naar

5

5-23. J. F. van Royen, *Maneschijn* (Moonlight) by Arthur van Schendel, double-page spread, 1916, 21.5 × 15.5 cm. Published by the Kunera Pers; initials and design by Van Royen; set in the Zilvertype of De Roos. Collection, University of Amsterdam.

PRESENTATION DE LA BEAUCE A NOTRE DAME DE CHARTRES

ETOILE DE LA MER voici la lourde nappe
Et la profonde houle et l'océan des blés
Et la mouvante écume et nos
    greniers comblés.
Voici votre regard sur cette immense chape

Et voici votre voix sur cette lourde plaine
Et nos amis absents et nos cœurs dépeuplés.
Voici le long de nous nos poings désassemblés
Et notre lassitude et notre force pleine.

Etoile du matin, inaccessible reine,
Voici que nous marchons vers votre illustre cour.
Et voici le plateau de notre pauvre amour,
Et voici l'océan de notre immense peine.

Un sanglot rôde et court par delà l'horizon.
A peine quelques toits font comme un archipel.
Du vieux clocher retombe une sorte d'appel.
L'épaisse église semble une basse maison.

Ainsi nous naviguons vers votre cathédrale.
De loin en loin surnage un chapelet de meules,
Rondes comme des tours, opulentes et seules
Comme un rang de châteaux sur la barque amirale.

16

Deux mille ans de labeur ont fait de cette terre
Un réservoir sans fin pour les âges nouveaux.
Mille ans de votre grâce ont fait de ces travaux
Un reposoir sans fin pour l'âme solitaire.

Vous nous voyez marcher sur cette route droite,
Tout poudreux, tout crottés, la pluie entre les dents.
Sur ce large éventail ouvert à tous les vents
La route nationale est notre porte étroite.

Nous allons devant nous, les mains le long des poches,
Sans aucun appareil, sans fatras, sans discours,
D'un pas toujours égal, sans hâte ni recours,
Des champs les plus présents vers les champs les plus proches.

Vous nous voyez marcher, nous sommes la piétaille.
Nous n'avançons jamais que d'un pas à la fois.
Mais vingt siècles de peuple et vingt siècles de rois,
Et toute leur séquelle et toute leur volaille

Et leurs chapeaux à plume avec leur valetaille
Ont appris ce que c'est que d'être familiers,
Et comme on peut marcher, les pieds dans ses souliers,
Vers un dernier carré le soir d'une bataille.

Nous sommes nés pour vous au bord de ce plateau,
Dans le recourbement de notre blonde Loire,
Et ce fleuve de sable et ce fleuve de gloire
N'est là que pour baiser votre auguste manteau.

c 17

5-24. J. F. van Royen, *La Tapisserie de Nôtre Dame* by Charles Peguy, double-page spread, 1929, 25.7 × 19 cm. Kunera Press; title, initials and design by Van Royen; set in the Disteltype of Lucien Pissarro. Collection, Antiquariaat Schuhmacher, Amsterdam.

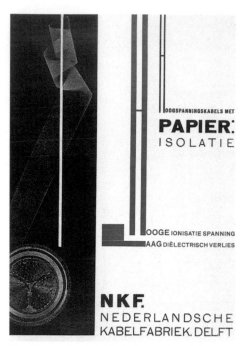

Piet Zwart, Laga advertisement for rubber flooring, card, 1923, 10.8 × 15.2 cm. Collection Ex Libris, New York. © Estate of Piet Zwart/VAGA, New York, 1991.

Piet Zwart, *Papier Isolatie* (Paper insulation), N.K.F. advertisement using photograms, circa 1925, 30 × 21.3 cm. Collection Ex Libris, New York. © Estate of Piet Zwart/VAGA, New York, 1991.

Piet Zwart, *Tentoonstelling Bouwkunst en Kunstnijverheid* (Architecture and Applied Arts Exhibition), poster, 1930. Collection Ex Libris, New York. © Estate of Piet Zwart/VAGA, New York, 1991.

Piet Zwart, *Vertinde Gevlochten Koper Kabel* (Tin coated braided copper cable), *N.K.F. Nomalieënboekje* (N.K.F. Normalization Booklet) page, 1924, 16 × 11.5 cm. Collection Ex Libris, New York. © Estate of Piet Zwart/VAGA, New York, 1991.

Piet van der Hem, *Spyker Autos,* poster, before 1914, 112×84 cm. Collection Gallery Van Voorst van Beest, The Hague.

C. A. Lion Cachet, *Jaarbeurs Utrecht* (Utrecht Trade Fair), poster, 1917, 100×68 cm. Collection Bernice Jackson, Concord, Massachusetts.

J. W. (Willy) Sluiter, *Naar Keulen via Kesteren Nijmegen* (To Cologne via Kesteren and Nijmegen), poster, 1914, 90×70 cm; Collection Bernice Jackson, Concord, Massachusetts.

Richard Nicolaus Roland Holst, *Raden Arbeid* (Labor Councils), poster, 1920, 110×80 cm. Collection Bernice Jackson, Concord, Massachusetts.

Vilmos Huszár, *Ruimte, Jaarboek van Nederlandsche Ambachts en Nijverheidskunst* (Space, Yearbook of Dutch Trade and Industrial Art) by W. F. Gouwe, book cover, 1929, 25.5 × 17.8 cm. Collection Ex Libris, New York.

Albert Pieter Hahn, *Stemt Rood, Kiest de Kandidaten der Soc. Dem. Arb. Partij* (Vote Red, Choose the Candidates of the Socialist Democratic Labor Party), poster, 1919. Collection Bernice Jackson, Concord, Massachusetts.

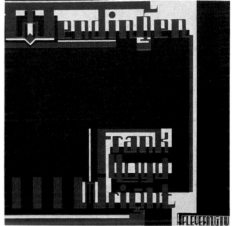

H. Th. Wijdeveld, *Wendingen* VII, no. 3–9, cover, Frank Lloyd Wright issue, 1925–26, 33 × 33 cm. Collection Antiquariaat Schuhmacher, Amsterdam.

Theo van Doesburg, *De Stijl* Vol. 6, no. $^{10}/_{11}$, 1925, 21.7 × 27 cm. Collection Antiquariaat Schuhmacher, Amsterdam.

Piet Zwart, page from advertising booklet for the printer Nijgh en Van Ditmar, 1931, 17.5 × 25 cm. Collection Ex Libris, New York. © Estate of Piet Zwart/VAGA, New York, 1991.

Piet Zwart, *Serie Monografieën over Filmkunst, no. 2: Dertig Jaar Film door L. J. Jordaan* (Series of Monographs on Film Arts, No. 2, Thirty Years Film by L. J. Jordaan), cover, 1931, 22.5 × 18.5 cm. Published by W. L. and J. Brusse, Rotterdam. Collection Antiquariaat Schuhmacher, Amsterdam. © Estate of Piet Zwart/VAGA, New York, 1991.

Paul Schuitema, P. van Berkel Ltd., Rotterdam, Holland, Superior Dutch Ham, poster, circa 1925, 50 × 50 cm. Collection Schuitema, Wassenaar.

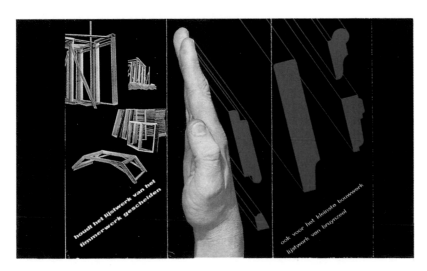

Piet Zwart, Bruynzeel folder, circa 1935, 21.9 × 28 cm. Collection W. Michael Sheehe, New York. © Estate of Piet Zwart/VAGA, New York, 1991.

Johann Georg van Caspel, *Boon's geillustreerd magazijn* (Boon's Illustrated Magazine), poster, circa 1900, 65 × 50 cm. Collection Bernice Jackson, Concord, Massachusetts.

H. P. Berlage, *Harwich—Hoek van Holland,* poster, 1893, 100 × 64 cm.

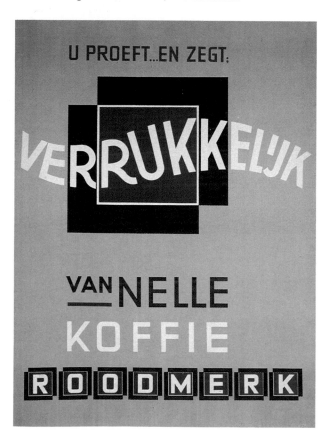

(Above) Jan Ros, *Blooker's Cacao*, poster, 1895, 86 × 63 cm. Collection Alston W. Purvis, Boston.

(Left) Jacob (Jac.) Jongert, *Van Nelle Koffie,* poster, circa 1930, 78 × 63 cm. Collection Bernice Jackson, Concord, Massachusetts.

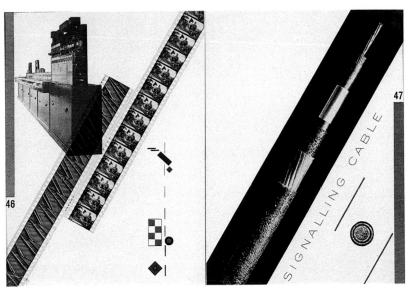

Piet Zwart, NKF English catalog, pages 46 and 47, 1928–29, 29.8×21 cm. © Estate of Piet Zwart/VAGA, New York, 1991.

Piet Zwart, N.K.F. Catalog, page 26, 1928, 29.8×21 cm. Collection W. Michael Sheehe, New York. © Estate of Piet Zwart/VAGA, New York, 1991.

Piet Zwart, *Gij, Nu* (You, Now), back of brochure for experimental theater, 1925, 29.2×21.2 cm. Collection Ex Libris, New York. © Estate of Piet Zwart/VAGA, New York, 1991.

Piet Zwart, NKF English catalogue, page 25, 1928–29, 29.8×21 cm. Collection W. Michael Sheehe, New York. © Estate of Piet Zwart/VAGA, New York, 1991.

Piet Zwart, NKF catalog, double-page spread, 1933, 21 × 16 cm. © Estate of Piet Zwart/VAGA, New York, 1991.

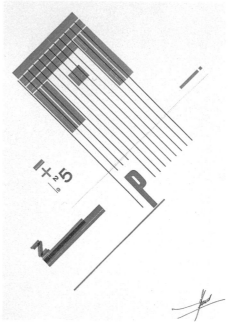

Piet Zwart, *Homage to a Young Woman*, typographic composition, 1925, 21 × 16 cm. Collection Antiquariaat Schuhmacher, Amsterdam. © Estate of Piet Zwart/VAGA, New York, 1991.

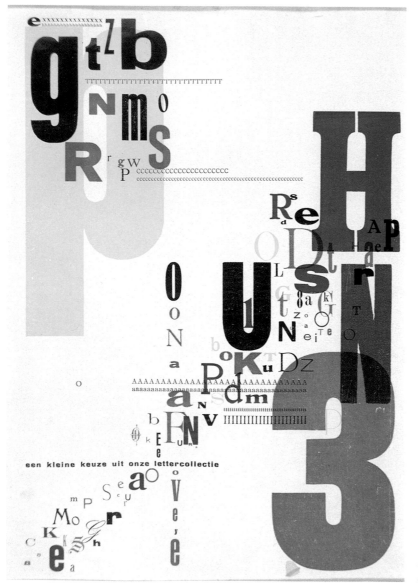

(Above) Piet Zwart, ITF, International Film Festival, poster. 1928, 85.5 × 61 cm. Collection Bernice Jackson, Concord, Massachusetts. © Estate of Piet Zwart/VAGA, New York, 1991.

(Left) Piet Zwart, Drukkerij Trio (Trio Printers catalog), page, 1931, 31 × 22 cm. © Estate of Piet Zwart/VAGA, New York, 1991.

H. Th. Wijdeveld, *Internationale Economisch-Historische Tentoonstelling* (International Economics and History Exhibition), poster, 1929, 65×60 cm. Collection W. Michael Sheehe, New York.

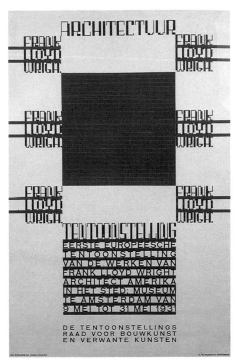

H. Th. Wijdeveld, Frank Lloyd Wright Exhibition, poster, 1931, 78×50 cm. Collection W. Michael Sheehe, New York.

Vilmos Huszár, *Wendingen* X, no. 3, cover, Diego Rivera issue, 1929, 33×33 cm. Collection Antiquariaat Schuhmacher, Amsterdam.

Fré Cohen, *La suppression des taudis et des quartiers insalubres à Amsterdam* (The Elimination of Slums and Unhealthy Districts of Amsterdam), cover, 1930, 24.3×15.2 cm. Collection Antiquariaat Schuhmacher, Amsterdam.

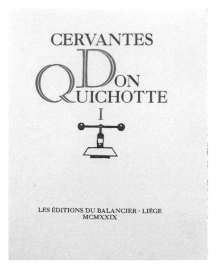

Charles Nypels, *Don Quichotte*, title page,
1929–1931, 30 × 23 cm. Collection Antiquariaat Schuhmacher, Amsterdam.

A. A. M. Stols, *Nieuwe Loten* (New Cuttings) by Marie Cremers,
double-page spread, 1923, third book from the Trajectum ad
Mosam series. Collection Antiquariaat Schuhmacher,
Amsterdam.

Charles Nypels, *Balans, Algemeen Jaarboek der
Nederlandsche Kunsten* (Balance, General
Dutch Art Annual), title page, 1930–31,
27.5 × 20 cm, cover by Schuitema, text and
title page by Nypels. Publisher, Leiter Nypels,
Maastricht. Collection Antiquariaat Schuhmacher, Amsterdam.

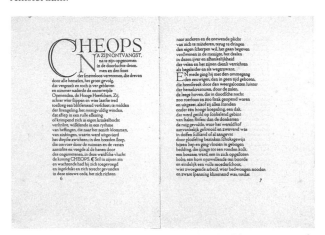

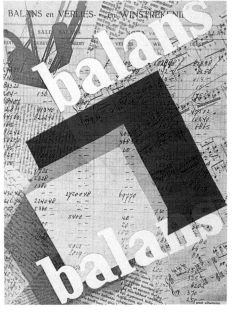

J. F. van Royen, *Cheops* by J. H. Leopold, double-page spread,
1916, 24 × 17 cm.; initials and titles by De Roos. Designed by
Van Royen, set in the Zilvertype of De Roos. Publisher, De
Ziverdistel. Collection Antiquariaat Schuhmacher, Amsterdam.

Paul Schuitema, *Balans, Algemeen Jaarboek der
Nederlandsche Kunsten* (Balance, General
Dutch Art Annual), book cover, 1930–31,
27.5 × 20 cm. Collection Antiquariaat
Schuhmacher, Amsterdam.

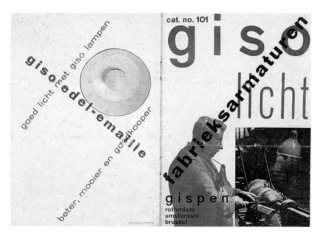

(Above) Paul Schuitema, Giso Catalogue no. 150, cover and back, 1930, 29.6 × 21.1 cm. Collection Schuitema, Wassenaar.

Paul Schuitema, Giso Catalogue no. 101, cover, 1930, 21.1 × 14.8 cm. Collection Schuitema, Wassenaar.

Paul Schuitema, Filmliga, advertising card, 1930, 20.2 × 14.5 cm. Collection Schuitema, Wassenaar.

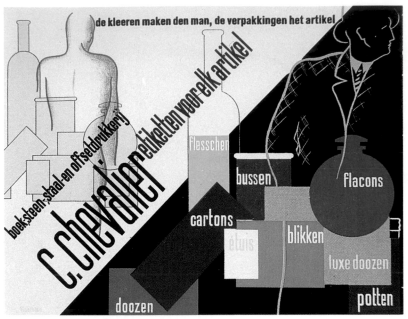

Paul Schuitema, C. Chevalier Etiketten, blotting paper advertisement, 1933, 16.5 × 21.2 cm. Collection Schuitema, Wassenaar.

Paul Schuitema, *Stad* (City) by B. Stroman, cover, 1932, 21.6 × 16.5 cm. Published by W. L. and J. Brusse, Rotterdam. Collection Antiquariaat Schuhmacher, Amsterdam.

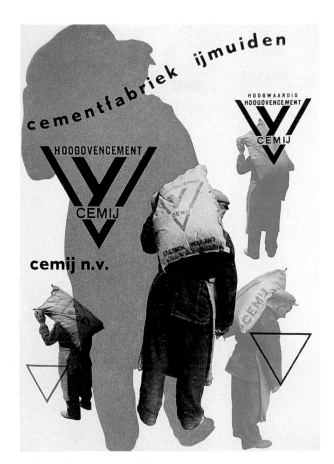

Paul Schuitema, Boele & van Eesteren, page from advertising brochure, 1936, 28.5 × 21.4 cm. Collection Antiquariaat Schuhmacher, Amsterdam.

Paul Schuitema, *Cementfabriek IJmuiden* (Cement Factory IJmuiden), advertising brochure, 1936, 29.3 × 20.7 cm. Collection Antiquariaat Schuhmacher, Amsterdam.

H. N. Werkman, *Preludium,* cover, 1938,
23.3 × 15.3 cm. Collection Alston W. Purvis,
Boston.

H. N. Werkman, Cover for De Ploeg publication, 1927,
36.5 × 23.8 cm. Collection Dr. Robert Polak, Amsterdam.

H. N. Werkman, one of 10 bookplate designs
for M. C. v.L., 1934, 11 × 7 cm. Photograph
courtesy Jan Martinet, Amsterdam.

H. N. Werkman, bookplate P. J. Hiemstra,
1938, 11.1 × 8 cm. Collection Alston W.
Purvis, Boston.

Paul Schuitema, *de 8 en Opbouw,* Vol. 12, No. 2, cover, 1941, 28.7 × 22.1 cm. Collection Schuitema, Wassenaar.

Paul Schuitema, Berkel Rindless Cheese, Showcard advertisement, circa 1930, 43.3 × 26.5 cm. Collection Schuitema, Wassenaar.

Paul Schuitema, *De V.B.P. 8,* advertisement, 1929. 28.9 × 21 cm, Collection Schuitema, Wassenaar.

Paul Schuitema, *Centrale Bond 30,000 Transportarbeiders* (Central Union, 30,000 Transport Workers), poster, 1930, 115 × 76 cm. Collection Ex Libris, New York.

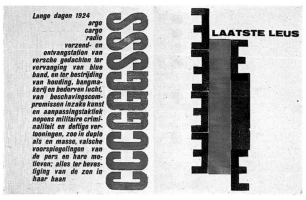

The Next Call 5, pages 4 and 5, double-page spread, 1924, 27.2 × 21.5 cm. Collection Dr. Robert Polak, Amsterdam.

Piet Zwart, poster for greeting telegrams, 1931, 70 × 49 cm. the four forms depicted from top to bottom are by George Rueter (1924), Jac. Jongert (1931), Jan Sluyters (1931), and Fokko Mees (1931). Collection Ex Libris, New York. © Estate of Piet Zwart/VAGA, New York, 1991.

H. N. Werkman, The Next Call 1, cover, 1923, 27.4 × 21.5 cm. Collection Dr. Robert Polak, Amsterdam.

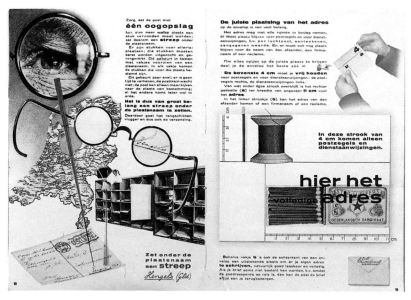

Piet Zwart, Het Boek van PTT (PTT Book), double-page spread, 1938, 25 × 17.5 cm. Collection Antiquariaat Schuhmacher, Amsterdam. © Estate of Piet Zwart/VAGA, New York, 1991.

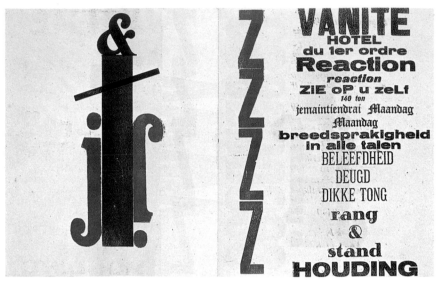

H. N. Werkman, *The Next Call* 5, pages 2 and 3, double-page spread, 1924, 27.2 × 21.5 cm. Collection Dr. Robert Polak, Amsterdam.

H. N. Werkman, *The Next Call* 6, cover, 1924, 27.4 × 21.5 cm. Collection Dr. Robert Polak, Amsterdam.

H. N. Werkman, *The Next Call* 9, cover and back, 1926, 35 × 21.4 cm. Collection Dr. Robert Polak, Amsterdam.

H. N. Werkman, 1926 De Ploeg calendar, November 1925, 45.8 × 28.4 cm. Collection Dr. Robert Polak, Amsterdam.

S. H. de Roos, *Hand and Soul* by Dante Gabriël Rossetti, double-page spread, 1929, 21.5 × 15.5 cm. Heuvel Press (Hill Press), Collection University of Amsterdam.

(Above left) Jan van Krimpen, *Idylle* by Andre Jolles, Palladium no. 19, double-page spread, 1924, 25.5 × 18 cm. Collection Antiquariaat Schuhmacher, Amsterdam.

(Above right) Jan van Krimpen, *Het Zatte Hart* (The Drunken Heart) by Karel van de Woestijne, Palladium No. 25, double-page spread, 1926, 25.5 × 17.5 cm. Collection Antiquariaat Schuhmacher, Amsterdam.

Charles Nypels, *'t Voorhout ende 't kostelijke Mal* by Constantin Huygens, double-page spread, 1927, 24.4 × 16 cm. Typeface Grotius and initials designed by De Roos. Collection Antiquariaat Schuhmacher, Amsterdam.

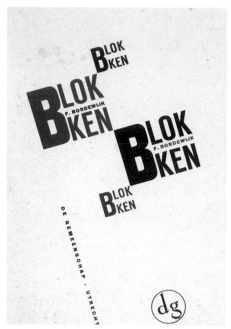

A. Oosterbaan, *Blokken* (Blocks) by
F. Bordewijk, title page, 1931,
20 × 14.4 cm. Published by de Gemeenschap,
printed by Lumax. Collection Antiquariaat Schuhmacher, Amsterdam.

Unknown, ASB, *Tentoonstelling van Architectuur, Schilderkunst en Beeldhouwkunst,
Stedelijk Museum Amsterdam.* (Architecture, Painting and Sculpture Exhibition),
cover, circa 1930, 30.8 × 24.5 cm. Collection Antiquariaat Schuhmacher,
Amsterdam.

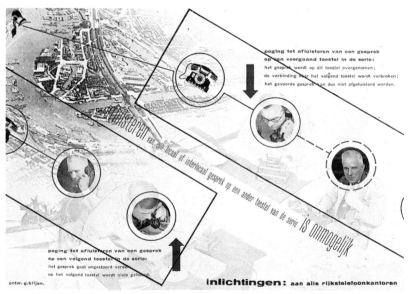

Gerard Kiljan, PTT booklet, page, 1933, 14.8 × 20.8 cm.

Wim Brusse, *Sterk door werk* (Strong for
work), poster, 1936, 100 × 60 cm.

Henny Cahn, advertisement or label for Lüschen's Sportbeschuiten (Lüschen's Sport Biscuits) circa 1937, 29 × 16 cm. Collection Antiquariaat Schuhmacher, Amsterdam.

P. A. H. Hofman, Annual Utrecht International Industrial Fair poster, 1930, 79 × 62 cm. Collection Bernice Jackson, Concord, Massachusetts.

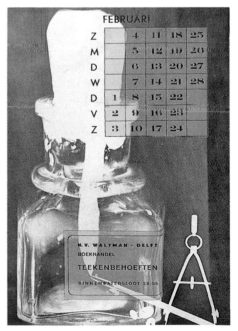

Dick Elffers, April page from calendar for the technical book dealer and printer J. Waltham, Jr., 1934, 29 × 21.2 cm.

Dick Elffers, *De Rimpel* (The Wrinkle), cover, 1933, 31.1 × 21.2 cm.

Dick Elffers, *De Niederlande* (The Netherlander) cover, circa 1938, 14.3 × 22.4 cm. Collection Antiquariaat Schuhmacher, Amsterdam.

A. A. Balkema, *Zehn kleine Meckerlein,* page from booklet 1943, text smuggled out of a concentration camp, 14.2 × 12.3 cm. Collection Antiquariaat Schuhmacher, Amsterdam.

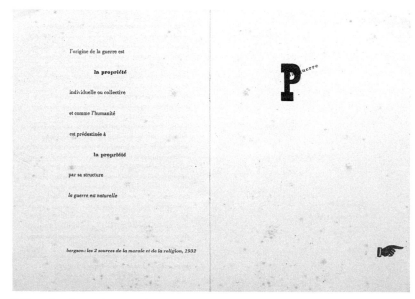

Nicolaas P. de Koo, *AVO Zomer Feesten* (AVO Summer Festivals), poster, 1938, 61.5 × 29 cm. Collection Alston W. Purvis, Boston.

Willem Sandberg, *lectura sub aqua, experimenta typographica 1,* double-page spread, 1944, 21 × 15 cm. Collection Antiquariaat Schuhmacher, Amsterdam.

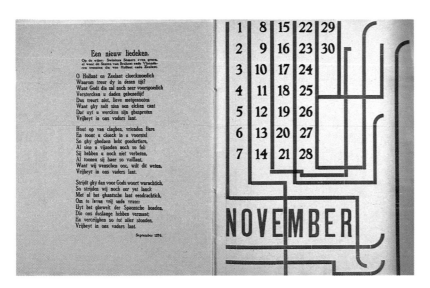

H. N. Werkman, *Turkenkalender* (Turkish calendar), cover, 1941, 32.7 × 25 cm. Collection Dr. Robert Polak, Amsterdam.

H. N. Werkman, *Alleluia*, old Dutch Easter hymn, inside spread for *De Blauwe Schuit* 3, 1941, 24.9 × 19.1 cm. Collection Antiquariaat Schuhmacher, Amsterdam.

H. N. Werkman, *Gesprek* (conversation), cover and back page for *De Blauwe Schuit* 9, 1942, 31.7 × 22.2 cm. Collection Antiquariaat Schuhmacher, Amsterdam.

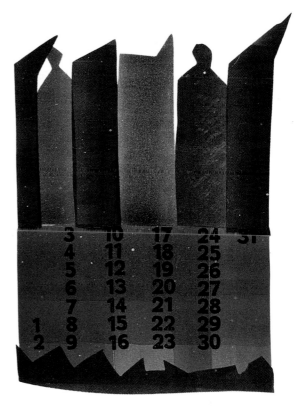

H. N. Werkman, 1944 calendar, November 1943, 32 × 24.5 cm. Collection Dr. Robert Polak, Amsterdam.

artists and designers were involved, and by the end of the 1920s they included the Constructivists Zwart and Schuitema.

Van Royen's relationship with De Roos was always correct, but somewhat reserved. This coolness probably occurred because De Roos felt he had not received sufficient credit for his part in some of De Zilverdistel and Kunera Pers publications. Additionally, Van Royen's own bibliophile printing contradicted his personal philosophy which, unlike that of De Roos, enthusiastically embraced the Industrial Revolution. Van Royen was optimistic about the use of machinery and often referred to what had been achieved in Germany with modern printing methods. He also advocated better ties between the manufacturing and arts sectors. De Roos knew and respected Van Royen as a master of traditional typography and as partner in the crusade to achieve perfection. Now Van Royen was actually accepting those hideous "aberrations" of Zwart and others of the same ilk, even going so far as to give them assignments for the PTT! For De Roos, this was impossible to accept. To him compromise was out of the question, the equivalent of artistic and professional sedition.[46]

From 1920 onward the PTT began to devote much attention to advertising and information, and stickers, folders, posters, booklets, and instruction manuals were produced in great quantity. All sections of the PTT were either directly or indirectly affected by the changes—lettering on cars, forms, stamps, furniture, telephone booths, mailboxes, and architecture. Even though it drew accusations of "official anarchy" from the press, the PTT grew rapidly after 1925, and the volume of design increased as well. New departments needed symbols and logos. During the 1920s their advertisements were limited to a few standard messages, one of the most important involving airmail service between The Netherlands and the Indonesian colonies (the first flight took place in 1924). Another emphasized the necessity of telephone service for all Dutch households. International calls were also promoted along with the telex for businesses.

In 1924 Van Royen, Gouwe, and W. Penaat, director of the Museum van Kunstnijverheid (Museum of Industrial Art) in Haarlem, created, together with a group of enlightened industrialists, the BKI (Association for Art in Industry). Its objective was to encourage well-designed and well-produced industrial products. Many prominent people in the industrial sector became BKI members, including Joh. Enschedé en Zonen and the Rotterdam publisher W. L. and J. Brusse. This proved to be an ideal connection for Van Royen in his campaign to raise the standards of PTT products.

Informing the public about various services became an important objective, and in 1927 a special division, the PPD (Press and Propaganda Service), was created specifically for this purpose. The

director of the PPD, P. G. de Pater, acted mainly as a go-between. Whenever there was a design project, he would ask Gouwe, director of the ISN (Institute of Decorative and Industrial Art), to recommend a suitable designer. For this service the ISN would receive a 10 percent commission. Although Van Royen had the power to countermand their decisions, he usually agreed with their choices. Van Royen made an effort to involve the entire staff at the PTT in the decision-making process, and his influence was felt at all levels.

In spite of Van Krimpen's well-known low opinion of De Zilverdistel, Van Royen solicited his collaboration on stamp designs in 1923, beginning an association that would last until 1937. The first assignment was lettering for stamps designed by W. van Konijnenburg to celebrate Queen Wilhelmina's Silver Jubilee. Another designer who played a major role within the PTT was N. P. de Koo. He received an interior design assignment from the PTT as early as 1918, and in the 1930s he worked for them principally as a graphic designer. He was largely responsible for the PTT's image during this period, and was influential in his position as secretary of the V.A.N.K., where he also worked closely with Van Royen (Fig. 5-25).

In 1929 Van Royen gave Zwart his first PTT commission. In addition to stamps, his assignments included brochures, posters, forms, and displays. Van Royen clearly preferred the classic approaches of Van Krimpen and De Roos, but he was enlightened enough to exploit the talents of the more experimental designers as well. Zwart's first piece for the PTT was a four-page advertising brochure for Scheveningen Radio using photomontage and photograms. Small photographs of the ticker tape machines are contrasted with a large photogram derived from the punched paper tape itself (Figs. 5-26, 5-27). What is small becomes large, and what is large becomes small. The total image of opposing diagonals soon became a typical Zwart device. Ironically, Zwart discarded the very kinds of typefaces Van Royen admired, stating that "the typefaces to avoid are those which have a conceited, personal and particular touch; the more uninteresting the letter the more useful it is typographically. A typeface is more uninteresting in proportion to its having less historical leftovers and comes more out of the exact tense spirit of the 20th century."[47]

Zwart designed the booklet to promote air mail titled *ook post voor U* (also post for you) in 1929 (Fig. 5-28). The left-hand pages have only text while the right-hand pages are made up of diagonals and horizontals to create a dynamic grid in two colors. His exclusive use of lowercase letters precipitated a controversy, and while such use was consistent with the new international style, people in general simply considered it to be a blatant desecration of the Dutch language (Figs. 5-29, 5-30). Zwart retorted by saying that he "could not have predicted that there would be such a close

5-25. Nicolaas P. de Koo, *Rijks Telefoondienst* (Post Office Telephone Service), advertisement, 1935, 20.9 × 9.7 cm. Collection, Antiquariaat Schuhmacher, Amsterdam.

semblance between Roman capital letters and pure, undiluted Dutch blood."[48] During the same year in a similar situation, Zwart caused a stir when he designed an invitation card and other printed pieces for a PTT convention, also in lowercase. For some reason, some of the delegates found it demeaning to be invited in lowercase, and to Zwart's amusement and disdain, the invitation was subsequently reprinted in uppercase letters.

At the end of the summer of 1931, Zwart designed his first two postage stamps, the first to employ photomontage as a technique. For these he reluctantly agreed to use a mundane state portrait of Queen Wilhelmina as the central pictorial element. For the following two stamps, however, Zwart chose his own material. The asymmetrical composition and the absence of borders make them unique in stamp design. Even more exciting were his rejected sketches for the purely typographic 1½ cent stamps. In 1939 Zwart expressed his own views on the function of the postage stamp:

[It] is a document of the times. In the first place it does not pose an aesthetic problem and has nothing in common with a painting. The only "true" postage stamp is the one which displays the attributes of the period from which it comes, which is the synthesis of the idea from which it is created and which is produced using contemporary technological meth-

5-26. Piet Zwart, *Via Scheveningen Radio* (PTT Prospectus for Scheveningen Radio), cover, 1929, 29.7 × 21 cm. Collection, Antiquariaat Schuhmacher, Amsterdam. © Estate of Piet Zwart/VAGA, New York, 1991.

5-27. Piet Zwart, PCH, *Via Scheveningen Radio,* prospectus cover, 1929, 29.7 × 21.1 cm. Collection, Antiquariaat Schuhmacher, Amsterdam. © Estate of Piet Zwart/VAGA, New York, 1991.

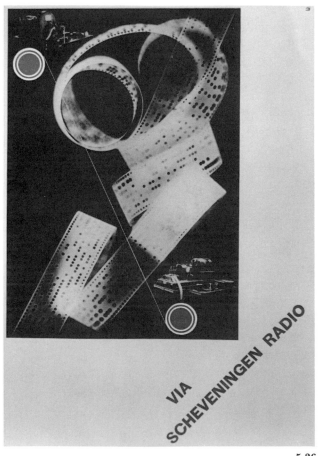

5-26

5-27

dit boekje wordt aangeboden door het
hoofdbestuur der posterijen, telegrafie en telefonie

5-28. Piet Zwart, *ook post van U* (also post for you), cover, 1929, 14.9 × 21 cm. Collection, Antiquariaat Schuhmacher, Amsterdam. © Estate of Piet Zwart/VAGA, New York, 1991.

ods. Any other basis is false and unworthy. . . . For the rest the consumer stamp is a part of a larger whole, the postal article, and thereby loses its independence. The conventional composition, namely a symmetrical image along a vertical axis (in some cases horizontal), grants the stamp an autonomy which is not its due. Therefore, the composition on my stamps is dynamic, and in addition I have made use of the photographic and the photo-technical reproduction methods so representative of our time. Beautiful? Ugly? That is of little consequence.

He often challenged the two terms *beautiful* and *ugly:* "These beliefs are prone to be accepted as standards. Appropriateness is the only proper standard."[49]

Zwart, Schuitema, and others of the period considered (or at least claimed that they did) the term *esthetic* to be a malediction and an anachronism, an outworn name for a discarded and discredited past. Yet they did, knowingly or unknowingly, create a new esthetic in graphic design, in effect a replacement for what they so vehemently denounced.

It is not known when Van Royen actually raised the subject of *Het boek van PTT* (The PTT Book) with Zwart, but it was probably as early as 1929. The publication did not appear until 1938. Zwart had provided the PTT with a rough sketch by 1930, even going so far as to list the number of photographs.[50] Various ideas were then bandied about for eight years; what finally emerged was an unusual concoction indeed. *Het boek van PTT,* written by Zwart himself, was intended to be an instruction manual for schoolchildren on how to use the services of the PTT. It is an interesting publication because it reflects so many aspects of Zwart's previous work as well as some of the new modes of the 1930s. In one package we find a swirling ferment of Functionalism and Dadaism, traditional and modern trends. Zwart mustered every possible

5-29. Piet Zwart, *PTT instructions on designing envelopes for more efficient machine stamping,* circa 1929, 19.5 × 22.2 cm. Collection, W. Michael Sheehe, New York. © Estate of Piet Zwart/VAGA, New York, 1991.

5-30. Piet Zwart, *Geef uw telegrammen telefonisch op* (Give your telegrams by phone), PTT advertisement, 1932, 24.7 × 17.5 cm. The caption for the man walking is *Dit is veloren tijd* (This is lost time). Collection, Antiquariaat Schuhmacher, Amsterdam. © Estate of Piet Zwart/VAGA, New York, 1991.

technique, source, influence, nuance, and typographic experiment, and the methods included collage, pen and ink, black chalk, montage, colored pencil, puppets, a plethora of typefaces in countless sizes and weights, and actual handwriting. He also included images of real objects, some produced exclusively for the project. Other objects were found pieces such as a box of matches. Although these methods had all been used by designers of that period, they had never before been brought together in such a mélange.[51] The printing method was rotogravure, which provided more opportunities for color nuances. With *Het boek van PTT,* Zwart extended this process beyond previous limits.

As it was a book created specifically for children, he wanted to stimulate their curiosity through all available visual means. The text is accented throughout with different typefaces and condensed and expanded letters. Elffers, who was working for Zwart at the time, also contributed illustrations. He was much less of a diehard Constructivist than Zwart, leaning more toward Surrealism, but the illustrations were kept under Zwart's strict control.[52] Two handcrafted paper puppets recall the type figures in Lissitsky's 1928 *4 regels voor de rekenkunst* (4 rules for the rule art), one of the typographic figures from Werkman's *The Next Call,* and

5-31. Gerard Kiljan, *Koopt weldadigheids postzegels en briefkaarten ten bate van het misdeelde kind* (Buy charity stamps and postcards on behalf of the handicapped child), card, 1932, 49 × 32 cm.

5-32. Gerard Kiljan, PTT booklet, cover, 1933, 14.8 × 20.8 cm.

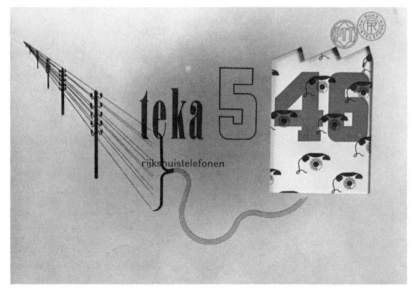

5-33. Henny Cahn, *Teka 5*, brochure, 1938, 15 × 21 cm.

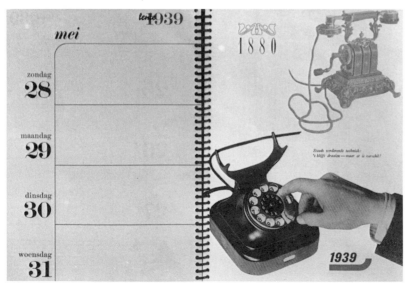

5-34. Wim Brusse, PTT Office Agenda, double-page spread, 1939, 20.7 × 15 cm. Collection, Antiquariaat Schuhmacher, Amsterdam.

5-35A. Piet Zwart, Postage stamps, 1931 and 1932, 3×2 cm.

5-35B. Paul Schuitema, Postage stamps, 1932, 3.5×2.5 cm.

5-35C. Gerard Kiljan, Postage stamps, 1931, 2.5×2 cm.

the collaborative children's book *Die Scheuche* by Van Doesburg, Schwitters, and Steinitz. They are also strongly reminiscent of paper puppets and animals that Rodchenko made in 1926 for the children's poems of S. Tretjakow. Zwart had most likely seen photographs of these when they were on display at the FIFO Exhibition at Stuttgart in 1929.[53] All in all, *Het boek van PTT* is a typographic anomaly and differs radically from Zwart's earlier work. With this publication, he ended the major phase of his contribution to Dutch graphic design.

Kiljan's 1931 stamps devoted to disabled children were among his strongest works, but his unorthodox use of photographs of actual disabled children provoked an outburst of criticism (Fig. 5-31). Each stamp is limited to two colors, which helps to unify the series. In 1932 he designed a booklet showing how to use the telephone. Here typography is combined with montage, symbols, and geometric forms (Figs. 5-32 to 5-34). Henny Cahn was another of the younger and more talented designers who produced work for the PTT shortly before World War II. In 1932 Van Royen commissioned Schuitema to design a series of stamps, and, like Zwart, he made use of the montage technique (Fig. 5-35). Apparently, though, Schuitema did not feel at home working in such a small format, and the stamps have a claustrophobic appearance. This was most likely the reason Schuitema was not given any more PTT assignments until 1950.[54]

The new image of the PTT was largely the result of the work and initiative of one imaginative and talented man, and Van Royen's position gave him a unique forum to improve design standards on an official level. Design at the PTT has never been the same again, and Dutch stamp design has been second to none since Van Royen confronted the state bureaucracy. It was through his efforts that the PTT became the preeminent public patron of graphic and industrial designers and a fervent supporter of pioneering graphic design. Most important, it was largely through his efforts that new typography in general gained broad acceptance in The Netherlands. Van Royen continued in this position until his death, during the German occupation in 1942.

Chapter 6
Hendrik Nicolaas Werkman

Hendrik Nicolaas Werkman was indeed the visionary, the master of the unexpected, and the unbridled force and outsider of Dutch graphic design. A reclusive and singular man whose existence was characterized by seclusion and introspection, he traveled only on rare occasions, and for most of his life remained in the semi-isolation of Groningen in the northern part of The Netherlands.

Werkman's output remained essentially pictorial, and he was never interested in abstraction for its own sake. Words were not used phonetically, as with Schwitters, Van Doesburg, and Van Ostaijen. The poetic, though, played a vital role, and Werkman's typography and text consistently mutually enhance one another. Much was always implied, and the audience was often asked to provide its own interpretation. As Werkman himself commented, "the hidden paths are the most beautiful." He lived in his own enchanted world, "the universe of a grown-up child."[1]

Despite the influence of Dada and Constructivism, Werkman always remained a phenomenon, a nonconformist, and a one-man show. Although Van Doesburg, Lissitsky, Marinetti, Tschichold, and others broke away from established typography, they were all, after their own fashion, striving for new canons. Werkman, on the other hand, rejected all formulas and did not attempt to introduce fresh ones.

There is no other work from this period to compare stylistically with Werkman's compositions. With few exceptions, most of the other avant garde publications of the time have a dated look, and when compared with *The Next Call* they seem more bound to the period in which they were made. Werkman's *druksels* (typographic prints) could not be placed in any previous categories and were, in effect, a new medium, born of necessity. For art historians, Werkman is an intriguing, yet vexing, paradox in that he fits into no comfortable niche and certainly no distinct sector of modern graphic design history.

Formative Years

Both the son and grandson of veterinarians, Werkman was born on the 29th of April, 1882, in Leens, a village in the northern

province of Groningen. This is in an area known as The Marne, and as Werkman's biographer Hans van Straten observed, in some ways it resembles parts of Ireland, having the same characteristics of hunger, religious fundamentalism, resistance to authority, superstition, and a substantial immigration to America.[2] Werkman's father died as the result of an accident in 1891. The family remained in Leens until 1893, and after a brief stay in Assen moved permanently to the city of Groningen.

Werkman's first full-time job was at the printing, publishing, and bookselling establishment of Borgesius in the nearby town of Sappemeer. He probably started out as a type sorter or "printer's devil." In addition, he wrote a few pieces for the Borgesius newspaper *Oost-Gorecht* and later helped to set type for the paper. A few of his photographs survive from this period; he regarded his work seriously enough to print a business card on a toy press: H.N. Werkman Amateur-Fotograaf Groningen (Fig. 6-1).[3]

In 1903, this first phase came to an end when he began writing for the newspaper *Het Groninger Dagblad.* All that survives of his writing are about fifty short pieces signed with the pseudonym Farao, representing his abortive attempt to escape from the routine tedium of journalism. Werkman said very little about this interval, but later he wrote: "For four years I also worked as a correspondent, first with Oppenheim and then at the *Nieuwe Groninger Courant.* It was a dog's occupation for little money, and when I finally left I could not even look at a newspaper for an entire year."[4] After Werkman left the *Groninger Dagblad* for the *Nieuwe Groninger Courant,* it was clear that his newspaper career was reaching an end. He resigned from his final newspaper position and eventually ended up as foreman at a printing company. The next year he managed to set up his own small printing establishment in Groningen.

In 1909 he married Jansje Cremer, daughter of a prosperous bourgeois family that owned a local iron factory. But with no money and apparently little chance of making any, Werkman was

6-1. H. N. Werkman, *H. N. Werkman Amateur-Fotograaf Groningen,* card, circa 1901, 6 × 12 cm. Photograph courtesy of Jan van Loenen Martinet, Amsterdam.

not viewed as an exemplary husband for their daughter. With the financial backing of the Cremer family, however, his firm flourished, and when in 1917 the number of employees reached 27, it was one of the largest such enterprises in that part of The Netherlands. But even though Werkman appeared on the surface to be a typical Groningen businessman, he had little regard for financial matters. He was constantly annoyed when the Cremer family insisted on a regular examination of the balance sheets, but this did keep the company on a sound financial footing.

Although Werkman was a capable printer his early typography was in no way redolent of what was to come, and there was little to differentiate his products from those of comparable establishments of the same period. Often the printing jobs were handled by subordinates. Only the book of poetry printed for his brother M. H. Werkman, *Museum van Plastische Verzen* (Museum of Plastic Verses), displays any real individuality, and for this period the style is distinctive. Jugendstil embellishments are used, together with a new German typeface, Tiemann Medieval, and the proportions are carefully controlled.

On April 2, 1917, Werkman's wife died suddenly of a stroke, leaving him with three young children. Six months later, he married again. At the same time he began to pay less attention to the running of the printing business, a prelude to fiscal disaster. He had a permanent rupture with members of the Cremer family, who objected to his remarrying so soon after the death of their daughter. He was forced to borrow money at a high rate of interest to buy them out. Their departure also meant that their financial expertise would no longer be available to administer the business.
In 1918 the Groningen art circle, De Ploeg, was inaugurated in a café, the objective being to "bring artists together and stimulate local art."[5] Among others, charter members included Jan Wiegers, Johan Dijkstra, Jan Altink, and the photographer Simon Steenmeijer. Later they were joined by Jan G. Jordens, Jan van der Zee, Hendrik de Vries, Johan Faber, and Wobbe Alkema. Werkman, who had begun to paint in 1917, became a member in 1920. His original inspiration had come from a visit to a Van Gogh exhibition in 1896, and throughout his life Van Gogh would remain one of his principal idols.

From October 1921 until March 1922, Werkman published at considerable personal expense a monthly art magazine called *Blad voor Kunst* (Publication for Art).[6] With woodcuts and reproductions of their drawings and paintings, it furnished an overview of early work by members of De Ploeg and a forum for his own views on contemporary art. One of the issues contains a review of Van Ostaijen's *Bezette Stad,* whose influence would soon surface in Werkman's own work. The last publication of *Blad voor Kunst* is of particular interest because it included an abstract cover by Werkman that suggests how his work would later manifest itself

6-2. H. N. Werkman, *Blad Voor Kunst* no. 6 (Magazine for Art), cover, 1921, 30.5 × 27.5 cm. Collection, Antiquariaat Schuhmacher, Amsterdam.

(Fig. 6-2). It was a woodcut in red, yellow, and blue, inspired by an exhibition of work by Huszár, Van Doesburg, and Van der Leck at the Groningen Pictura Gallery in February 1922.

It came as no surprise when the printing concern finally failed in 1923, largely because of his casual attitude toward business affairs. Willem Sandberg described Werkman as someone for whom anything utilitarian was beyond comprehension. Forced to dismiss all but one employee, Wybren Bos, he moved what was left of the operation to a garret workshop reached by climbing several flights of stairs above a warehouse on a canal called the Lage der A. Although he managed to earn a modest living from jobs such as wedding and birth announcements, invitations, brochures, stationery, and posters, the new business did not prosper.

Ultimately, however, all these adversities were transformed into a form of liberation, or in the words of his friend Job Hansen, "Werkman's art is the result of unemployment."[7] He later wrote that up until then his life had not been his own; he had been a captive of convention. From this time on he tried more and more to distance himself from anything and everything not related to the poetic, and even his commercial pieces reflected this attitude. Having used typographic elements for so many years to serve his clients, he arrived at the realization that he had never before exploited them as he wanted to. For the next twenty-two years, he immersed himself in a world of type, form, and color.[8]

The Next Call

In Groningen on the morning of September 12, 1923, Werkman's friends discovered a mysterious pamphlet in their mailboxes. Commencing with the phrase "GRONINGEN BERLIN PARIS MOSCOW 1923—Beginning of a Violet Season," it promulgated the avant garde publication *The Next Call,* and in unambiguous language proclaimed the birth of a new era in the arts. It stated: "It must be attested and affirmed. . . . Art is everywhere." Berlin, Paris, and Moscow were then centers of new art movements, and by having Groningen head the list, Werkman contended that similar achievements could and would take place there. At first it was unclear who the author was. It was signed "Travailleur & Cie" ("Workman & Others" in French), which provided a clue to the writer's identity. Some of the recipients realized that it was Werkman's creation because of the address Lage der A 13 at the bottom.[9]

The first issue of *The Next Call,* the esoteric title of which has always remained a riddle, was put in the mail two weeks later on September 22 (Figs. 6-3 to 6-5). In large, rough, uppercase sans serif letters on the bottom and right-hand sides of three pages, it boldly displayed a phrase that would reflect Werkman's philosophy for the rest of his life:

EEN RIL DOORKLIEFT
HET LIJF DAT VREEST
DE VRIJHEID VAN DE GEEST

[A CHILL SEEPS THROUGH
THE BODY THAT FEARS
THE FREEDOM OF THE SPIRIT][10]

Including the cover and back, the first issue consisted of 8 pages measuring 27.5 × 21.5 cm. The cover is one of Werkman's first

6-3. H. N. Werkman. *The Next Call 1,* double-page spread, 1923, 27.4 × 21.5 cm. Collection, Dr. Robert Polak, Amsterdam.

6-4. H. N. Werkman, *The Next Call 1*, double-page spread, 1923, 27.4×21.5 cm. Collection, Dr. Robert Polak, Amsterdam.

6-5. H. N. Werkman, *The Next Call 1*, double-page spread, 1923, 27.4×21.5 cm. Collection, Dr. Robert Polak, Amsterdam.

nonobjective typographic creations. Two lowercase *r*s and a larger lowercase *e* are combined with the impression of a lockplate from the side of a door. The letters are not used for any explicit message, and the lockplate takes on a new identity as an uppercase *E*. The composition is inventive, direct, and playful, controlled and at the same time relying on the intervention of chance. It concludes with the enigmatic text:

JOY OF
LIFE

Pray for Anguish
No Languishing from love;
Wasting worry,
Luxury of Woe.

Loathe triumph
Horseman's glow
Tomorrow the regret
Death in the cup.[11]

With this issue of *The Next Call* Werkman began to combine traditional printing with a new and unorthodox method. The technique itself was deceptively simple: the paper was placed face up on the bed of the handpress, which allowed him freely to arrange and vary previously inked design elements. Every print that resulted from this combined creative and printing approach was unique. The procedure could be repeated indefinitely with an unlimited number of shapes and colors, and in this way his printing technique resembled a form of painting. He pushed the handpress beyond its previous limits, allowing every nuance to assume a role—the individual and inherent idiosyncrasies of wood grains, the scratches on damaged pieces of type, the thickness of ink, the disparate methods of inking, and the paper textures. Werkman had become enraptured with the printing process itself and often referred to his materials as if they were animate beings: "There is paper so beautiful that one only wants to caress it and otherwise leave it unblemished. . . . Ink is an even more delicate creature."[12]

Groningen, still a parochial and somewhat insular city, was both geographically and psychologically removed from the more urbane centers of Amsterdam, Rotterdam, Utrecht, and The Hague. In 1924 Werkman wrote to his correspondent, the Belgian artist Michel Seuphor, pseudonym of F. Berckelaers, publisher of *Het Overzicht* (The Review): "Much to my regret I have to admit that Groningen sits in a corner which almost no sound penetrates."[13] The people of Groningen were by disposition skeptics,[14] exemplifying one of the many popular Dutch aphorisms *Wat de boer niet kent, dat vreet hij niet* (What the farmer doesn't know, he doesn't eat), and the inaugural issue of *The Next Call* did little to impress even his colleagues in De Ploeg. His friend Hansen, who contributed to three of the issues, was the only one of them who really seemed to understand what Werkman was trying to do. The rest reacted mainly with bewilderment and curiosity rather than affinity, dubious about the sudden plunge of someone whom they considered to be an amateur painter into the avant garde.[15] Werkman later wrote: "In spite of the fact that many of the things produced in this period seem somewhat mad in retrospect, *The Next Call* was never intended to be a joke. Otherwise, with vacillating self-confidence, I would never have been able to continue."[16] Irrespective of the reactions of his contemporaries, Werkman believed in his work and continued with the tenacity of a medieval monk.

The second number of *The Next Call* appeared on October 6, 1923 (Figs. 6-6 to 6-8). It included a pungent and anarchistic text by Werkman and the Groningen painter Wiegers in which they bemoaned the condition of current society: "All merchants, bailiffs, conceited constables and clerks of court, all those who wear caps and gowns shall be compelled to heed the laughter of the accused and prosecuted, and the tumult will be so loud in their court-

6-6. H. N. Werkman, *The Next Call 2*, cover, 1923, 27.4×21.5 cm. Collection, Dr. Robert Polak, Amsterdam.

6-7. H. N. Werkman, *The Next Call 2,* double-page spread, 1923, 27.4 × 21.5 cm. Collection, Dr. Robert Polak, Amsterdam.

6-8. H. N. Werkman, *The Next Call 2,* double-page spread, 1923, 27.4 × 21.5 cm. Collection, Dr. Robert Polak, Amsterdam.

rooms that, after stupidly gazing, they will never be able to shut their jaws again."[17]

The cover again utilized a lockplate as the dominant design element. This is printed in black on top of a yellow rectangle, with *The Next Call,* which consummates the composition, in a triangular arrangement. On page 2 an image of a man is assembled from pieces of type with small and large *o*s forming his head and torso and an upside-down *L* and *T* his legs and feet. A *J* lying on its side is converted into a walking stick. On page 4 a similar puppet figure appears to be standing halfway inside a doorway. Pages 5 and 6 are typographic interpretations of the words *CHAGALL UN FILS DU COSMOS* and *BOULEVARD,* and the author is listed as *TRAVAILLEUR ET CIE* in a vertical column on the back page.

On page 6 the word *Paris* is printed above *BOULEVARD* and then casually covered over with a piece of paper, indicating a late deci-

sion in the design process. Werkman's printed pieces were frequently in a continuous state of transition, a major difference between him and contemporaries such as Schuitema and Zwart. They were all committed to liberating typography from its established functions, but while the latter two often followed predetermined schemes, Werkman, a master of serendipity, delighted in the guided accident, in discovering his configurations through the printing procedure itself. With Werkman, design did not precede typesetting and printing; the three processes were combined into a single creative procedure.

Throughout the entire series, no two copies of *The Next Call* are exactly alike. The printing is deliberately irregular, the letter-spacing arbitrary, and the inking inconsistent. Werkman was not overly concerned with the esthetic qualities of the typefaces themselves and merely utilized what happened to be on hand in his printing shop. He was never an accomplished typographer in a conventional sense, and although his production before 1923 confirms that he was indeed an expert printer, he was never interested in pressmanship in itself. Details assumed a subordinate role, the end result remaining the crucial factor, and he was prepared to use any means necessary to achieve the desired result. No previous guidelines applied, and each circumstance invoked its own solution, or as Werkman later wrote, "the subject proclaims itself and is never sought."[18]

At the same time that he published *The Next Call*, Werkman produced many larger monotypes using similar methods. In 1923 he printed his first series of over six hundred *druksels*, a derivative of the Dutch word *drukken* meaning "to print." By applying different thicknesses, impressions, and viscosities of ink, he was able to create an intricate pattern of tone and depth, and by using a rough paper he provided an opportunity to experiment with textures that emerge through the layers of ink. They bring to mind the abstract prints Zwart was producing at the same time. It is unlikely, though, given Werkman's isolation in Groningen, that one was cognizant of what the other was doing. A principal difference between the two is that Werkman used the traditional printing methods of the previous century while Zwart, as much as possible, utilized new technology. Unlike Werkman, the idiosyncrasies of wooden type faces did not interest Zwart in the least. Also, Werkman often relied on the accidental, while Zwart maintained absolute control from conception to the end product.

Typographical elements were also assuming new functions in Russian Constructivism, Futurism, Cubism, Dadaism, and Surrealism, and the use of letters as elements in paintings was nothing new. Werkman's *druksels* could be defined as printed collages, and in this way analogous to what Schwitters, Hausmann, and others were doing in Germany during the same period. Both worked with existing prefabricated elements, Schwitters using cut paper

and other found elements and Werkman relying upon the various odds and ends available in the type shop—rules, numbers, letters, backs of poster types, and punctuation marks. Although Werkman's approach to typography was in most respects not functional, there is a similarity between his method and that of Zwart. Albeit in different ways, both were using type as collage. Werkman was far less influenced by De Stijl, but by emphasizing the innate qualities of printing elements, he did come close to the constructivist belief that art should reflect the nature of its material.[19] Zwart's work was more linear, analytical, and exact; Werkman approached his with the instincts of a painter. "He used common things in a completely uncommon manner and in this way achieved a very uncommon, very innate artistic form."[20]

In addition to the *druksels,* between 1926 and 1927 Werkman produced a series of typographic drawings created on the typewriter. These were called *tiksels,* a play on the word *tikken,* meaning "to type" in Dutch (Fig. 6-9). Almost at the same time, typewriter images were published in *De Stijl,* volume VII, numbers 75/76 and 77, 1926–27 by Pietro (de) Saga. They were similar in technique but quite different in imagery. Much of Werkman's production stemmed from economic necessity, and this was probably one of those cases. His questionable credit rating did not help his position with paper suppliers, and he sometimes had to resort to printing on wrapping paper. Often it is possible to date Werkman's *druksels* by the colors of the inks. Due to his ever-precarious financial position, he was often forced to buy a limited number of colors, and until they were depleted, this would determine the colors of the printed pieces.

On January 12, 1924, Werkman distributed the third number of *The Next Call,* visually the least provocative of the nine issues. A similar lock structure forms a yellow vertical band through the

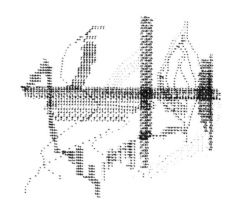

6-9. H. N. Werkman, *Tiksel,* 1923–1929, 27 × 21 cm, photograph courtesy of Jan van Loenen Martinet, Amsterdam.

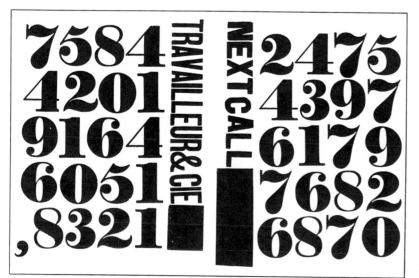

6-10. H. N. Werkman, *The Next Call 4,* cover and back, 1924, 27.4 × 21.5 cm. Collection, Dr. Robert Polak, Amsterdam.

center of the cover, and printed on top of this is a drypoint by Jan Wiegers depicting the incongruous combination of a drawing of a steamroller and a quotation from Walt Whitman.[21]

The fourth issue of *The Next Call* was circulated at the end of January 1924. Its motif was a Dada text by Job Hansen alluding vaguely to the inception of Constructivism:

flying machine
TODAY
Art and fabrications XX century
Beginning of appreciation of flying
machine, motor

FINALLY

God conceived man
and man
creates the objects
Constructivist art
                        "   of ob-
jects (without subject)
ART AND TECHNIQUE
Brand-new and
timely[22]

Beginning with this issue, the typography became more experimental. The compositions are consistently humorous, ambiguous, active, and rhythmical, and are filled with movement and tension (Figs. 6-10 to 6-13). Both the cover and back page are made up of a grid of numbers. The title *The Next Call* and "Travailleur & Cie" are printed vertically next to the fold. Page 6 alludes to an imaginary machine and recalls a 1920 collage by Moholy-Nagy. Bold contrasts of type style, direction, and size are employed to produce compositions that seem to have fallen into place at random. In this issue, the harmony of double-page spreads became more pronounced, and defects in the wood types clearly indicate that some letters were printed separately. (For example the same worn down *M* is used on both pages 2 and 3.)

On the second and third pages, Lenin's death on January 21 is solemnized with two columns of type built from *O*s and *M*s, giving the impression of soldiers escorting a cortège. Like many artists and writers of that period, he was keenly aware of the extraordinary achievements of the Russian avant garde and viewed the Russian Revolution as a potential catalyst in a postwar renaissance. Also, in Dutch the word *OOM* means "uncle," although perhaps this is merely a coincidence and one should not attribute a single special meaning to it—it is a common error to read too much into Werkman's compositions.

The fifth issue followed in June 1924 with the now-familiar lock plate appearing on the cover for the last time. This is the most

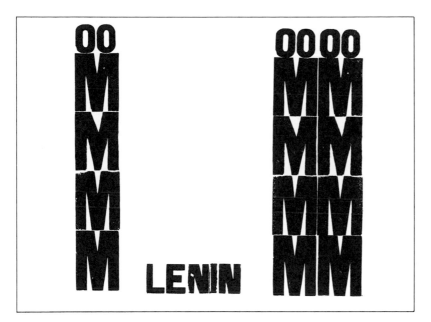

6-11. H. N. Werkman, *The Next Call 4,*
double-page spread, 1924, 27.4 × 21.5 cm.
Collection, Dr. Robert Polak, Amsterdam.

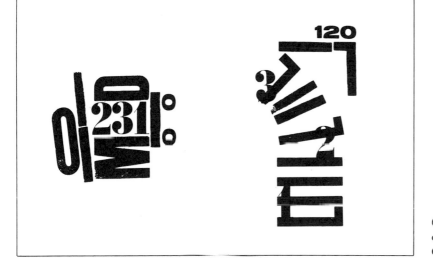

6-12. H. N. Werkman, *The Next Call 4,*
double-page spread, 1924, 27.4 × 21.5 cm.
Collection, Dr. Robert Polak, Amsterdam.

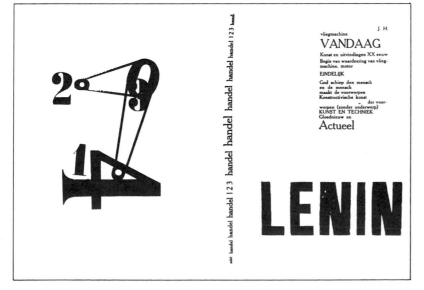

6-13. H. N. Werkman, *The Next Call 4,*
double-page spread, 1924, 27.4 × 21.5 cm.
Collection, Dr. Robert Polak, Amsterdam.

colorful number, with a bold use of orange, blue, and black. The typography is even more inventive and animated, as the pages alternate between text and image (Fig. 6-14). Page 2 displays an ampersand perched on top of a vertical rectangle like a typographic potentate or parrot. Two lowercase *j*s support the base and repeat the curves of the form above. Page 3 combines a vertical column of *z*s with a Dada text. He juxtaposes almost every typeface in his shop, and in spite of this incongruous assortment, he manages to attain a semblance of harmony. The similar slant to *The Next Call* and "Travailleur et Cie" indicates that cover and back page were printed as a unit.[23]

This number was distributed far beyond Groningen. Among others, there was a response from Bonset, Van Doesburg's Dada alter ego who, having missed the point of Werkman's use of Travailleur & Cie, rejoined with his familiar humility:

When and however it would be plausible to restructure your magazine in a more dadaistic path I would be glad to help you, also in sending it to addresses of conceivable interest such as: Picabia, Tzara, Arp, Schwitters, Richter, etc. . . . Typographically I find a lot to admire in your publication, notably page 4. However, it does not make a good impression when you neglect to mention the names of the collaborators at the beginning of your magazine. Every clandestine action is a priori rejected.[24]

That this criticism came from someone who was himself using two pseudonyms is perhaps indicative of Van Doesburg's iconoclastic and ironic wit.

Pretentious as they might have been, Van Doesburg's remarks may have had some effect, and in the sixth issue Travailleur et Cie was quietly supplanted by "Edit.—Publisher H. N. Werkman, Lage der A 13, Groningen, Holland."[25] By then Werkman had probably given up hope of getting much cooperation from his colleagues in De Ploeg, and this may have been another reason for his dropping "Travailleur et Cie."

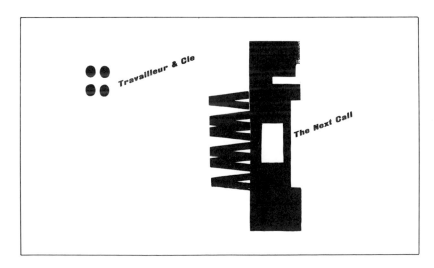

6-14. H. N. Werkman, *The Next Call 5,* cover and back, 1924, 27.4 × 21.5 cm. Collection, Dr. Robert Polak, Amsterdam.

The sixth issue was mailed on the first of November, 1924. The cover is particularly intriguing in that now the collage technique is also used. Fragments of typographic posters are pasted on the tops of both the front and back pages, adding to the individuality of each copy. The title is enclosed in a grid of rules on top of a thin layer of red ink printed from the back of a large wood type, a motif repeated on the envelope.

This was the first of two foldout issues measuring 43×54.4 cm, and here we find the typographic construction, "Plattegrond van de Kunst en Omstreken" (Map of Art and Environs) (Figs. 6-15, 6-16). The pun originated from an observation by Hansen when he saw Werkman busy with the composition: "It looks like a map of art and its perimeters."[26] Werkman then heightened the association with words and blocks forming pieces of land, lines indicating streets and rivers, and an arc of letters depicting the word *omstreken* (perimeters).

The second page contains a tightly structured composition built from the backs of carefully interlocked pieces of printing lock-up furniture. The text, set in a typeface imitating that of a typewriter, again parodies the bourgeois and begins with the sentence: "He has his Sundays, every week six, except Sunday. Sunday is the blank page in expectation of every Monday morning. He has his diversions. His motorboat and his pedigreed dog and his newspaper as convocation. . . ."[27]

The text on the back page confirms that Werkman was now in touch with other international avant garde publications. It lists:

Het Overzicht, F. Berckelaers and Josef Peeters, Antwerp
De Stijl, Theo van Doesburg, Leiden

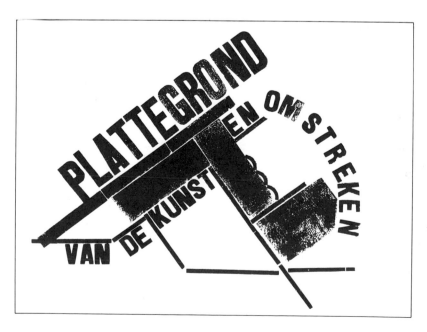

6-15. H. N. Werkman, *The Next Call 6,* unfolded, 1924, 43×54 cm. Collection, Dr. Robert Polak, Amsterdam.

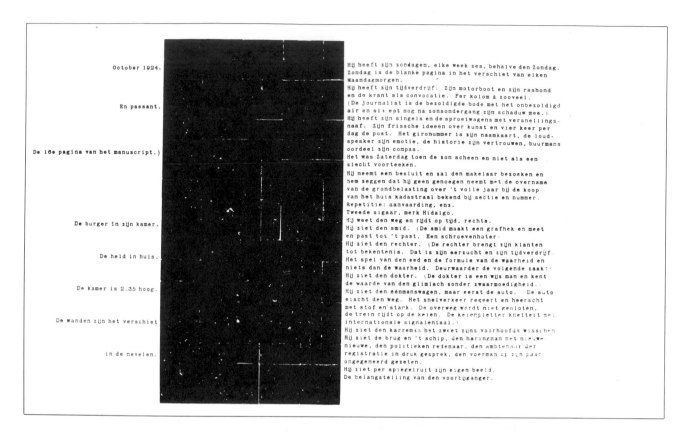

Mécano, I.K. Bonset, Paris
Merz, Kurt Schwitters and El Lissitsky, Hanover
La Zone, A. Cernik, Brünn Julianov, Belgrade
Zenith, L. Mitzitch, Belgrade
Blok, H. Stazewski and others, Warsaw
Disk, K. Teige, Prague, and many others

6-16. H. N. Werkman, *The Next Call 6,*
double-page spread, 1924, 27.2 × 21.5 cm.
Collection, Dr. Robert Polak, Amsterdam.

Again printed on a single sheet, the seventh issue of *The Next Call* was distributed in February 1925 (Fig. 6-17). Unfolded in the center of the verso is a large image by Werkman composed of rectangles, lines and *O*s. On the left and right are linoleum cuts by two Ploeg members, Van der Zee and Alkema, and a photographic print of a painting by Van der Zee. The paper was folded twice horizontally and then again in the middle. When partially folded, a composition composed from two columns of words is revealed, and in order to further emphasize the symmetry, the left column is set flush left and the right column flush right (Fig. 6-18). There are two versions of the cover, one composed of vertical and horizontal shapes and the other of diagonals, and two variations of Werkman's composition on the center spread. The back contains a whimsical composition using *O*s, heavy rules, and the backs of wood type.[28]

The eighth number is dated September 1925, but according to the postage cancellation was not mailed until February 1926. The typography has an implied association with industry, and the cover

6-17. H. N. Werkman, *The Next Call 7*, cover and back, 1925, 27.2 × 21.5 cm. Collection, Dr. Robert Polak, Amsterdam.

6-18. H. N. Werkman, *The Next Call 7*, half unfolded, 1925, 27.3 × 43 cm. Collection, Dr. Robert Polak, Amsterdam.

suggests a factory. Some of the constructions depict machinery: the composition on page 2 resembles a forklift and the one on the back page a truck. There are fewer letters and numbers and a less generous use of white space. Dissimilar copies show minute changes in the arrangement of type, which again reveals Werkman's constantly evolving creative process. A cryptic and sardonic "credit" and "debit" list alludes to the ever-dismal state of his business affairs (Fig. 6-19):

Per 1 Sept   ember 1925

Debit	Credit
Balance: inventory	constancy
pessimism (in a boundary of purple and green)	exercise in apa- thy
Olympiad	tyranny
sin (yet with repentance)	joyfulness
achievement: achievement ignored	undervalued silence
system: (followed principal)	constantcy
miserable game of ready-made agitation	independence
speakers	semi-automatic mimiographs and cash registers
(singular talk automats)	
selfishness- and utilities	unmasking
coefficient (pro memoria)	
coincidence (speculative)	determination of the misconstrued
cahs (recieved with gratitude)	offerings[29]

Typographically, however, this is the most mature issue. Pages 2, 3, and 7 are filled with contrasting vertical and horizontal texts, with the overall textures broken intermittently by larger type (Figs. 6-20 to 6-22). The superb center spread on pages 4 and 5, constructed with large lowercase *a*s and heavy black rules, is melodic in feeling, as the type forms seem to ramble freely through the white space. It closes with the following wistful lines, almost pure nostalgia:

6-19. H. N. Werkman, *The Next Call 8*, double-page spread, 1926, 27.3 × 21.5 cm. Collection, Dr. Robert Polak, Amsterdam.

once when the earth
was still not round
once when
art was still *not*
art
once when the ant
was not yet diligent
once when he
was still *young*
once when she
was still small
once when my
mother *still sang*
once when it
was summer
once when it was still
the day before yesterday
once when yesterday
was not yet today[31]

Werkman had become increasingly disillusioned with the conservative stance of some of his colleagues in De Ploeg, and a principal objective of *The Next Call* was to send a signal warning them against the risks of complacency. Johan van Zweden wrote in 1945: "For members of De Ploeg Werkman served a kind of artistic conscience; he protected them from becoming bourgeois too soon and with his astute vision he breached the limitations of a menacing parochialism."[32] Werkman's eloquent appeal never ignited the spark that he desired; most of his friends found his work too subjective and never really understood what he was doing. Even though there was some respect for his originality, they were still confused by its unusual manifestation. Or, as his friend Hendrik de Vries wrote in 1945, "his colleagues in De Ploeg had as much admiration for him as their pedestrian states of mind would allow."[33]

6-20. H. N. Werkman, *The Next Call 9,*
double-page spread, 1926, 35 × 21.4 cm.
Collection, Dr. Robert Polak, Amsterdam.

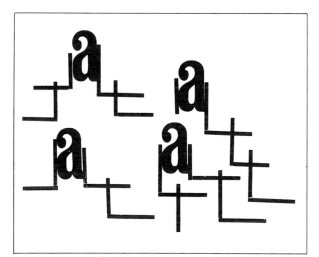

6-21. H. N. Werkman, *The Next Call 9,*
double-page spread, 1926, 35 × 21.4 cm.
Collection, Dr. Robert Polak, Amsterdam.

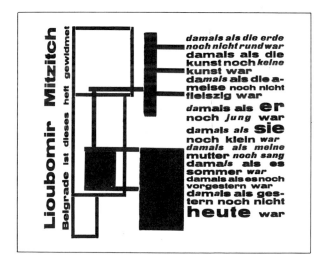

6-22. H. N. Werkman, *The Next Call 9,*
double-page spread, 1926, 35 × 21.4 cm.
Collection, Dr. Robert Polak, Amsterdam.

In addition to being the unsolicited conscience for De Ploeg, *The Next Call* served three additional purposes: as an outlet for Werkman's various manifestos regarding the new art, as a means to explore and exhibit his experimental typography, and as a channel to communicate with the international avant garde. While *The Next Call* was being published, Werkman continued to produce other typographic material in a similar style. These were mainly posters and invitations for De Ploeg, birth announcements, posters, calendars, bookplates, and cards (Fig. 6-23). The most consistent unifying element was the combination of Werkman's playfulness, innocence, and boldness. It would be misleading to label this a style: it has a transcendent quality that makes Werkman's creations immediately recognizable as his own and goes beyond the obviously technical into another, almost impenetrable and ineffable, realm.

Hot Printing

After 1927, the art circle De Ploeg followed a more conservative and traditional path, but in spite of this digression, Werkman, who was never really accepted by De Ploeg, remained involved and kept up his friendships with the other members. It was around that time that he experienced a longing to return to the basics of life, and inspired by Gauguin, seriously contemplated immigrating to Tahiti. Werkman made his first and only trip abroad in 1930 when he was invited by Seuphor to participate in a group exhibition in Paris that would include Kandinsky and Arp. The trip to Paris and Cologne, however, was a disappointment—he was not able to see any of the artists themselves, not even Seuphor. Even the language and food were not to his liking.[34]

6-23. H. N. Werkman, Invitation for a De Ploeg drawing exhibition, 1928, 10.6 × 14.4 cm. Photograph courtesy of Jan van Loenen Martinet, Amsterdam.

With a few interruptions, the next ten years were among Werkman's most productive. He experimented with new techniques, and his work alternated more and more between figurative and abstract compositions. In 1929 he began to use the ink roller as a drawing and painting instrument, applying it directly to the paper, and in 1934 he introduced the stencil technique. This consisted of rolling ink on papers out of which forms had been cut. He incorporated a stamping method where elements such as pieces of wood type were separately inked and pressed onto the paper surface. Jazz was also an inspiration. In 1935 he named this new stencil-inspired series of *druksels* "Hot Printing" after hot jazz. He later explained his technique in a letter to his friend, the Reformed Minister F. R. A. Henkels: "I use an old handpress for my prints; so the impression is done vertically, and the impression can be regulated instinctively. Sometimes you have to press hard, sometimes very lightly, sometimes one half of the block is heavily inked, the other half sparsely. Also, by printing the first layer of ink on another sheet of paper, you then get a paler shade which is used for the definitive version. Sometimes a single print goes under the press fifty times."[35] Virtually all his prints combine several techniques as he tried to produce as many effects as possible from the basic printing process.

His work, while not losing any of its candid, almost primitive, vitality, became increasingly more refined. The 1931 poster for De Ploeg and the Proclamatie manifestos showed this subtle change. The compositions from 1931 have some of the same sense of balance, movement, and innocence of Alexander Calder's mobiles. His 1933 poster for *De Rekenmachine* (The Adding Machine), a drama by the progressive playwright Elmer L. Rice, inventively depicted an adding machine constructed out of typographic material (Fig. 6-24). Years later Rice saw the poster for the first time at a Werkman exhibition at the Stedelijk Museum in Amsterdam. The *Proclamatie* manifestos were attempts to begin a new version of *The Next Call*, but never got beyond this stage. Also notable was his ten-part series of bookplate designs made for M.C.v.L. in 1934. Each version, partially built out of printing "furniture," was a different interpretation.

Preludium, published in September 1938, was one of the few pieces printed, illustrated, and written by Werkman. Another was *3 Syllabijnen, 2 Vocaletten* (3 Syllables, 2 Vocalettes), published in 1944. *Preludium* was sent to friends in De Ploeg as a protest against an attempt by some of them to accept twelve new members whom Werkman and some others feared would be a bourgeois and conservative influence. The only result of this effort was that some of the more progressive members left De Ploeg. On the cover the type is used as an accordion, and the images are printed with stencils.

6-24

6-25

As De Ploeg eventually became known outside Groningen, its members were invited to have exhibitions in Leeuwarden, Rotterdam, Hilversum, and the Stedelijk Museum in Amsterdam. Certain critics referred to Werkman's *druksels* as "abracadabra," and Werkman seized upon the word as a slogan and used it as a basis for his *Proclamatie 2* (Fig. 6-25). In 1931, 1938, 1939, and 1940, Werkman produced complete calendars that were in line with his other experimental typography. In the last two calendars he began to use illustrations as well, and these anticipate the calendars and other pieces proaduced during the occupation years of World War II.

In 1936, with the beginning of the Spanish Civil War and the occupation of the Rhineland by Germany, ominous signs of war appeared throughout Europe. When Werkman married in that year for the third time, his printing company was still operating, but only on a shoestring. His career would finally come to a brilliant and climatic conclusion with his clandestine publications produced during the German occupation of the Netherlands from 1940 to 1945.

6-24. H. N. Werkman, *De Rekenmachine,* poster for performance of Elmer L. Rice's *The Adding Machine,* 1928, 10.6 × 14.4 cm. Photograph courtesy of Jan van Loenen Martinet, Amsterdam.

6-25. H. N. Werkman, *Proclamatie 2,* 1932, 57.7 × 48 cm. Photograph courtesy of Jan van Loenen Martinet, Amsterdam.

Chapter 7
The 1930s

Oppression and Involution

As in most parts of the world, the 1930s in Europe presented a depressing picture. The uncertain and deteriorating economic and political climate had a stagnating effect on the optimism and idealism of the 1920s, and as National Socialism grew in Germany, as well as in The Netherlands, the climate became increasingly uneasy for the artistic avant garde. Invigorating and propitious international contacts became less frequent, and a feeling of bleak isolation began to take hold in the artistic community. Although Dutch society remained essentially intact during the thirties, it became more fractured as the depression gained momentum, bringing with it mass unemployment and the collapse of the international currency exchange market in Europe.

As the enervating political and economic problems of the period took hold, a new and sometimes decadent realism in painting developed alongside Constructivism. On one hand, there was an increasing appetite for a sense of security—though it was a false security—through technology, and on the other there was a growing skepticism, in which the elation of a regained confidence was gradually transformed into unhealthy feelings of indifference, despair, and irony. In one way this was exemplified through Surrealism. This movement signaled a surrender to the subconscious and a cynicism about the erratic values of an unsound culture. In architecture there was also a reactionary movement against functionalism.

The political and social situation affected graphic design as well. Innocuous and profuse embellishment, which had been assigned to the dustbin during the 1920s, began to creep back in, and traditional illustration began to encroach on some of the turf it had lost to photography. The exhibition "Art et Technique," which was held as a part of the Paris World Fair in 1937, showed little of the achievements of the 1920s and early thirties.

As many graphic designers began to adapt themselves more to the proclivities of their clients, and as the field became more benign, it became more mundane as well. By the beginning of World War II, some of the few exceptions to this regression were Werkman, Cohen, and the architects and designers associated with the magazine *De 8 en Opbouw,* such as Zwart and Schuitema.

Of the independent graphic designers whose careers began to ascend during the thirties in The Netherlands, the most prominent were Willem Sandberg, Gerard Kiljan, Wim Brusse, Hendrik Josef Louis (Henny) Cahn, Nicolaas de Koo, and Dick Elffers. There were also many anonymous designers, especially at the advertising agencies, who deserve a place in this book (Fig. 7-1). Unfortunately, there are few records, and because advertising was not at that time considered to be worth collecting, only a fraction of their work survives. Another important and often overlooked contributor was the printer Lumax in Utrecht, which produced many of the books for De Gemeenschap. The manager of Lumax, A. M. Oosterbaan, also supervised the design of many of their publications (Figs. 7-2, 7-3). He was a naturally gifted typographer, and

e r i c   v a n
d e r   s t e e n

g e m e n g d e
b e r i c h t e n

de gemeenschap
u t r e c h t   1 9 3 2

7-2. A. Oosterbaan, *Gemengde berichten* (Mixed Messages) by Eric van der Steen, cover, 1928. Published by de Gemeenschap, printed by Lumax, 22.9 × 15.3 cm. Collection, Antiquariaat Schuhmacher, Amsterdam.

7-1. Unknown, *Socialistische Kunst.heden* (Socialist Art Today), Amsterdam, 1930, cover for Stedelijk Museum catalog. 24.5 × 15.6 cm. Collection. Antiquariaat Schuhmacher.

7-3. A. Oosterbaan, *8.100.000 m3 Zand* by M. Revis, cover, 1932. Published by de Gemeenschap, printed by Lumax. 20.5 × 13.7 cm. Collection, Antiquariaat Schuhmacher, Amsterdam.

many of his books, such as *Blokken* (Blocks) by F. Bordewijk, rank among the most innovative book designs of the period.

Willem Sandberg

Although Sandberg's major contribution to Dutch graphic design would not come until after World War II, his accomplishments up until then are significant. Before that time he covered much territory, both as a graphic designer and a museum curator.

Willem Jacob Henri Berend Sandberg was born on October 24, 1897, in Amersfoort. Like many others in his generation, he had a traditional Calvinist upbringing, but by the time he was 16 had already dissociated himself from religion. Throughout his life he tried deliberately to distance himself from this early orthodox environment.[1] He initially wanted to become a painter, a difficult option for his family, which for generations had been lawyers and civil servants. In 1919 he entered the Rijksacademie in Amsterdam, but left after only six months, having become disenchanted

with the art school environment in general. He had also found it difficult to make friends among the other students and considered it annoying to have the teachers make corrections directly on his drawings.[2]

After marrying in 1920, Sandberg traveled with his wife to Italy to see the art of the Renaissance. He also traveled to Switzerland and Germany and studied at the Académie de la Grande Chaumière in Paris. By 1923 he had discarded any residual painting ambition, feeling that he possessed neither the necessary enjoyment nor talent. He later commented that Mondrian had already realized what he wanted to achieve anyway.[3] Filled with uncertainty and constantly in search of new paths, Sandberg returned to Holland, where he studied law and eventually he ended up with a law degree. He also took courses in philosophy, art history, psychology, and statistics in both Vienna and Utrecht.[4]

Becoming a graphic designer almost by default during the late twenties, Sandberg came into contact with progressive young designers in the V.A.N.K., the Dutch arts and crafts organization. He was introduced to the architectural group De 8 en Opbouw, which included internationalist architects and graphic designers such as Zwart, Stam, and Van Eesteren who, either directly or indirectly, had been influenced by recent developments in Germany and Russia. They were all committed to producing well-conceived and well-designed industrial products, residences, and interiors in

7-4. Willem Sandberg, *Nederlands Muziek Feest 1935* (Dutch Music Festival 1935), cover. 20.5 × 16.5 cm. Collection, Antiquariaat Schuhmacher, Amsterdam.

Vereeniging tot bevordering van het

Onderwijs in Kinderverzorging en Opvoeding

K en O

*doel
opleiding
tijdschriften
cursussen
werk van gediplomeerden
plaatsingsbureau
adressen*

7-5. Willem Sandberg, *Ver. K en O* (K and O Society), page from brochure, 1936, 15 × 11 cm. Collection, Antiquariaat Schuhmacher, Amsterdam.

the interest of society. Sandberg had much respect for Stam's vision, and Stam played a dominant role in the development of Sandberg's philosophy. After 1934, Stam and Sandberg collaborated on exhibitions, and during the war they worked together in the resistance.

Sandberg designed his first printed piece in 1927, a calendar for the publisher Ploegsma. Like Zwart, Schuitema, and others he had no previous education in graphic design except for his brief stay at the Rijksacademie, his work with statistics in Vienna, and a few months as a typesetting assistant in 1921. He was initially influenced by De Stijl, Constructivism, and Dada, yet developed a unique and intensely free vision that stressed the experimental, spontaneity, and intuition. He never started with a preconceived idea, and as with Werkman, the result grew out of the design process itself (Figs. 7-4 to 7-7).

In 1928 he designed his first piece for the Stedelijk Museum, a statistics chart for an exhibition called Work for the Disabled, as well as pieces for the State Insurance Bank, the Economic Information Service, and the PTT. In 1931 he designed a series of 12

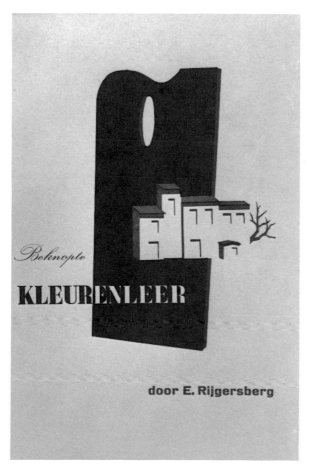

7-6

7-7

geography charts for the publisher Nijgh & Van Ditmar and in 1933 began planning the PTT display windows in The Hague, a task previously handled by Piet Zwart. In 1935 he began serving as an exhibition consultant for the Stedelijk Museum, and the following year, at the age of 39, he accepted a position as curator. In 1938 he was hired as a conservator and went on to design most of the exhibition catalogs. The catalog for the 1939 exhibition *Rondom Rodin, Honderd Jaar Fransche Sculptuur* (Around Rodin, A Hundred Years of French Sculpture) became a prototype for the catalogs after the war.

In the winter of 1938–39 Sandberg first became acquainted with the work of Werkman and in a later interview recalled his initial encounter:

7-6. Willem Sandberg, *Beknopte Kleurenleer* (Condensed Color Principles) by E. Rijgersberg, cover, 1938. 22 × 15 cm. Collection, Antiquariaat Schuhmacher, Amsterdam.

7-7. Willem Sandberg, *'t Woonhuys*, catalog cover. 1938. 31 × 19.2 cm. Collection, Antiquariaat Schuhmacher, Amsterdam.

It came about in that I was a friend of the painter Jan Wiegers. Originally from Groningen, he had worked for a time in Switzerland and Germany and had become friends with Kirchner. He was instrumental in bringing expressionism to Groningen. I had not been at the museum very long before he arrived with a portfolio under his arms and said: "I have a few things here that I don't know quite what to do with. You do a bit with typography and design and will like them." He then produced the large sheets by Werkman. . . . I was so curious and intrigued by these large pieces that I wanted to actually see the man and learn about the other things he was doing. Shortly afterwards I took a train to Groningen and looked him up at his small home. I then encountered a reserved Groninger with whom it was not easy to start a conversation. A really taciturn person. Having grown up under the shadow of Groningen in Assen I understand this type. After the first cigarette things went better and, I believe, we became friends on that day. . . . I was fascinated by him and by his work. And then to think that this man was once the head of a book printing establishment.[5]

From that moment on Werkman would become the major influence on Sandberg, who considered him to be his mentor. Also, as with Werkman, the occupation years 1940–45 would prove for Sandberg to be a productive period and a time of spiritual and artistic renewal.

Gerardus Kiljan

From 1904 until 1907, Gerard Kiljan (1891–1968) studied "decorative drawing" at the Quellinus School of Applied Arts at Amsterdam and from 1909 until 1911 lithography at the Steen-en Boek Drukkerij Faddegon (Faddegon Litho and Book Printers). Afterward he worked as a draftsman and retoucher at the Van Leer Printing Company, and at the same time took evening courses at the Rijksacademie from 1914 to 1916. After teaching at various technical schools in Amsterdam, he was appointed to a position at the Academy of Fine Arts at The Hague in 1918 and in 1920 began teaching at the Rotterdam Academy as well. This was his first contact with Zwart, who had started teaching there a year earlier.[6]

Although design education occupied most of his time, Kiljan began to take on his own design assignments in 1926. However, his output was limited; he directed his interest toward theory and photography, which he began to use in 1928, systematically investigating the possibilities of a maximum tonal scale.[7] His actual design production was mainly restricted to the brochures, advertising, and stamps for the PTT.

From the outset, Kiljan's designs reflect esthetic developments of the time, constructed from basic elements and sans serif letters and employing the high contrasts so exploited by Zwart during the same period (Fig. 7-8). His work is further characterized by an

7-8. Gerard Kiljan, *Carl Dreyer, Jeanne d'Arc,* card, 1932, 12 × 10 cm. Collection, Antiquariaat Schuhmacher, Amsterdam.

architectural structure, overprinting, an acceptance of the role of photography as an important design element, and the use of graduated tones of gray and color. Unlike Zwart and Schuitema, Kiljan was never very touched by Constructivism and Dada; instead, his inspiration came more from the Bauhaus.[8] Indeed, Kiljan wrote in 1935: "This devotion (to functionalism) is hardly of value . . . whenever we really need it, without a doubt the next day it would again be modified both in the theoretical and practical aspects and the next day again, and further on. That is evolution."[9]

In 1930 the board of directors at the Koninklijke Academie van Beeldende Kunsten (Royal Academy of Fine Arts) at The Hague officially approved Kiljan's plan to establish a Department of Advertising. This was virtually an academy within an academy, so removed was it from the traditional emphasis of the school.[10] It received the active support of the enlightened director, Dr. Ir. J. H. Plantenga, and was the first design program in The Netherlands based on functional principles and the first department at an official government art school where photography was a pivotal course.[11] As a teacher in the drawing and painting department, Kiljan had already begun to introduce students to photography by having them experiment with montage using magazine photographs.[12] The Weimar point of view was represented at the academy by the former Bauhaus student Paul Guermonprez.

Schuitema came often as a guest instructor in 1929 and was officially hired as a teacher in 1931. Although Schuitema did not have the appropriate academic credentials, he received an appointment because of his "special capacities."[13] Although critics of the department referred to them contemptuously as the "maniacs,"[14] together with Zwart they formed the vanguard of Dutch graphic design education. Both Schuitema and Kiljan remained on the faculty until the 1960s and were instrumental in training a new generation of designers and photographers. Among the more prominent ones were Cahn, Brusse, and Gerard de Vries. The latter taught photography there until his retirement in 1980.

Wim Brusse

Brusse (1910–1978) studied at the Royal Academy of Fine Arts at The Hague from 1928 until 1933, and although he did not actually study in their department, he was influenced by Schuitema and Kiljan. A year after leaving the academy, he became an assistant to Schuitema and at the same time worked on his own as an independent graphic designer. Among his clients were the Rotterdam publisher W. L. and J. Brusse, the Spain Help Commission, and the PTT. His close family connection with the publisher Brusse made it possible for him to obtain some early book cover assignments.[15] These were clearly affected by his association with

Schuitema and Kiljan, yet his style soon moved in a freer and more independent direction.

This shift was partially due to the magnetism of Elffers, who was also working with Schuitema at the time.[16] Along with Elffers, Brusse put together the controversial 1939 "Grafiesnummer" of the architectural magazine *De 8 en Opbouw,* which was a direct assault on Constructivism.

Hendrik Josef Louis (Henny) Cahn

Cahn (b. 1908) was born in Hengelo. From 1930 to 1934 he studied at the Royal Academy of Fine Arts at The Hague under Kiljan and Schuitema.

Cahn began his professional career as a freelance designer and in 1934 began working as an independent photographer and graphic designer. His major clients included the PTT, the N.V. Nederlandsche Huistelefoon Mij (Dutch Home Telephone Company), the N.V. Handelmaatschappij Reforma (Commercial Company Reforma), and the Dutch Communist Party (Figs. 7-9, 7-10). In 1937 he helped with the design of the Dutch Pavilion at the World Exhibition in Paris, where he received a gold medal for his photo montages.

Cahn clearly exhibits the influence of his two teachers, but like Kiljan, he never became a disciple of Constructivism. He used drawings together with photographs, and like Kiljan, he made wide use of overprinting and graduated shades of color. Zwart's devices of guiding the viewer through the composition and extreme contrasts in size and direction also became part of Cahn's

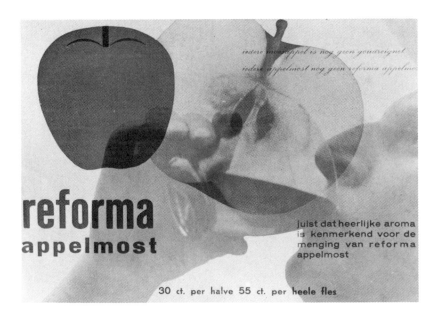

7-9. Henny Cahn, Label for Reforma Applesauce, 1937, 10.6×15 cm. Collection, Antiquariaat Schuhmacher, Amsterdam.

7-10. Henny Cahn, *Reformhuis* (Health-food Shop), 1937. 25.8 × 19.5 cm.

visual vocabulary. From 1942 until 1947, he taught at the Ecole d'Humanité in Schwarzsee and Goldern in Switzerland. He then returned to The Netherlands where he continued his work in graphic and industrial design.

Nicolaas P. de Koo

De Koo (1881–1960) is probably the least known of all the Dutch graphic designers who played a role between the two world wars, and much of his work has remained unknown. Some was lost, and the rest has remained stored in archives.

De Koo came from a family of intellectuals. His father was a minister in a Friesian village until forced to resign because of his unorthodox views. He then became the editor of a literary journal and also wrote plays that enjoyed reasonable success.[17] De Koo

attended the State School for Applied Arts in Amsterdam from 1902 to 1907, where he was trained as an interior designer. During the 1910s he moved to Rotterdam. He worked mainly as a graphic designer, having found it difficult to make a living solely as an interior designer. His letterhead, though, read simply "interior designer."[18] During this period he was also active in helping to organize exhibitions having to do with typography.

In addition to his work for the PTT, De Koo's other important clients included the Rotterdamse Schoolvereniging (Rotterdam School Association), for which he designed various kinds of printed material, including stationery and reports, and the Phoenix Brewery, for which he designed the entire corporate image. His illustrative charts for the city of Rotterdam are noteworthy for their fresh and lively approach.

De Koo's manner of working was very different from that of Zwart or Schuitema, and his typography was not experimental in itself. He preferred traditional illustration techniques and never used photographs as design components. His 1938 poster for the AVO Zomerfeesten (Arnhem, Velp, and Oosterbeek Summer Festivals) is especially striking in its simplicity and liveliness (Figs. 7-11 to 7-18).

7-11. Nicolaas P. de Koo, *Architectuur en kunstnijverheid tentoonstelling Leerdam* (Architecture and Applied Arts Exhibition Leerdam), poster, 1929, 100 × 58.5 cm. Collection, Bernice Jackson, Concord, Massachusetts.

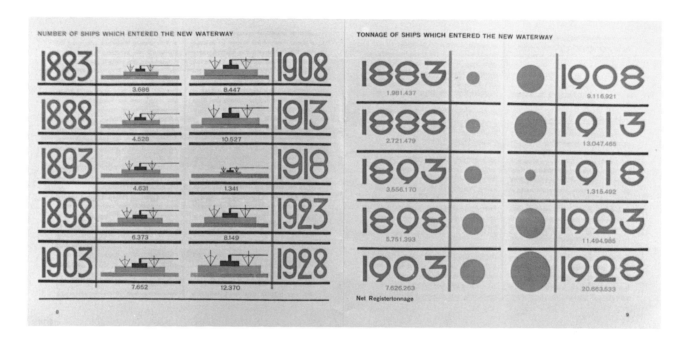

NUMBER OF SHIPS WHICH ENTERED THE NEW WATERWAY

TONNAGE OF SHIPS WHICH ENTERED THE NEW WATERWAY

7-12. Nicolaas P. de Koo, International Chamber of Commerce Rotterdam, booklet, double-page spread, 1929, 22.5 × 22 cm. Collection, Antiquariaat Schuhmacher, Amsterdam.

7-13. Nicolaas P. de Koo, *Phoenix Pullen Bier*, poster, 100 × 60 cm. Collection, Brattinga, Amsterdam.

7-14. Nicolaas P. de Koo, *RSV. Jaarverslag N. V. Rotterdamsche Schoolvereeniging 1932–1933* (*RSV.* (Annual Report Rotterdam School Association 1932–1933), advertisement, 1933, 14.8×21 cm. Collection, Antiquariaat Schuhmacher, Amsterdam.

7-15. Nicolaas P. de Koo, *Phoenix Dortmunder Bier,* blotter, 15.2×10.5 cm. Collection, Antiquariaat Schuhmacher, Amsterdam.

7-16

7-17

7-18

Poster Design in the Late Twenties and Thirties

With the usual exceptions, poster design in The Netherlands, although at times associated with other movements, for the most part remained outside the mainstream, often constituting a style (or collection of styles) within itself. There were Constructivist overtones in some and De Stijl and *Wendingen* traits in others, but in the final analysis the poster designers stayed in their own respective domains. The political turmoil of the 1930s created a fertile setting for political posters, especially those of the Left. They were designed mainly for Socialist organizations such as the NVV (Dutch Federation of Trade Unions) and the SDAP (Social Democratic Workers Party). Although some looked dated when compared to the work of the Constructivists and other avant garde designers, they possessed a raw strength and energy that generally hit the target at which they were aiming. Of the two positions mentioned in the Prologue, "shout" and "information," theirs was definitely the former (see Figs. 7-19 through 7-26).

The most significant of these designers was the uncompromising Meijer Bleekrode, who designed posters until 1935, when he began to devote all of his time to painting. Like Cohen, his family was in the Amsterdam diamond trade, and also like Cohen his death was a direct result of the war. Arrested by the Nazis, he died at age 47 in the Sobibor concentration camp on April 23, 1943, less than two months before Cohen.

Other designers active in the political arena were Schuitema, Cohen, J. Walter, Albert Hahn Jr., Louis Frank, and Samuel Schwarz. Schwarz died at Auschwitz on November 19, 1942.

Many of the other poster designers who had begun their careers in the early 1920s, such as P. A. H. Hofman (1885–1965), contin-

7-16. Nicolaas P. de Koo, *Hertbier*, vignette, circa 1930.

7-17. Nicolaas P. de Koo, *Phoenix Bier*, vignette, circa 1930.

7-18. Nicolaas P. de Koo, *Phoenix Bok Bier*, vignette, circa 1930.

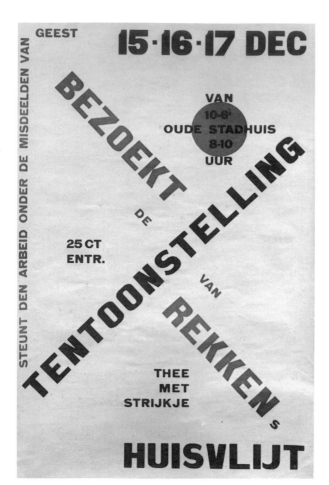

7-19

7-20

7-21

7-19. Ravesteyn, Sybold van, *Bezoek de Tentoonstelling van Rekken* (Visit the Rekken Exhibition), poster, circa 1927, 101×66 cm.

7-20. Hahn, Albert Pieter Jr., *Gemeenteraads Verkiezing 1927* (Municipal Council Election 1927), poster, Carrying a flag and armed with a pick, the laborer stands triumphant as two capitalist bats hover around his feet, 1927. 78×54 cm. Collection, Brattinga, Amsterdam.

7-21. Hahn, Albert Pieter Jr., *NVV Koopt het, Steun Zegal Troelstra Oord* (The Dutch Federation of Trade Unions Buys It, Support Stamp Troelstra Region), poster, circa 1931, 80×55 cm. Collection, Brattinga, Amsterdam.

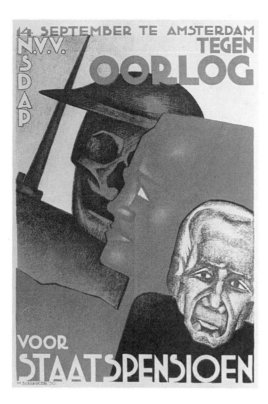

7-22. Bleekrode, Meijer, *S.D.A.P., N.V.V. Tegen Oorlog, Voor Staatspension* (S.D.A.P., N.V.V. Against War, For State Pension), poster, 1930, 79 × 55 cm. Collection, Brattinga, Amsterdam

7-23. Bleekrode, Meijer, *Werkverruiming, SDAP Werkloozenzorg* (Providing More Work, SDAP Unemployment Care), poster, 1930, 79 × 55 cm. Collection, Brattinga, Amsterdam.

7-24. J. Walter, *SDAP Kiest Rood* (Choose Red), poster, 1929, 79 × 55 cm. Collection, Brattinga, Amsterdam.

7-25. P.A.H. Hofman, *Narcissus op Vrijers-voeten* (Narcissus Courting) by S. Vestdijk, Bookbinding, 1938, 20.5×12.5 cm. Collection, Antiquariaat Schuhmacher, Amsterdam.

7-26. Nijgh, H., Heemaf, *Ook Uw Motor* (Heemaf, Also Your Motor), poster, 1936, 28×21 cm.

7-27. E. M. ten Harmsen van Beek, *Carnaval Hamdorff,* poster, 1935, 68×96 cm, Collection, Brattinga, Amsterdam.

7-28. E. M. ten Harmsen van Beek, *Carnaval op Broadway,* poster, 1936, 68×96 cm. Collection, Brattinga, Amsterdam.

ued to work into the late 1930s. Notable new arrivals were Wim
ten Broek (b. 1905) and Herman Nijgh (b. 1909). The illustrator
E. M. ten Harmsen van Beek remained completely out of any
mainstream with his lively and colorful carnival posters for the
Hotel Hamdorff in Laren (Figs. 7-27, 7-28).

The Immigrants

After 1930, when the social climate in Russia and Germany had
clearly changed for the worse, intellectuals and artists migrated
to The Netherlands with new ideas that greatly enriched Dutch
typography. The German refugees such as Henri Friedlaender
(Fig. 7-29), Susanne Heynemann, Helmut Salden, Hajo Rose, and
Otto Treumann brought with them a new spirit and outlook. A
number of publishing companies provided work for immigrant
designers such as Friedlaender; two of the most notable were
departments of the publishers Albert de Lange and Querido.[19]

After Friedlaender, Salden was probably the most important of
the immigrant designers. He fled Germany in 1934 by way of

7-29. Friedlaender, Henri, *Anders en Eender*
(Other and the Same) by Arthur van Schendel, title page, 1939. Published by L.J.C.
Boucher, The Hague, 21.4 × 12.7 cm. Collection, Alston W. Purvis, Boston, Massachusetts.

Spain and then went to Switzerland when the Spanish Civil War broke out. He eventually settled in The Netherlands and during the war was arrested for refusing to serve in the German Army. In 1933 Hajo Rose settled in Amsterdam, where he taught at the Nieuwe Kunst School set up by Paul Citroen in 1933 to fill the void left by the closing of the Bauhaus. Rose was responsible for advertising and typography, and his lessons were based on the Bauhaus principles that every design has a social purpose and that form must be approached with clarity and a specific direction. Because of students such as Treumann and Benno Premsela, his influence was strongly felt even after the war.[20] Photography was taught by Paul Guermonprez. In 1935 Citroen and Guermonprez, both former Bauhaus students, began teaching at the Royal Academy of Fine Arts at The Hague and brought in the Bauhaus influence.

Dirk Cornelis (Dick) Elffers

Elffers was another Rotterdamer who was active in many different fields—graphic design, interior and architectural design, monumental plastics and reliefs, wall hangings, ceramics, photography, illustration, and painting. Wim Crouwel later referred to Elffers as *een grensbewoner* (one living on the border) who "lives in the no-man's land between the professions."[21] Like Werkman, Elffers stood apart and was always looking for new possibilities. Difficult to categorize, he was one of the few influential designers who did not formulate his ideas into specific theories and manifestos, quite unlike Zwart and Schuitema.[22]

After briefly attending the evening school at the Rotterdam Academy, Elffers was accepted by the day school of Decorative and Industrial Arts in 1927, and studied under Jongert, Zwart, and Kiljan. To make ends meet during his student days, he made and decorated consumer products such as lampshades and even artistic coatings for coffins.[23]

A crucial component in Elffers' development was his contact with Jongert, who had been teaching decorative art and industrial arts since 1918 at the Rotterdam Academy where the onerous responsibility of revitalizing the department had fallen upon his shoulders. He eventually chose the intermediate ground between the adamant Constructivists like his classmate Zwart and traditionalists who considered graphic design to be an art form first with functionality having a secondary status.[24]

Jongert was an outspoken advocate of subjectivity, and resolutely maintained that the designer's individuality was imperative for any real creativity. He felt that beautiful form was a direct result of the designer's personal input and that the subjective approach

went much further than what he considered to be a simplistic arrangement of functional components. Consequently, he was continually in disagreement with colleagues such as Zwart. For Zwart, appropriateness was the only acceptable path, and according to his theories true functional design left no room for personal expression. Appropriateness and expressionism became the slogans of the two opposing camps.[25]

Elffers soon became a protegé of Jongert, who in turn put him in touch with many artists and clients involved with social issues.[26] During his last year at the academy he began working as an assistant in the Rotterdam studio of Schuitema who, like Zwart, represented the functional viewpoint. Elffers profited from both factions, and throughout his life one of his stronger traits was his capacity to move easily in disparate circles. For Elffers it was quite simple: with constructivism he required room for personal expression and with Expressionism he felt the need for the practical.[27] Although Schuitema began as a painter himself, he downgraded any such leanings on the part of Elffers and instead treated it more as a hobby: "Painting is something that you do in your spare time." For Elffers, this was definitely not the case. During his student years he took painting very seriously and soon was exhibiting his work.[28]

Somewhat of a prodigy, Elffers began to acquire design assignments while still a student and in 1929 won a prize for a book cover design at the age of nineteen.[29] He was invited to teach at the Rotterdam Academy only a year after graduation and at the instigation of Schuitema joined De 8 en Opbouw during the same year.[30]

Elffers' cover for the magazine *De Rimpel* showed that he had not fallen under the Constructivist spell: He combined typography and a self-portrait made from a photograph and a drawing, some-

7-30. Dick Elffers, advertising card for Simon's Bakery, circa 1931, 10.4 × 14.9 cm.

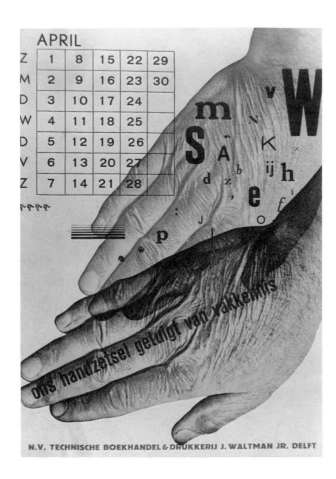

7-31 Dick Elffers, April page from calendar for the technical book dealer and printer J. Waltham, Jr., 1934, 29 × 21.2 cm.

thing that was strictly against the Constructivist guidelines of Schuitema and Zwart.[31] The simplicity and whimsical quality that characterized his work from the beginning is very evident here (Figs. 7-30, 7-31).

After working with Schuitema from 1931 until 1934, Elffers became an assistant in Zwart's studio. He had known Zwart earlier as an art history teacher at the Rotterdam Academy. Until 1937, he performed every kind of design task and also worked with Zwart on one of his best-known and controversial projects, *Het boek van PTT*, in addition to producing some of the illustrations. Elffers' overt aversion to the more dogmatic facets of functionalism must have played a prominent role in the decided "nonfunctionality" of *Het boek van PTT* which, in most respects, was very "nonZwart." According to Elffers, Zwart let his assistants come up with ideas and sketches and would then use whatever elements appealed to him, and in later years Elffers could not recall who had done this or that drawing. The final renderings were always done by Zwart himself.[32]

For the exhibition "Foto 37," Elffers wrote an article for the magazine *Prisma der Kunsten* about the pioneer work of Kiljan, Zwart, and Schuitema, clearly stating his views on the limitation of the photograph as the only appropriate visual element for modern graphic design:

Although it was logical to overrate the value of photography in the discovery of the new design possibilities, we consider it of interest to point out that with photography no renewal in design has taken place. . . . We would like to see photography placed on the same level with all the other techniques and suggest that in the future the visual artist or designer, will, for example, use photography in contrast with other techniques in the same image. How the image came into being is not so important to the observer; what it says to him is the decisive factor.[33]

This was a direct blast at his former employer Schuitema, who considered photography to be the central element in modern graphic design. It was also a strike at Zwart and Kiljan, both of whom considered drawing to be an outdated technique, another factor that makes *Het boek van PTT* all the more mysterious. To drive home his point, Elffers accompanied the article with a collage illustration for Ben Stroman's book, *Hannibal Boontje's Ascension,* composed from a drawing, part of an old engraving, and a full-length photographic self-portrait.[34]

7-32 Dick Elffers, *Bouwkunst Tentoonstelling, Museum Boymans Rotterdam* (Architecture Exhibition, Museum Boymans Rotterdam), poster, 1941, 34.8×59.8 cm.

This salvo was reciprocated in the next issue by Zwart, Schuitema, Kiljan, and Cahn. They accused the "young Turks" Elffers, Sandberg, Brusse, and others of clinging to the past.

Do the hearts of these juniors have *such* small desires? If the answer is yes, then it is to hope that these young ones are not *The* young ones, for this does not raise great expectations. . . . In spite of the fact that modern art generates new symbols there is still a great shortage, according to Elffers. Common sense says that the "young ones" still have enough to do in filling this shortage, or have they lost confidence in modern art? Or would they rather evoke the past?[35]

In a piece for the 1939 "Graphics Number" for *De 8 and Opbouw,* Elffers replied by saying he was pleased to be distinguished as a "young one" by Zwart but no longer wanted or needed that with which Zwart was scoring such a great success. As a final barb, Elffers added that *Het boek van PTT* was far too overwhelming and heavy.[36]

Elffers was well into his career when the war started (Fig. 7-32). Sadly, much of his earlier work was lost when his house and studio were destroyed during the bombing of Rotterdam in May 1940, bringing to an abrupt end his first period with the Rotterdam avant garde.[37]

The 1930s closed with the same kind of inconclusive and quixotic ideological battles that characterized the earlier decades of the century. Ironically and tragically, it would take a war to resolve them.

Chapter 8
War and Aftermath

Occupation and Resistance

On April 20, 1940, Hitler's birthday, an exhibition of German art opened at the Stedelijk Museum in Amsterdam. Organized by the Deutsch-Niederländische Gesellschaft (German-Dutch Union) and the Kölnnische Kunstverein (Cologne Art Club), it was intended to encourage mutual understanding of the Dutch and German cultures. However, given Hitler's zealous campaign against the so-called decadent art in Germany, there was little of note to be seen.[1] The exhibition ended abruptly three weeks later when, in the early morning hours of May 10, more than half of the 125 planes of the Dutch Air Force were destroyed without warning while still on the ground. On May 13, Queen Wilhelmina reluctantly followed her family to England, in spite of her request to be taken to another part of Dutch-held territory. Although Hitler had expected the "matter" to be settled in one day, on May 14 the Dutch army was still resisting. On that same day the center of Rotterdam was subjected to saturation bombing. The Netherlands surrendered the following day, beginning a five-year occupation, one of the harshest of the European war.[2]

Overnight, artists and writers found themselves in the unusual position of having to salvage what was left of intellectual freedoms and individual liberties and expression, things that had, as in so many places, been taken for granted. In a positive sense, the occupation bolstered their conviction that the general good should come before individual interests. For many it was a period of spiritual renewal in which it became easier to distinguish essentials from issues of marginal significance.

In his foreword to *Het Vrije Boek in Onvrije Tijd* (The Free Book in Unfree Times), Professor H. de la Fontaine Verwey wrote:

In our literary history there is perhaps no period in which literature has had such a broad and deep effect. One can say that literature was one of the forces that awakened the people and drove them to resist. Not in a direct sense: only a small portion of the books listed here could be called seditious and directly tied to the resistance. . . . However, never before has literature been so defiant, so national and so topical as during the years of the resistance; the power of poetry as human expression was seldom so strongly felt as in these years, not only by the youth who up until then knew little about it. Those in prison cells experienced its liberating effect, and its meaning was also revealed for countless others for whom it had previously been a closed book.[3]

At first government departments, municipalities, businesses, offices, and schools continued to function without significant interruption, and it seemed that daily life would continue as it had before the occupation. It was soon dramatically evident that this was not to be the case, and each day brought with it new inexorable constraints, crimes, perfidies, conspiracies, and indignities. The German administration was headed by Reichskommissar Authur Seyss-Inquart, the infamous Austrian lawyer who had made a major contribution to the annexation and Germanization of his own country.[4] One of his first targets was to reduce Dutch Jews to the status to which German Jews had been relegated in 1933—nonpersons—and by the autumn of 1940 an official decree had been issued banning Jews from the civil service. With the exception of those connected with the NSB (the Dutch Nazi Party) all student organizations protested, and 50 percent of the university professors signed a letter of protest which was delivered to Seyss-Inquart himself. In addition to the universities, this protest involved, among others, the major political parties, trade unions, churches, industrialists, businessmen, lawyers, artists, farmers, writers, musicians, and doctors.[5]

To present a stronger front against the Germans after the invasion, Van Royen of the PTT attempted to align all Dutch artists into a single organization, an ambition he had entertained even before the war. This organization was to be in addition to the V.A.N.K. and the Exhibition Council for Architecture and Related Arts, and was to be called the Nederlandsche Organisatie van Kunstenaars (Dutch Artists Organization) or the N.O.K. It was strongly opposed by many artists like Sandberg, who felt that it would only be playing into the hands of the Nazis, giving them even more control by having everyone on one list. By the autumn of 1941, Van Royen realized that in the long run the N.O.K. would have an adverse effect, and in 1941 he desperately attempted to dismantle the very organization he had tried to set up. At the end of 1941 it was officially dissolved by the Germans, who had plans to set up a similar union, the Kultuurkamer (Culture Chamber), which was officially constituted in November of that year. All artists who wanted to perform, exhibit, publish, or in any way practice their professions were required to join, and any infraction of the rules was considered a criminal offense. Many, including Sandberg, defiantly ignored the order. Werkman also refused, saying that he was exempt since he was a printer and not an artist. Jews were banned outright and thus not allowed to work anyway.[6]

Over 2,700 artists signed a letter of protest, which was delivered to Seyss-Inquart. Even though Van Royen was not behind this particular action, he received the blame and was arrested on the fourth of March 1942. He was taken to the German concentration camp at Amersfoort, where his health rapidly deteriorated. He died at the camp on the tenth of June.[7]

By the summer of 1942 it had become impossible for Fré Cohen to work at her studio in Amsterdam, and she was forced to go underground to avoid arrest and deportation as a Jew. She stayed with friends, among them Pieter Brattinga, and moved from place to place to avoid capture. From the end of 1942 until March 1943 she bravely continued to produce work from a hiding place in Diemen. On June 12, 1943, she was arrested at Borne and committed suicide two days later.[8]

The Underground Press

Publishing in general was subjected to every conceivable kind of rule and obstacle. Legitimate literary life, in effect, came to a halt, and any work by the collaborator writers and publishers was boycotted by both book dealers and a majority of the reading public. However, from the very outset the Germans had gravely underestimated the Dutch propensity for defiance. Clandestine presses were abundant, and this was a surprisingly productive period. The underground press basically served three purposes: to keep alive the population's spirit of defiance and endurance, to provide necessary printed material for the resistance, and to earn money for the resistance.[9]

Actual books soon began to appear from these underground publishers. Some of the presses dealt with the occupation, while others were directed toward assisting illegal resistance groups. It was very risky to produce more than very small editions, and distribution was an even greater risk. It was hard to find appropriate manuscripts, and there was little contact with the world outside. There were also some open, legal publications, but commercial design in The Netherlands came more or less to a standstill. Most of the typography was conventional and badly printed, but given the circumstances, content rather than esthetics was the first consideration. Production options were very limited, and simply getting anything printed at all became more and more difficult. Paper became harder to obtain and poorer in quality, and printers were forced to relinquish part of their lead type to be melted down for ammunition.

One of the many schemes used by the Nazis to control printing was a special registry that listed the owners of various typefaces. This registry was largely ineffective, however, because De Roos' still popular typeface Hollandsche Mediaeval was used by so many printers that it was impossible for the Gestapo to use that particular typeface to trace which printer was involved when a clandestine publication appeared.[10]

Although there are undoubtedly many other printers and publishers who deserve mention, the most prominent underground

presses were in The Hague, Groningen, Utrecht, Leiden, and Amsterdam. One of the most important was the De Bezige Bij (The Busy Bee) in Amsterdam, which used its profits for a fund to assist those in special need.[11] Writers for the most part donated their works and wrote under pseudonyms. Many of the clandestinely printed books were texts by important Dutch writers and were distributed by underground means. Various names for publishers were used, and sometimes the publisher was not mentioned at all. De doezende Dar (The Dozing Drone) and l'Abeille Laborante were both pseudonyms for The Busy Bee.

The Amsterdam book dealer A. A. Balkema continued to produce bibliophile work and, together with Van Krimpen and W. G. Hellinga began the Vijf Ponden Pers (Five Pounds Press), which turned out some of the best designed and printed clandestine publications during and directly following the occupation. The name of the press was a sardonic reference to the maximum paper weight permitted by the occupying powers for unofficial printing. He also published a number of books under his own name. Two of the finest examples from the Vijf Ponden Pers were *Huit Sonnets par Edgar Degas* (Eight Sonnets by Edgar Degas) and *Doortocht, Gedichten, 1883–1943* door H. W. J. M. Keuls (Passage, Poems, 1883–1943 by H. W. J. M. Keuls). Both were printed in 1943 and designed by Dick Elffers (Figs. 8-1, 8-2). Another designed for Balkema by Van Krimpen in the same year was *De Pendule* (The Mantelpiece Clock) by Jacobus van Looy (Fig. 8-3). One of Balkema's most dangerous publications was *Zehn kleine Meckerlein* (Ten Little Nuisances), printed in 1943 by Balkema himself in an edition of forty. The satirical text by an unknown

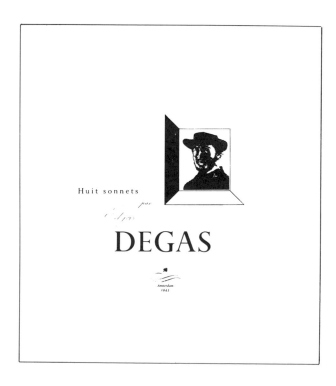

8-1. Dick Elffers, *Edgar Degas, Huit Sonnets,* cover, 1943, 25 × 22.3 cm. Illegal publication from A. A. Balkema's Vijf Ponden Pers (Five Pounds Press). Collection, Antiquariaat Schuhmacher, Amsterdam.

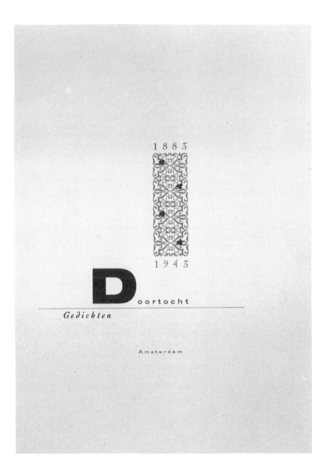

8-2. Dick Elffers, *Doortocht. Gedichten* (Passage. Poems) by H. W. J. M. Keuls, title page, 1943, 24.2 × 16.1 cm. Illegal publication from A. A. Balkema's Vijf Ponden Pers (Five Pounds Press). Collection, Antiquariaat Schuhmacher, Amsterdam.

8-3. Jan van Krimpen, *De Pendule* (The Mantelpiece Clock) by Jac. van Looy, title page, 1943, 20.2 × 10.4 cm. Illegal publication from A. A. Balkema's Vijf Ponden Pers (Five Pounds Press). Collection, Antiquariaat Schuhmacher, Amsterdam.

author was smuggled out of a concentration camp. Its simple design and direct method of printing recall some of the pieces Werkman would produce for De Blauwe Schuit (Figs. 8-4, 8-5).

In Leiden there was the Molenpers of Jan Vermeulen. Dr. K. Heeroma published his own work as well as that of other Protestant poets. In The Hague there was the Mansarde Pers, which would later be called the Final Stage Press. In Groningen there was In Agris Occupatis for which Werkman designed and printed many of the publications. Stols published 60 books under the cloak of invented publishers, printers, places, pen names, and dates of publication (Figs. 8-6 to 8-8). Typographically, this was some of his most interesting work. Even though it was not actual literature against the occupation, some of the texts were by writers classed as "decadent" by the Nazis. In addition, the occupation introduced and, through underground work, even helped to train a new generation of graphic designers. It also rejuvenated some of the older ones. Many graphic designers, including Stam, Sandberg, and Treumann, used their skills in successfully making false identity and ration cards and passport stamps, and courageous printers such as Frans Duwaer risked and eventually gave their lives in helping them. Simulating the water marks was an especially difficult challenge, but this was ultimately met by using two thin sheets of paper glued together.

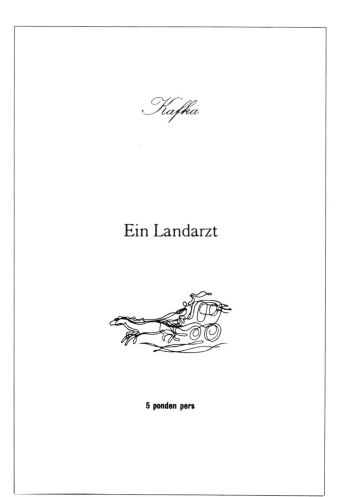

8-4. A. A. Balkema, *Ein Landarzt* by Franz Kafka, title page, 1943, 25×16.5 cm. Illegal publication from A. A. Balkema's Vijf Ponden Pers (Five Pounds Press). Collection, Antiquariaat Schuhmacher, Amsterdam.

8-5. A. A. Balkema, *Zehn kleine Meckerlein* (Ten Little Nuisances), booklet (back) 1943, text smuggled out of a concentration camp, 14.2×12.3 cm. Collection, Antiquariaat Schuhmacher, Amsterdam.

Roulant dans la splendeur lunaire;
Oh, regarde en silence, te pressant contre moi,
Femme dédiée à la ville!

64

L'INNOMMABLE

Quand je serai mort, quand je serai de nos
    chers morts,
(Au moins, me donnerez-vous votre souvenir, pas-
sants
Qui m'avez coudoyé si souvent dans vos rues?)
Restera-t-il dans ces poëmes quelques images
De tant de pays, de tant de regards, et de tous
    ces visages
Entrevus brusquement dans la foule mouvante?
J'ai marché parmi vous, me garant des voitures
Comme vous, et m'arrêtant comme vous aux
    devantures.
J'ai fait avec mes yeux des compliments aux Dames;
J'ai marché, joyeux, vers les plaisirs et vers la
    gloire,
Croyant dans mon cher cœur que c'était arrivé;
J'ai marché dans le troupeau avec délices,
Car nous sommes du troupeau, moi et mes aspi-
    rations.

65

Treumann's skills were particularly valuable, because he had learned to write the German letters as a boy. In addition to duplicating official stamps on passports and other government documents, he copied actual banknotes by hand, which were then laundered by bankers working for the resistance. For the most part the designers were very successful in deceiving the authorities, and Sandberg later said he considered this to be the greatest compliment he ever received for his typography.[12]

Sandberg joined the Dutch resistance soon after the German invasion. In October 1942 he and others conceived a plan to attack and destroy the population registry in Amsterdam. These extensive records, listing a large part of the population, made it much easier for the Nazis to identify Jews and track down members of the resistance. The plot took shape over the next several months, and on March 27, 1943, it was implemented with great success.[13] Although the registry was not completely demolished, many of the records were destroyed.

A few days before, Sandberg had given a tour of the Stedelijk Museum to some Amsterdam police officers, and since it was felt

8-6. A. A. M. Stols, *Les Poésies de A. O. Barnabooth,* title page, 1944, issued as a clandestine publication *Les Poésies de a. O. Barnabooth, Dévotions particulières, Poésies diverses. Copenhague. Pour les amis Danois de Maxime Claremoris 1941* (actually printed by Stols at The Hague), 20.2 × 12.8 cm. Collection, Antiquariaat Schuhmacher, Amsterdam.

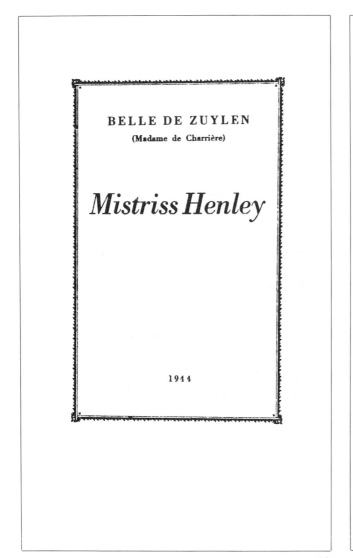

BELLE DE ZUYLEN

(Madame de Charrière)

Mistriss Henley

1944

8-7

I

Awake! for Morning in the Bowl of Night
Has flung the Stone that puts the Stars to Flight:
And Lo! the Hunter of the East has caught
The Sultan's Turret in a Noose of Light.

II

Dreaming when Dawn's Left Hand was in the Sky
I heard a Voice within the Tavern cry,
'Awake, my Little ones, and fill the Cup
Before Life's Liquor in its Cup be dry.'

8-8

he might be recognized, he was not involved in the actual assault. A 10,000 guilder reward was posted for anyone who could provide information on the incident, and soon afterward seven of the eight who actually carried out the operation were arrested. On July 1, thirteen of those involved were shot. Sandberg was not at home when his house was searched, and afterward he went into hiding.[14]

From April 22 until the end of the war, Sandberg carried the identity papers of Henri Willem van den Bosch. The isolation of this period gave him an opportunity for reflection, and between December 1943 and April 1945 he produced his *experimenta typografica,* nineteen booklets containing illustrations and handwritten typographic interpretations of quotations and thoughts. The texts, written in Dutch, German, French, and English, touched upon such subjects as the causes of war, individuality, reality, art, love, culture, belief, typography, and education. The first booklet, *lectura sub aqua,* was issued by A. A. Balkema and printed in an

8-7. A. A. M. Stols, *Mistriss Henley* by Belle de Zuylen, double-page spread, 1944, clandestine publication by Claude Sézille (pseudonym of A. A. M. Stols), Paris (actually printed by Trio Printers at The Hague), 17.3 × 11.1 cm. Collection, Antiquariaat Schuhmacher, Amsterdam.

8-8. Jan van Krimpen, *Rubáiyát* by Omar Khayyám, page, 1945, published by A. A. Balkema, 19.4 × 11.3 cm. Collection, Antiquariaat Schuhmacher, Amsterdam.

edition of 200 by Duwaer in 1944 (Fig. 8-9). It begins with an introduction by Sandberg, the first line reading "Some Dutch are living under water." Duwaer set the type for another one, *gnothi se auton* (know thyself), but because Duwaer was executed in 1944, it was not printed until after the war in 1945 by the Vijf Ponden Pers. Only five of the *experimenta typographica* were ever published, the last as late as 1968 by the Gallery Der Spiegel in Cologne. The typography was an interpretation of the content, as the text and image became one and the same. Capital letters appeared only rarely as decorative elements. Handwriting is used throughout, and Sandberg utilized every graphic device available: combinations of typefaces in different weights and styles, and collage.

In April 1945, shortly before the liberation, Sandberg returned to Amsterdam and on May 5, Liberation Day, Henri Willem van den Bosch again became Willem Jacob Henri Berend Sandberg.[15]

Like Sandberg and the others, Elffers used his design skills to make false identity and ration cards, and together with a trusted archivist helped to alter family registers at the state records office in Haarlem by changing Jewish names to those that sounded more Dutch.[16] At the same time, he managed to paint and produce some design work, one piece being a jubilee folder for the United Shoe Dealers and, of course, the book designs for Balkema. In 1944 he designed a calender that was published illegally by Balkema's Vijf Ponden Pers and printed by Duwaer, de Hoop & Meijer (Fig. 8-10).

The occupation was also a difficult time for Dutch museums. After the invasion of Poland in 1939, a secret storage bunker was begun in the dunes near Castricum and finished just before the

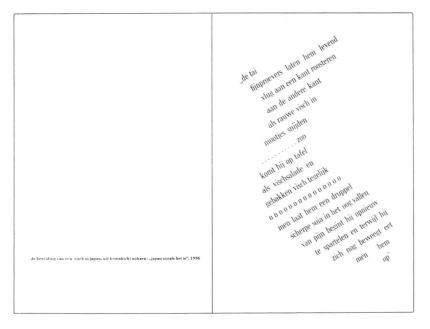

8-9. Willem Sandberg, *lectura sub squa*, experimenta typografica, double-page spread, 1944, 21 × 15 cm. Collection, Antiquariaat Schuhmacher, Amsterdam.

invasion of The Netherlands. It was filled with the most valuable works from the municipal museums on the very same day that The Netherlands surrendered. David C. Röell, the director of the Stedelijk Museum in Amsterdam, tried to replace the museum's main collection, which had been transferred to the storage bunker, with exhibitions to keep the Nazis from bringing in their own.[17] However, the replacement exhibitions were not always successful, as evidenced by one in the winter of 1943 called "Kunstenaars zien de Arbeidsdienst" (Artists See the Labor Service). According to a Dutch Nazi Party member, this was an effort to "bring the Labor Service to the artist and the artist to the labor service." The poster for the exhibition showed the typical blond Aryan.

The Blauwe Schuit

From the standpoint of graphic design, by far the most notable series of clandestine publications were the 40 issues of *De Blauwe Schuit* (The Blue Barge) printed by Werkman, the magnificent culmination of what he had begun in the early 1920s.[18] Standing apart from other underground publications of the time, *De Blauwe Schuit* followed its own course, and Werkman was one of the few who used artistic means as a tool during the occupation.

The ramifications of World War II had a great effect on Werkman, and from 1939 until May 1941 he was almost completely immobilized by the events that were taking place. As the solitude and pessimism that had been with him since his childhood increased in intensity, he became even more indifferent toward his business and took on jobs as they came. Except for some commercial work done with the aid of his helper Wybren Bos, what remained of his business came to a standstill. It was at this time that he met a man who would be the most profound and inspiring friend of his life, the Reformed Minister F. R. A. Henkels from Winschoten. The intense correspondence between the two provides a rare glimpse into Werkman's iconoclastic nature.

At the end of November 1940, Henkels attended a gathering together with the chemist Dr. A. J. Zuithof and the German language teacher Mevrouw Adri Buning. During the meeting, they decided to publish something to bolster the morale of the Dutch people during the occupation. Henkels then remembered the printer Werkman and a few days later traveled to Groningen to meet him. They discussed items such as printing costs and other details for the first issue of *De Blauwe Schuit,* and plans were made for publication. The 40 issues of *De Blauwe Schuit* that were published consisted of booklets in various formats ranging in size from 4 to 50 pages. There were few costs involved, and they were printed on whatever was available. The kinds and sizes of typefaces were also very limited. It was not an attempt to reach large numbers of people; the booklets were distributed inside a small circle.

8-10. Dick Elffers, calendar, 1944, 34.8 × 24.8 cm. Illegal publication from A. A. Balkema's Vijf Ponden Pers (Five Pounds Press), printed at Duwaer. Collection, Antiquariaat Schuhmacher, Amsterdam.

It is unclear how *De Blauwe Schuit* came to be used on the colophon, but most likely it came from the painting by Jerome Bosch called *Die blau scute,* which had recently been shown at the Boymans Museum in an exhibition of northern Netherlandish primitives. Printed before Christmas 1940, the first number of *De Blauwe Schuit* was distributed among friends as a New Year's gift in 1941, and an identical edition was published the following September. The text was Martinus Nijhoff's poem *Het Jaar 1572* (The Year 1572), written on the occasion of Princess Juliana's 25th birthday in 1934.

The second issue, *die Predigt des Neuen Jahres* (The Sermon of the New Year), a Hasidic legend by Martin Buber, appeared in March 1941. The cover depicts a city with towers and a wall lit by moonlight. There were 8 pages and an edition of 60, which was produced by the stencil and ink-roller. The third issue was *Alleluia,* an Easter message, the typography of which recalls some of the pages from *The Next Call.* The next was *Sabbatgesänge,* songs by the Jewish poet Jehuda Halevi, translated by Franz Rosenzweig. Henkels then asked Werkman if he would do a ten-print series of the *Chassidische Legenden* (Hasidic Legends) as well.

In October 1941 Werkman began the *Turken Kalendar* (Turkish Calendar) which would appear between Christmas and the New Year 1942. Inspired by the Turkish Calendar of Gutenberg published in 1454 as a warning against a Turkish invasion of Europe, the *Turken Kalendar* was done in the same spirit as Werkman's calendars made during the 1920s and 1930s. All his accumulated techniques were utilized, and he seemed to have been delighted with the fact that he had broken with every previous typographic principle. Afterward, he jokingly wrote that he hoped professional typographers would not see the calendar, as his life would be in danger for all the sins he had committed against the rules of typography. In March 1942, *Het Gesprek* (The Conversation) appeared. This was a description by Henkels of a 1938 painting by Werkman of the same title. It was followed in April by *Bij het Graf van den Onbekenden Nederlandschen Soldaat* (By the Grave of an Unknown Dutch soldier), a poem by M. Nijhoff.

De Blauwe Schuit was not taken seriously by the Nazis and was left untouched by the continuous crackdowns. The best cloak was its straightforwardness. *De Blauwe Schuit* and Werkman's name were always clearly visible on each publication, although the numbers of the editions were sometimes jumbled and the names of some of the living poets were omitted.

Henkels introduced Werkman to the world of Hasidic Judaism, and sent him the book *Hasidic Legends* by Martin Buber. Werkman, always an admirer of folk legends, was captivated by these stories. Werkman was not a religious man in the conventional sense, but the *Hasidic Legends* touched him deeply. In August 1942 the first

8-11. H. N. Werkman, *Chassidische Legenden* (Hasidic Legends, Suite no. 1), label, 1942, 17 × 12.7 cm. Photograph courtesy of Jan van Loenen Martinet, Amsterdam.

Hasidic Legends portfolio was completed and exhibited in a school-room at the local seminary (Fig. 8-11). It was well received and for a price of 75 guilders, 16 of the 20 copies were sold within two months. It is said that a young painter even sold his bicycle to buy one; considering the value of such transportation during the war years, this was no small sacrifice.

For Christmas 1942, *De Blauwe Schuit* issued the *Gedichtje van St. Nicolaas* to provide some cheer for Dutch children on December 5, the Sinterklaas (Santa Claus) evening. *Paul Robeson zingt* (Paul Robeson sings) and the second portfolio of the *Hasidic Legends* were published in December 1943 (Fig. 8-12). The last printing for *De Blauwe Schuit* was Boutens' *Reizang van Burgers* (Chorus for Citizens), printed by Werkman in anticipation of an early libera-tion. By this time there was almost no electricity available in Groningen, and without heat in the printshop, ink became too hard to use. Also, as happened to other printers, a large part of his lead type had been confiscated. As a result of these impossible working conditions, Werkman's printing activities virtually ceased by the beginning of 1944.

The Tenth Man

The failure of the British landing at Arnhem in September 1944 delayed the liberation of the rest of The Netherlands until May 5, 1945. During the winter of 1944, the Allies were advancing rapid-ly across France and Belgium, and to impede their advance the Germans took all of the fuel supplies from Holland. That winter was an especially severe one, and in The Netherlands over 15,000 people died of starvation and exposure. The situation had wors-

8-12. H. N. Werkman, *Chassidische Legenden* (Hasidic Legends, Suite 2–8), De Sabbat der Eenvoudigen (The Sabbath of the Humble), 1943, 51.1 × 32.8 cm. Collection, Dr. Robert Polak, Amsterdam.

ened to such an extent that a large part of the Dutch population was living in hiding, and it became difficult to trust anyone other than close acquaintances. On the morning of March 13, 1945, Werkman and his friend Henkels were arrested and brought to the Scholtenhuis in Groningen, where the SS had its headquarters. All of his work in the house and printshop were seized as Bolshevik art, as shown by the works of "subversive" writers such as Dostoevsky on his bookshelf.[19]

Throughout the war Werkman had consistently refused to print illegal material not out of fear for his own safety, but because his shop was in a building with other businesses, other people could have been compromised as well. Although he had sheltered several Jews in his house, this had never been detected. His arrest was probably a combination of several factors, but it was most likely his identification with the Jews through the *Hasidic Legends*. In addition to the pieces for *De Blauwe Schuit,* Werkman also printed some work for De Bezige Bij; and this could have been an another reason for his arrest. By this time the war in Europe was drawing to an end. Allied armies had crossed the Rhine, and Canadian units were already moving toward Groningen through the eastern Dutch provinces of Gelderland, Overijsel, and Drente.

What happened on the eighth, ninth, and tenth of April 1945 has always remained a partial mystery. According to the Dutch War Crimes Commission, an order came from the SS headquarters at The Hague to execute three groups of ten prisoners as a reprisal against underground activities and the Canadian advance. On Sunday the first group of ten were taken to Anlo and executed, and the next day the second contingent met a similar fate.[20] When the third group of prisoners were being driven to the execution site on April 9, one of them leapt from the truck and escaped. The truck then returned to Groningen with the remaining nine. The next morning the same nine prisoners were taken from their cells, and Werkman was selected to replace the one who had escaped on the previous day. He was the tenth man. On the morning of April 10, Werkman was executed with the other nine near the town of Bakkeveen.[21] Two days later, the Canadian army entered Groningen. The tragedy continued unabated when on April 15 the Scholtenhuis was destroyed by an ammunition explosion in the heavy fighting for the city. With it was lost all of the work and documents seized at Werkman's arrest, almost half of his life's work.

Aftermath and Transition

To some of the traditional designers, the war demonstrated a necessity for change, and to the avant garde it showed how necessary it was to maintain the rudiments of culture. Former topics such as

8-13. Wim Brusse, *Het vrije boek in onvrije tijd* (The Free Book in Unfree Times), poster, 1945, 100 × 62 cm.

whether to use sans serif or serif type, symmetry or asymmetry, machine or craft, photography or traditional illustration, all became irrelevant. During these five years the most important concerns became the preservation of human life and dignity, the protection of intellectual and artistic freedoms, and the deliverance of the Dutch nation. Whatever it took to achieve these objectives was considered appropriate for the moment.

Van Royen's crusade to rehabilitate government design was made official in 1945 with the appointment of an esthetic advisor to head a new government branch called the Dienst Esthetische Vormgeving (Esthetic Design Service). In 1946 one of Van Royen's former colleagues, Gouwe, was appointed to this position, thus ensuring that Van Royen's earlier efforts had not been in vain.[22] Gouwe worked with dedication and insight and continued the tradition of providing opportunities for many young and talented designers. His energies were directed toward all aspects of the PTT, including graphic, furniture, industrial, and interior design. New designers involved with the PTT included the master calligrapher P. J. J. van Trigt and the typographer P. C. Cossee.

In September 1945 Sandberg was appointed director of the Stedelijk Museum in Amsterdam, and under his enlightened leadership the museum became one of the leading supporters of the avant garde. Sandberg took chances with unknown artists, many of whom owe their success to him. He designed over three hundred catalogs for the museum that were essentially a continuation of his *experimenta typographica.* Lowercase letters were used almost exclusively, and he was intrigued by the negative inner forms of letters. His museum publications helped to establish a new standard for similar institutions throughout the world (Figs. 8-13, 8-14). Sandberg possessed a unique ability to delegate, and many of the museum catalogs and posters were actually designed by his devoted staff following his suggestions during meetings.[23]

Sandberg held a Werkman retrospective at the Stedelijk Museum in the fall of 1945, and with this event the first Werkman catalog was published. At the end of 1946 Balkema published Henkel's *Logboek van De Blauwe Schuit,* designed by Elffers (Fig. 8-15), and a year later an English/Dutch book on Werkman was published. During his lifetime Werkman had been greatly underestimated, but from the early fifties on, his influence on twentieth-century graphic design would become increasingly apparent. One can detect his inspiration in the work of many modern graphic designers.

In 1945 prizes were established by the city of Amsterdam in memory of two printers who had died during the war, Werkman and Duwaer. The first Werkman prize was posthumously awarded to Werkman himself for the *Turken Calendar,* and the first Duwaer prize went to Van Krimpen.[24]

In addition to being director of the Stedelijk Museum, Sandberg became involved after the war with the rehabilitation of Dutch art in general and was elected chairman of the Gebonden Kunsten Federatie, the G.K.F. (the Aligned Arts Federation), a post he would fill until 1948.[25] This new organization was the fulfillment of one of Van Royen's dreams and a successor to the V.A.N.K. However, the G.K.F. was even broader in scope than the V.A.N.K. and embraced disciplines such as film, dance, graphic design, photography, and theater. In the beginning, it was overshadowed to some extent by politics, and its outlook was influenced by some of the Left-leaning members. For example, those who worked for advertising agencies were not accepted because they were too closely aligned with capitalist industry and in 1948 they formed their own group, the V.R.I. (Association of Advertising Designers and Illustrators).[26]

Many principal figures in modern Dutch graphic design died as a direct result of the second world war. Among them were Werkman, Van Royen, Bleekrode, Lebeau, Cohen, Guermonprez, and the printer Duwaer. Designers whose careers had been inter-

8-14. Willem Sandberg, Stichting 40–45, Zwitsersche Affiches (Foundation 40–45. Swiss Posters), poster, 1946, 99 × 65 cm.

8-15. Dick Elffers, *Logboek van de Blauwe Schuit* (Logbook of the Blue Barge) by F. R. A. Henkels, cover, 1946, 23.7 × 15.7 cm. Published by A. A. Balkema. Collection, Alston W. Purvis, Boston, Massachusetts.

rupted by the war rose to prominence immediately after 1945. The German refugees Henri Friedlaender, Susanne Heynemann, Helmut Salden, and Otto Treumann, who had all begun their careers in the thirties, survived the war and continued to enrich Dutch typography after 1945.

One of the former students of Schuitema and Kiljan who emerged after the war was the designer and photographer Gerard de Vries. His 1946 work for the Coöperatieve Melkcentrale (Cooperative Milk Exchange) was one of the first complete design programs for a Dutch company and included logo design, brochures, packaging, labels, and lettering on cars and trucks.

In 1946 Elffers designed the poster for *Weerbare democratie* (Defensible Democracy), inaugurating a new painterly style in his work (Fig. 8-16). Created for an exhibition organized by Sandberg on Wartime Dutch art, the poster shows a melancholy civilian in a hat, carrying a rifle and standing against a background of red and brown; the typography is deliberately unpolished and written like a slogan on a wall. The person's face seems to exhibit bravery, ter-

8-16. Dick Elffers, *Weerbare democratie* (Defensible democracy), poster, 1946, 100.5 × 70 cm. Collection, Antiquariaat Schuhmacher, Amsterdam.

ror, and surprise, and looks very much like a self-portrait of Elffers. He later said that the war had destroyed his idealism. "In that time I came to the conclusion that one must not work from a closed principle but instead be open, letting in doubts. I never again wanted to be caught in a net of dogmas." The naivete of the '30s was brought into broad daylight after the war.[27]

In September 1946 the first issue of the international magazine *Open Oog* appeared, an avant garde publication on visual design edited by Stam, Rietveld, Kloos, Jaffé, Brusse, and Sandberg, who designed the now familiar cover (Fig. 8-17).[28]

At the close of the 1930s, the term and profession "graphic designer" had begun to be taken more seriously. Before, they were for the most part referred to as "advertising" draftsmen. This change was to a large extent due to the uncompromising attitude of Zwart and Schuitema. Before the war there were few publishers who hired book designers as such, but after 1945 this position became an essential part of a company's structure. The book designer was no longer thought of as a luxury but instead was a necessary staff member.[29]

The end of the war offered a new beginning for Dutch graphic design, and the first decade after liberation was a vital period of rejuvenation, reflection, and searching. The significance of the link between the traditionalists and the avant garde became much clearer to the new generation of designers. Before that time, personal enmities had encumbered any real reconciliation between the two philosophies.[30] Most important, after the war the younger designers were not interested in the endless ideological skirmishes of the prewar innovators. Like many of the designers during the resistance, they instead selected and used whatever theories seemed applicable for the task at hand. Members of the old vanguard were now seen as respected masters and part of a rich heritage rather than revolutionary leaders of particular movements. Even though the foundations of postwar Dutch graphic design can be seen in the work of these early pioneers, that which would eventually be produced by their "students" would be quite different from anything ever envisioned by either De Roos and Van Krimpen, or by Zwart and Schuitema.[31]

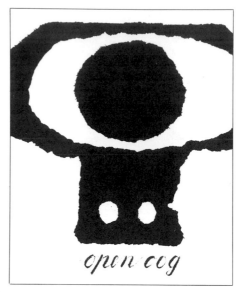

8-17. Willem Sandberg, *Open Oog* (Open Eye), cover, 1946, 25.8 × 19 cm. Collection, Antiquariaat Schuhmacher, Amsterdam.

Notes

Chapter 1

1. Jaffé, H. L. C. 1956. *De Stijl/1917–1931*. Amsterdam: Meulenhoff/Landshoff, page 81.

2. Jaffé, H. L. C. 1956. *De Stijl/1917–1931*. Amsterdam: Meulenhoff/Landshoff, page 80.

3. Jaffé, H. L. C. 1956. *De Stijl/1917–1931*. Amsterdam: Meulenhoff/Landshoff, page 82.

4. Schama, Simon. 1988. Foreword. In *The Netherlands and Nazi Germany* by Louis de Jong. The Erasmus Lectures, 1988. Cambridge: Harvard University Press, page x.

5. Brattinga, Pieter. 1987. *Influences on Dutch Graphic Design, 1900–1945*.

6. Jaffé, H. L. C. 1956. *De Stijl/1917–1931*. Amsterdam: Meulenhoff/Landshoff, page 83.

7. Jaffé, H. L. C. 1956. *De Stijl/1917–1931*. Amsterdam: Meulenhoff/Landshoff, page 83.

8. Jaffé, H. L. C. 1956. *De Stijl/1917–1931*. Amsterdam: Meulenhoff/Landshoff, page 83.

9. Ovink, G. W. 1965. 100 Years of Book Typography in The Netherlands. In *Book Typography, 1815–1965 in Europe and The United States of America,* ed. Kenneth Day. Chicago: University of Chicago Press, page 251.

10. Jaffé, H. L. C. 1956. *De Stijl/1917–1931*. Amsterdam: Meulenhoff/Landshoff, page 3.

11. Jaffé, H. L. C. 1956. *De Stijl/1917–1931*. Amsterdam: Meulenhoff/Landshoff, page 3.

12. Radermacher Schorer, M. R. 1951. *Bijdrage tot de Geschiedenis van de Renaissance der Nederlandse Boekdrukkunst*. Utrecht, page 8.

13. Ovink, G. W. 1965. 100 Years of Book Typography in The Netherlands. In *Book Typography, 1815–1965 in Europe and The United States of America,* ed. Kenneth Day. Chicago: University of Chicago Press, page 230.

14. Radermacher Schorer, M. R. 1951. *Bijdrage tot de Geschiedenis van de Renaissance der Nederlandse Boekdrukkunst*. Utrecht, page 8.

15. Radermacher Schorer, M. R. 1951. *Bijdrage tot de Geschiedenis van de Renaissance der Nederlandse Boekdrukkunst*. Utrecht, page 4.

16. Ovink, G. W. 1965. 100 Years of Book Typography in The Netherlands. In *Book Typography, 1815–1965 in Europe and The United States of America,* ed. Kenneth Day. Chicago: University of Chicago Press, page 248.

17. Ovink, G. W. 1965. 100 Years of Book Typography in The Netherlands. In *Book Typography, 1815–1965 in Europe and The United States of America,* ed. Kenneth Day. Chicago: University of Chicago Press, page 249.

18. Ovink, G. W. 1965. 100 Years of Book Typography in The Netherlands. In *Book Typography, 1815–1965 in Europe and The United States of America,* ed. Kenneth Day. Chicago: University of Chicago Press, page 249.

19. Ovink, G. W. 1965. 100 Years of Book Typography in The Netherlands. In *Book Typography, 1815–1965 in Europe and The United States of America,* ed. Kenneth Day. Chicago: University of Chicago Press, page 249.

20. Blokker, Jan. 1989. *De Wond'ren Werden Woord en Dreven Verder,* Honderd Jaar Informatie in Nederland 1889–1989. Amsterdam: J. A. Blokker, page 151.

21. Blokker, Jan. 1989. *De Wond'ren Werden Woord en Dreven Verder,* Honderd Jaar Informatie in Nederland 1889–1989. Amsterdam: J. A. Blokker, page 152.

22. Blokker, Jan. 1989. *De Wond'ren Werden Woord en Dreven Verder,* Honderd Jaar Informatie in Nederland 1889–1989. Amsterdam: J. A. Blokker, page 152.

23. Dooijes, Dick and Pieter Brattinga. 1968. *A History of the Dutch Poster, 1890–1960.* Amsterdam: Scheltema & Holkema, page 36.

24. Radermacher Schorer, M. R. 1951. *Bijdrage tot de Geschiedenis van de Renaissance der Nederlandse Boekdrukkunst.* Utrecht, page 35.

25. Radermacher Schorer, M. R. 1951. *Bijdrage tot de Geschiedenis van de Renaissance der Nederlandse Boekdrukkunst.* Utrecht, page 35.

26. Ovink, G. W. 1965. 100 Years of Book Typography in The Netherlands. In *Book Typography, 1815–1965 in Europe and The United States of America,* ed. Kenneth Day. Chicago: University of Chicago Press, page 254.

27. Dooijes, Dick and Pieter Brattinga. 1968. *A History of the Dutch Poster, 1890–1960.* Amsterdam: Scheltema & Holkema, page 9.

28. Dooijes, Dick and Pieter Brattinga. 1968. *A History of the Dutch Poster, 1890 1960.* Amsterdam: Scheltema & Holkema, page 4

29. Dooijes, Dick and Pieter Brattinga. 1968. *A History of the Dutch Poster, 1890–1960.* Amsterdam: Scheltema & Holkema, page 9.

30. Dooijes, Dick and Pieter Brattinga. 1968. *A History of the Dutch Poster, 1890–1960.* Amsterdam: Scheltema & Holkema, page 10.

31. Dooijes, Dick and Pieter Brattinga. 1968. *A History of the Dutch Poster, 1890–1960.* Amsterdam: Scheltema & Holkema, page 11.

32. Aldus. 1989. *"Allemaal Flauwekul" en Andere Typografische Notities.* Amsterdam: De Buitenkant, page 65.

33. Kuitenbrouwer, Carel. July 1989. Graphic Holland, A Prominent Place. *Dutch Arts.* Dutch Ministry for Cultural Affairs. The Hague: SDU Publishers, page 21.

34. Dam, Peter van, and Pim Reinders. 1990. *Johann George van Caspel, Affichekunstenaar (1870–1928).* Amsterdam: Stadsuitgeverij, page 11.

35. Dooijes, Dick and Pieter Brattinga. 1968. *A History of the Dutch Poster, 1890–1960.* Amsterdam: Scheltema & Holkema, page 21.

36. Dam, Peter van, and Pim Reinders. 1990. *Johann George van Caspel, Affichekunstenaar (1870–1928).* Amsterdam: Stadsuitgeverij, page 19.

37. Dooijes, Dick and Pieter Brattinga. 1968. *A History of the Dutch Poster, 1890–1960.* Amsterdam: Scheltema & Holkema, page 24.

38. Dooijes, Dick and Pieter Brattinga. 1968. *A History of the Dutch Poster, 1890–1960.* Amsterdam: Scheltema & Holkema, page 26.

39. Bruinsma, Max, Lies Ros, and Rob Schröder. 1989. *Dick Elffers en de Kunsten.* Netherlands: Het Gerrit Jan Thiemefonds, page 14.

40. Lopes Cardozo, A., and A. Stroeve. 1987. Graphic Design Since 1945. In *Holland in Form. Dutch Design 1945–1987,* ed. Gert Staal and Hester Wolters. 's-Gravenhage: Stichting Holland in Vorm, page 248.

41. Broos, Kees. 1982. From De Stijl to a New Typography. In *De Stijl, 1917–1931, Visions of Utopia,* ed. Mildred Friedman. New York: Abbeville Press, page 147.

42. Broos, Kees. 1982. From De Stijl to a New Typography. In *De Stijl, 1917–1931, Visions of Utopia,* ed. Mildred Friedman. New York: Abbeville Press, page 147.

Chapter 2

1. Doesburg, Theo van. 1918. *De Stijl Vol. II,* page 2.

2. Doesburg, Theo van. 1918. *De Stijl Vol. IV,* page 126.

3. Berman, Merrill C. 1987. *Captured Glance, The Avant-Garde and Advertising in the Twenties.* New York: Helen Serger/La Boetie, Inc.

4. Jaffé, H. L. C. 1956. *De Stijl/1917–1931.* Amsterdam: Meulenhoff/Landshoff, page 4.

5. Doesburg, Theo van. 1917. *De Stijl Vol. I,* page 1.

6. Jaffé, H. L. C. 1956. *De Stijl/1917–1931.* Amsterdam: Meulenhoff/Landshoff, page 5.

7. Baljeu, Joost. 1974. *Theo van Doesburg.* London: Studio Vista, Cassell & Collier Macmillan, page 10.

8. Dooijes, Dick. 1988. *Wegbereiders van de Moderne Boektypografie in Nederland.* Amsterdam: De Buitenkant, page 61.

9. Baljeu, Joost. 1974. *Theo van Doesburg.* London: Studio Vista, Cassell & Collier Macmillan, page 20.

10. Baljeu, Joost. 1974. *Theo van Doesburg.* London: Studio Vista, Cassell & Collier Macmillan, page 24.

11. Dooijes, Dick. 1988. *Wegbereiders van de Moderne Boektypografie in Nederland.* Amsterdam: De Buitenkant, page 62.

12. Broos, Kees. 1982. From De Stijl to a New Typography. In *De Stijl, 1917–1931, Visions of Utopia,* ed. Mildred Friedman. New York: Abbeville Press, page 153.

13. Jaffé, H. L. C. 1956. *De Stijl/1917–1931.* Amsterdam: Meulenhoff/Landshoff, page 61.

14. Jaffé, H. L. C. 1956. *De Stijl/1917–1931.* Amsterdam: Meulenhoff/Landshoff, page 5.

15. Jaffé, H. L. C. 1956. *De Stijl/1917–1931.* Amsterdam: Meulenhoff/Landshoff, page 5.

16. Baljeu, Joost. 1974. *Theo van Doesburg.* London: Studio Vista, Cassell & Collier Macmillan, page 71.

17. Dooijes, Dick. 1988. *Wegbereiders van de Moderne Boektypografie in Nederland.* Amsterdam: De Buitenkant, page 62.

18. Neumann, Eckhard. 1967. *Functional Graphic Design in the 20's.* New York: Reinhold, page 39.

19. Schippers, K. 1974. *Holland Dada.* Amsterdam: Em. Querido's Uitgeverij B.V., page 30.

20. Neumann, Eckhard. 1967. *Functional Graphic Design in the 20's.* New York: Reinhold, page 25.

21. Schippers, K. 1974. *Holland Dada*. Amsterdam: Em. Querido's Uitgeverij B.V., page 30.

22. Shattuck, Roger. 1968. *The Banquet Years*. New York: Vintage Books, page 33.

23. Wright, Edward. 1967. Paul van Ostaijen. In *The Liberated Page*, ed. Herbert Spencer. San Francisco: Bedford Press, 1987, page 91.

24. Ades, Dawn. 1978. *Dada and Surrealism Reviewed*. London: Arts Council of Great Britain, page 125 (quote from Lagos Kassak. 1921–22. *MA*. Vienna).

25. Schippers, K. 1974. *Holland Dada*. Amsterdam: Em. Querido's Uitgeverij B.V., page 34.

26. Schippers, K. 1974. *Holland Dada*. Amsterdam: Em. Querido's Uitgeverij B.V., page 34.

27. Schippers, K. 1974. *Holland Dada*. Amsterdam: Em. Querido's Uitgeverij B.V., page 34.

28. Fitzgerald, F. Scott. 1945. *The Crack-Up*. New York: New Directions, page 69.

29. Schippers, K. 1974. *Holland Dada*. Amsterdam: Em. Querido's Uitgeverij B.V., page 32.

30. Neumann, Eckhard. 1967. *Functional Graphic Design in the 20's*. New York: Reinhold, page 33.

31. Schippers, K. 1974. *Holland Dada*. Amsterdam: Em. Querido's Uitgeverij B.V., page 37.

32. Doesburg, Theo van. 1921. Letter to Antonie Kok.

33. Schippers, K. 1974. *Holland Dada*. Amsterdam: Em. Querido's Uitgeverij B.V., page 37.

34. Schippers, K. 1974. *Holland Dada*. Amsterdam: Em. Querido's Uitgeverij B.V., page 39.

35. Broos, Kees. 1982. From De Stijl to a New Typography. In *De Stijl, 1917–1931, Visions of Utopia*, ed. Mildred Friedman. New York: Abbeville Press, page 159.

36. Ex, Sjarel and Els Hoek. 1985. *Vilmos Huszár, Schilder en Ontwerper 1884–1960*. Utrecht: Reflex, page 111.

37. Ex, Sjarel and Els Hoek. 1985. *Vilmos Huszár, Schilder en Ontwerper 1884–1960*. Utrecht: Reflex, page 111.

38. Ex, Sjarel and Els Hoek. 1985. *Vilmos Huszár, Schilder en Ontwerper 1884–1960*. Utrecht: Reflex, page 111.

39. Ex, Sjarel and Els Hoek. 1985. *Vilmos Huszár, Schilder en Ontwerper 1884–1960*. Utrecht: Reflex, page 113.

40. Ex, Sjarel and Els Hoek. 1985. *Vilmos Huszár, Schilder en Ontwerper 1884–1960*. Utrecht: Reflex, page 111.

41. Ex, Sjarel and Els Hoek. 1985. *Vilmos Huszár, Schilder en Ontwerper 1884–1960*. Utrecht: Reflex, page 126.

42. Dooijes, Dick. 1988. *Wegbereiders van de Moderne Boektypografie in Nederland*. Amsterdam: De Buitenkant, page 62.

43. Dooijes, Dick. 1986. *Boektypografische Verkenningen*. Amsterdam: De Buitenkant, page 126.

Chapter 3

1. Broos, Kees. 1982. From De Stijl to a New Typography. In *De Stijl, 1917–1931, Visions of Utopia,* ed. Mildred Friedman. New York: Abbeville Press, page 152.

2. Dooijes, Dick. 1988. *Wegbereiders van de Moderne Boektypografie in Nederland.* Amsterdam: De Buitenkant, page 72.

3. Dooijes, Dick. 1988. *Wegbereiders van de Moderne Boektypografie in Nederland.* Amsterdam: De Buitenkant, page 71.

4. Dooijes, Dick. 1988. *Wegbereiders van de Moderne Boektypografie in Nederland.* Amsterdam: De Buitenkant, page 71.

5. Oldewarris, Hans. 1975. Wijdeveld Typografie. Amsterdam: *Forum,* Vol. 25, no. 1, page 9.

6. Broos, Kees. 1982. From De Stijl to a New Typography. In *De Stijl, 1917–1931, Visions of Utopia,* ed. Mildred Friedman. New York: Abbeville Press, page 152.

7. Oldewarris, Hans. 1975. Wijdeveld Typografie. Amsterdam: *Forum,* Vol. 25, no. 1, page 15.

8. Oldewarris, Hans. 1975. Wijdeveld Typografie. Amsterdam: *Forum,* Vol. 25, no. 1, page 6.

9. Dooijes, Dick. 1988. *Wegbereiders van de Moderne Boektypografie in Nederland.* Amsterdam: De Buitenkant, page 72.

10. Unger, Gerard en Marjan Unger. 1989. *Dutch landscape with letters.* Utrecht: Van Boekhoven-Bosch bv grafische industrie, page 34.

11. Dooijes, Dick. 1988. *Wegbereiders van de Moderne Boektypografie in Nederland.* Amsterdam: De Buitenkant, page 73.

12. Ovink, G. W. 1965. 100 Years of Book Typography in The Netherlands. In *Book Typography, 1815–1965 in Europe and The United States of America,* ed. Kenneth Day. Chicago: University of Chicago Press, page 269.

13. Pannekoek, G. H., Jr. 1925. *De Herleving van de Nederlandsche Boekdrukkunst Sedert 1910.* Maastricht: Boosten & Stols, page 17.

14. Dooijes, Dick. 1977. Over Fré Cohen, de AJC en het Kunstgebeuren in de jaren '20. In *Fré Cohen, Rond Paasheuvel en Prinsenhof.* Amsterdam: Stadsdrukkerij van Amsterdam, page 12.

Chapter 4

1. Graatsma, William. No date. *Piet Zwart, Normalieënboekje,* Nuth: Drukkerij Rosbeek B.V., page 92.

2. Broos, Kees. 1982. *Piet Zwart, 1985–1977.* Amsterdam: Van Gennep, page 6.

3. Hefting, Paul. 1985. *Piet Zwart, Het boek van PTT* (facsimile). Den Haag: Staatsuitgeverij.

4. Broos, Kees. 1982. *Piet Zwart, 1985–1977.* Amsterdam: Van Gennep, page 16.

5. Hefting, Paul. 1985. *Piet Zwart, Het boek van PTT* (facsimile). Den Haag: Staatsuitgeverij (no page numbers).

6. Broos, Kees. 1982. *Piet Zwart, 1985–1977.* Amsterdam: Van Gennep, page 16.

7. Broos, Kees. 1982. *Piet Zwart, 1985–1977*. Amsterdam: Van Gennep, page 26.

8. Broos, Kees. 1982. *Piet Zwart, 1985–1977*. Amsterdam: Van Gennep, page 36.

9. Broos, Kees. 1982. *Piet Zwart, 1985–1977*. Amsterdam: Van Gennep, page 38.

10. Broos, Kees. 1982. *Piet Zwart, 1985–1977*. Amsterdam: Van Gennep, page 38.

11. Hefting, Paul. 1985. *Piet Zwart, Het boek van PTT* (facsimile). Den Haag: Staatsuitgeverij (no page numbers).

12. Graatsma, William. No date. *Piet Zwart, Normalieënboekje*. Nuth: Drukkerij Rosbeek B.V., page 89.

13. Dooijes, Dick. 1966. *Over typografie en grafische kunst*. Amsterdam: Lettergieterij en Machinehandel voorheen N. Tetterode, page 60.

14. Broos, Kees. 1982. *Piet Zwart, 1985–1977*. Amsterdam: Van Gennep, page 38.

15. Hefting, Paul. 1985. *Piet Zwart, Het boek van PTT* (facsimile). Den Haag: Staatsuitgeverij (no page numbers).

16. Jaffé, H. L. C. 20 November 1964. *Uitreiking van de David Röellprijs aan Piet Zwart. Een pictorale biografie van Piet Zwart door Pieter Brattinga*. Amsterdam: Prins Bernhard Fonds (no page numbers).

17. Broos, Kees. 1982. *Piet Zwart, 1985–1977*. Amsterdam: Van Gennep, page 44.

18. Hefting, Paul. 1985. *Piet Zwart, Het boek van PTT* (facsimile). Den Haag: Staatsuitgeverij (no page numbers).

19. Broos, Kees. 1982. *Piet Zwart, 1985–1977*. Amsterdam: Van Gennep, page 46.

20. Broos, Kees. 1982. *Piet Zwart, 1985–1977*. Amsterdam: Van Gennep, page 60.

21. Broos, Kees. 1982. *Piet Zwart, 1985–1977*. Amsterdam: Van Gennep, page 52.

22. Ovink, G. W. 1965. 100 Years of Book Typography in The Netherlands. In *Book Typography, 1815–1965 in Europe and The United States of America,* ed. Kenneth Day. Chicago: University of Chicago Press, page 269.

23. Dooijes, Dick and Pieter Brattinga. 1968. *A History of the Dutch Poster, 1890–1960*. Amsterdam: Scheltema & Holkema, page 36.

24. Dooijes, Dick and Pieter Brattinga. 1968. *A History of the Dutch Poster, 1890–1960*. Amsterdam: Scheltema & Holkema, page 39.

25. Broos, Kees. 1982. *Piet Zwart, 1985–1977*. Amsterdam: Van Gennep, page 74.

26. Maan, D. F. 1982. *De Maniakken, Ontstaan en ontwikkeling van de grafische vormgeving aan de Haagse academie in de jaren dertig*. Den Haag: Rijksmuseum Meermanno-Westreenianum, Museum van het boek, page 2.

27. Monguzzi, Bruno. November–December 1988. *Piet Zwart*. Graphis Magazine No. 258, page 57.

28. Maan, Dick and John van der Ree. 1986. *Paul Schuitema*. Rotterdam: Museum Boymans-van Beuningen (no page numbers).

29. Dooijes, Dick. 1966. *Over typografie en grafische kunst*. Amsterdam: Lettergieterij en Machinehandel voorheen N. Tetterode, page 64.

30. Maan, D. F. 1982. *De Maniakken, Ontstaan en ontwikkeling van de grafische vormgeving aan de Haagse academie in de jaren dertig*. Den Haag: Rijksmuseum Meermanno-Westreenianum, Museum van het boek, page 13.

31. Maan, D. F. 1982. *De Maniakken, Ontstaan en ontwikkeling van de grafische vormgeving aan de Haagse academie in de jaren dertig*. Den Haag: Rijksmuseum Meermanno-Westreenianum, Museum van het boek, page 13.

32. Schuitema, Paul. 1961. Neue Typografie um 1930. In *Neue Grafik*.

33. Schuitema, Paul. 1961. Neue Typografie um 1930. In *Neue Grafik*.

34. Schuitema, Paul. 1961. Neue Typografie um 1930. In *Neue Grafik*.

35. Schuitema, Paul. 1929. Gisteren en Vandaag. In *Schoonheid en Opvoeding*, page 1.

36. Maan, D. F. 1982. *De Maniakken, Ontstaan en ontwikkeling van de grafische vormgeving aan de Haagse academie in de jaren dertig*. Den Haag: Rijksmuseum Meermanno-Westreenianum, Museum van het boek, page 24.

37. Schuitema, Paul. 1961. Neue Typografie um 1930. In *Neue Grafik*.

38. Maan, D. F. 1982. *De Maniakken, Ontstaan en ontwikkeling van de grafische vormgeving aan de Haagse academie in de jaren dertig*. Den Haag: Rijksmuseum Meermanno-Westreenianum, Museum van het boek, page 22.

39. Schuitema, Paul (under the pseudonym S. Palsma). 1933. Foto als wapen in de klassestrijd. In *Links Richten*, page 21.

40. Dooijes, Dick. 1966. *Over typografie en grafische kunst*. Amsterdam: Lettergieterij en Machinehandel voorheen N. Tetterode, page 64.

41. Schuitema, Paul and Gerard Kiljan. 1933. Foto als beeldende element in de reclame. In *Reclame,* page 429.

42. Dooijes, Dick. 1966. *Over typografie en grafische kunst*. Amsterdam: Lettergieterij en Machinehandel voorheen N. Tetterode, page 65.

43. Dooijes, Dick. 1966. *Over typografie en grafische kunst*. Amsterdam: Lettergieterij en Machinehandel voorheen N. Tetterode, page 65.

44. Paul Schuitema. November 1928. Reclame. In *International Revue i10, No. 16, Volume I,* ed. Arthur Müller Lehning. Van Gennep, Amsterdam, 1979, page 73.

45. Maan, Dick and John van der Ree. 1986. *Paul Schuitema*. Rotterdam: Museum Boymans-van Beuningen (no page numbers).

46. Schuitema, Paul. 1961. Neue Typografie um 1930. In *Neue Grafik*.

47. Schuitema, Paul. 1961. Neue Typografie um 1930. In *Neue Grafik*.

48. Schuitema, Paul, and Gerard Kiljan. 1933. Foto als beeldende element in de reclame. In *Reclame,* page 429.

49. Schuitema, Paul. 1961. Neue Typografie um 1930. In *Neue Grafik*.

50. Schuitema, Paul. 1928. Talk for Arti et Industriae.

51. Doesburg, Theo van. 1918. *De Stijl II*.

52. Bool, Flip. De nieuwe typo- en fotografie. 1989. In *Voor Arthur Lehning,* ed. Toke van Helmond and J. J. Overstegen. Maastricht: Gerards en Schreurs, page 96.

53. Dooijes, Dick. 1966. *Over typografie en grafische kunst*. Amsterdam: Lettergieterij en Machinehandel voorheen N. Tetterode, page 65.

54. Rand, Paul. 1964. Een "type director." Interview in *"Allemaal Flauwekul"* en Andere Typografische Notities. 1989. Amsterdam: De Buitenkant, page 60.

Chapter 5

1. Ovink, G. W. 1965. 100 Years of Book Typography in The Netherlands. In *Book Typography, 1815–1965 in Europe and The United States of America,* ed. Kenneth Day. Chicago: University of Chicago Press, page 267.

2. Dooijes, Dick. 1988. *Wegbereiders van de Moderne Boektypografie in Nederland.* Amsterdam: De Buitenkant, page 7.

3. Ovink, G. W. 1965. 100 Years of Book Typography in The Netherlands. In *Book Typography, 1815–1965 in Europe and The United States of America,* ed. Kenneth Day. Chicago: University of Chicago Press, page 261.

4. Dooijes, Dick. 1966. *Over typografie en grafische kunst.* Amsterdam: Lettergieterij en Machinehandel voorheen N. Tetterode, page 62.

5. Dooijes, Dick. 1987. *Over de drukletterontwerpen van Sjoerd H. de Roos.* Zutphen: Bührmann-Ubbens Papier B.V., page 7.

6. Radermacher Schorer, M. R. 1951. *Bijdrage tot de Geschiedenis van de Renaissance der Nederlandse Boekdrukkunst.* Utrecht, page 43.

7. Unger, Gerard en Marjan Unger. 1989. *Dutch Landscape with Letters.* Utrecht: Van Boekhoven-Bosch bv grafische industrie, page 34.

8. Royen, J. F. van. 1913. De Hollandsche Mediaeval van S. H. de Roos. In *Onze Kunst 12,* page 132.

9. Dooijes, Dick. 1987. *Over de drukletterontwerpen van Sjoerd H. de Roos.* Zutphen: Bührmann-Ubbens Papier B.V., page 34.

10. Dooijes, Dick. 1959. *Traditie en vernieuwing, tien jaar Nederlandse drukkunst/1945–1955.* Amsterdam: Nederlandse Vereniging voor Druk-en Boekkunst, page 13.

11. Dooijes, Dick. 1986. *Boektypografische Verkenningen.* Amsterdam: De Buitenkant, page 241.

12. Dooijes, Dick. 1966. *Over typografie en grafische kunst.* Amsterdam: Lettergieterij en Machinehandel voorheen N. Tetterode, page 62.

13. Krimpen, Jan van. 1922. Palladium Prospectus.

14. Lommen, Mathieu. 1991. *De Grote Vijf.* Amsterdam. M. M. Lommen, page 20.

15. Krimpen, Jan van. 1922. S. H. de Roos, Boekkunstenaar en Letterontwerper. In *Nieuwe Arnhemsche Courant.*

16. Caflisch, Max. 1989. *Hoogtepunten van het letterontwerpen in Nederland:* Utrecht: Van Boekhoven-Bosch bv grafische industrie, page 20.

17. Lommen, Mathieu. 1991. *De Grote Vijf.* Amsterdam: M. M. Lommen, page 38.

18. Ovink, G. W. 1965. 100 Years of Book Typography in The Netherlands. In *Book Typography, 1815–1965 in Europe and The United States of America,* ed. Kenneth Day. Chicago: University of Chicago Press, page 268.

19. Radermacher Schorer, M. R. 1951. *Bijdrage tot de Geschiedenis van de Renaissance der Nederlandse Boekdrukkunst.* Utrecht, page 51.

20. Roos, S. H. de. 1955. Interview in Haarlems Dagblad.

21. Dooijes, Dick. 1966. *Over typografie en grafische kunst.* Amsterdam: Lettergieterij en Machinehandel voorheen N. Tetterode, page 62.

22. Ovink, G. W. 1965. 100 Years of Book Typography in The Netherlands. In *Book Typography, 1815–1965 in Europe and The United States of America,* ed. Kenneth Day. Chicago: University of Chicago Press, page 263.

23. Unger, Gerard en Marjan Unger. 1989. *Dutch Landscape with Letters.* Utrecht: Van Boekhoven-Bosch bv grafische industrie, page 34.

24. Krimpen, Jan van. 1930. Typography in Holland. In *The Fleuron,* No. 7, pages 5–7.

25. Roos, S. H. de. 1933. Holland. In *The Dolphin,* Vol. 1, page 336.

26. Dooijes, Dick. 1976. *Sjoerd H. de Roos, zoals ik mij hem herinner.* 's-Gravenhage: Rijksmuseum, Meermanno-Westreenianum & museum van het boek, page 30.

27. Rosmalen, Jo van. 1986. Uit een oud Maastrichts Drukkersgeslacht. In *Charles Nypels, Meester Drukker.* Maastricht: Charles Nypels Stichting, page 10.

28. Braches, Ernst. 1986. Nypels en de boekkunst in de jaren twintig. In *Charles Nypels, Meester Drukker.* Maastricht: Charles Nypels Stichting, page 29.

29. Dooijes, Dick. 1988. *Wegbereiders van de Moderne Boektypografie in Nederland.* Amsterdam: De Buitenkant, page 40.

30. Dooijes, Dick. 1988. *Wegbereiders van de Moderne Boektypografie in Nederland.* Amsterdam: De Buitenkant, page 39.

31. Dooijes, Dick. 1988. *Wegbereiders van de Moderne Boektypografie in Nederland.* Amsterdam: De Buitenkant, page 40.

32. Roos, S. H. de. 1933. Holland. In *The Dolphin,* Vol. I, page 336.

33. Krimpen, Jan van. 1930. Typography in Holland. In *The Fleuron,* No. 7, pages 1–2.

34. Dooijes, Dick. 1986. *Boektypografische Verkenningen.* Amsterdam: De Buitenkant, page 114.

35. Dooijes, Dick. 1988. *Wegbereiders van de Moderne Boektypografie in Nederland.* Amsterdam: De Buitenkant, page 40.

36. Dooijes, Dick. 1988. *Wegbereiders van de Moderne Boektypografie in Nederland.* Amsterdam: De Buitenkant, page 40.

37. Dooijes, Dick. 1988. *Wegbereiders van de Moderne Boektypografie in Nederland.* Amsterdam: De Buitenkant, page 49.

38. Ovink, G. W. 1965. 100 Years of Book Typography in The Netherlands. In *Book Typography, 1815–1965 in Europe and The United States of America,* ed. Kenneth Day. Chicago: University of Chicago Press, page 271.

39. Ovink, G. W. 1965. 100 Years of Book Typography in The Netherlands. In *Book Typography, 1815–1965 in Europe and The United States of America,* ed. Kenneth Day. Chicago: University of Chicago Press, page 271.

40. Dooijes, Dick. 1988. *Wegbereiders van de Moderne Boektypografie in Nederland.* Amsterdam: De Buitenkant, page 50.

41. Ovink, G. W. 1965. 100 Years of Book Typography in The Netherlands. In *Book Typography, 1815–1965 in Europe and The United States of America,* ed. Kenneth Day. Chicago: University of Chicago Press, page 265.

42. Lommen, Mathieu. 1991. *De Grote Vijf.* Amsterdam: M. M. Lommen, page 7.

43. Lommen, Mathieu. 1991. *De Grote Vijf.* Amsterdam: M. M. Lommen, page 11.

44. Lommen, Mathieu. 1991. *De Grote Vijf.* Amsterdam: M. M. Lommen, page 19.

45. Royen, J. F. van. 1912. De typographie van 's Rijks drukwerk. In *De Witte Mier.*

46. Dooijes, Dick. 1976. *Sjoerd H. De Roos, zoals ik mij hem herinner.* 's-Gravenhage: Rijksmuseum, Meermanno-Westreenianum & museum van het boek, page 29.

47. Broos, Kees. 1982. *Piet Zwart, 1985–1977.* Amsterdam: Van Gennep, page 74.

48. Zwart, Piet. 1929. In *Het Vaderland.*

49. Zwart, Piet. 1939. Timbres au profit des vitraux de Gouda et timbres-poste ordinaires. In *Les timbres-poste des Pays-Bas de 1929 à 1939.* Den Haag, page 17.

50. Hefting, Paul. 1985. *Piet Zwart, Het boek van PTT* (facsimile). Den Haag: Staatsuitgeverij.

51. Hefting, Paul. 1985. *Piet Zwart, Het boek van PTT* (facsimile). Den Haag: Staatsuitgeverij.

52. Hefting, Paul. 1985. *Piet Zwart, Het boek van PTT* (facsimile). Den Haag: Staatsuitgeverij.

53. Hefting, Paul. 1985. *Piet Zwart, Het boek van PTT* (facsimile). Den Haag: Staatsuitgeverij.

54. Forde, Gerard. 1991. *The Dutch PTT, 1920–1990, Design in the Public Service.* London: Design Museum, page 32.

Chapter 6

1. Shattuck, Roger. 1968. *The Banquet Years,* New York: Vintage Books, page 32.

2. Straten, Hans van. 1980. *Hendrik Nicolaas Werkman.* Amsterdam: Meulenhoff, page 1.

3. Straten, Hans van. 1980. *Hendrik Nicolaas Werkman.* Amsterdam: Meulenhoff, page 16.

4. Werkman, H. N. May 12, 1941. Letter to ds. F. R. A. Henkels. In *Brieven van H. N. Werkman, 1940–1945,* ed. Jan Martinet, page 28. Second edition, 1982. Uitgeverij, Amsterdam: De Arbeiderspers.

5. Straten, Hans van. 1980. *Hendrik Nicolaas Werkman.* Amsterdam: Meulenhoff, page 42.

6. Straten, Hans van. 1980. *Hendrik Nicolaas Werkman.* Amsterdam: Meulenhoff, page 55.

7. Straten, Hans van. 1980. *Hendrik Nicolaas Werkman.* Amsterdam: Meulenhoff, page 61.

8. Straten, Hans van. 1980. *Hendrik Nicolaas Werkman*. Amsterdam: Meulenhoff, page 66.

9. Werkman, H. N. 1923. Announcement for *The Next Call*.

10. Werkman, H. N. 1923. *The Next Call 1*.

11. Werkman, H. N. 1923. *The Next Call 1*.

12. Werkman, H. N. September 25, 1942. Letter to Paul Guermonprez.

13. Werkman, H. N. 1924. Letter to Michel Seuphor.

14. Straten, Hans van. 1980. *Hendrik Nicolaas Werkman*. Amsterdam: Meulenhoff, page 67.

15. Straten, Hans van. 1980. *Hendrik Nicolaas Werkman*. Amsterdam: Meulenhoff, page 67.

16. Straten, Hans van. 1980. *Hendrik Nicolaas Werkman*. Amsterdam: Meulenhoff, page 67.

17. Werkman, H. N. 1923. *The Next Call 2*.

18. Werkman, H. N. January 24, 1941. Letter to ds. F. R. A. Henkels. In *Brieven van H. N. Werkman, 1940–1945,* ed. Jan Martinet, page 16. Second edition, 1982. Uitgeverij, Amsterdam: De Arbeiderspers.

19. Straus, Monica. October 1989. Dutch Book Design, The Avant-Garde Tradition. In *Printing Arts in The Netherlands*. Fine Print, Vol. 15, No. 4, page 177.

20. Dooijes, Dick. 1966. *Over typografie en grafische kunst*. Amsterdam: Lettergieterij en Machinehandel voorheen N. Tetterode, page 72.

21. Werkman, H. N. 1924. *The Next Call 3*.

22. Werkman, H. N. 1924. *The Next Call 4*.

23. Werkman, H. N. 1924. *The Next Call 5*.

24. Doesburg, Theo van (I. K. Bonset). July 2, 1924. Letter to H. N. Werkman.

25. Straten, Hans van. 1980. *Hendrik Nicolaas Werkman*. Amsterdam: Meulenhoff, page 74.

26. Os, Henk van. 1989. *Hanson, Job*. Groningen: Wolters-Noordhoff/ Forsten, page 62.

27. Werkman, H. N. 1924. *The Next Call 6*.

28. Werkman, H. N. 1925. *The Next Call 7*.

29. Werkman, H. N. 1926. *The Next Call 8*.

30. Werkman, H. N. 1926. *The Next Call 9*.

31. Werkman, H. N. 1926. *The Next Call 9*.

32. Zweden, Johan van. December 1945. *Werkman, H. N., De Groningse Drukker-Schilder*. In *Apollo, I*. Den Haag: Uitgevers: N. V. Servire, page 29.

33. Vries, Hendrik de and Dr. A. J. Zuithoff. 1945. *Werkman, Drukker-Schilder*. Amsterdam: Stedelijk Museum, page 3.

34. Wiegers, Jan. ca. 1945. *De Buitenlandse Reis*.

35. Werkman, H. N. January 24, 1941. Letter to ds. F. R. A. Henkels. In *Brieven van H. N. Werkman, 1940–1945,* ed. Jan Martinet, page 16. Second edition, 1982. Uitgeverij, Amsterdam: De Arbeiderspers.

Chapter 7

1. Petersen, Ad and Pieter Brattinga. 1975. *Sandberg, A Documentary.* Amsterdam: Kosmos, page 11.

2. Petersen, Ad and Pieter Brattinga. 1975. *Sandberg, A Documentary.* Amsterdam: Kosmos, page 12.

3. Petersen, Ad and Pieter Brattinga. 1975. *Sandberg, A Documentary.* Amsterdam: Kosmos, page 16.

4. Petersen, Ad and Pieter Brattinga. 1975. *Sandberg, A Documentary.* Amsterdam: Kosmos, page 18.

5. Sandberg, Willem. Typografisch Ontwerper. 1981. In *Willem Sandberg, Portret van een Kunstenaar,* ed. Ank Leeuw-Marcar. Amsterdam: Meulenhoff Nederland B.V., page 63.

6. Maan, Dick and John van der Ree. 1990. *Typo-foto/Elementaire typografie in Nederland, 1920–1940.* Utrecht/Amsterdam: Veen/Reflex, page 19.

7. Maan, Dick and John van der Ree. 1990. *Typo-foto/Elementaire typografie in Nederland, 1920–1940.* Utrecht/Amsterdam: Veen/Reflex, page 19.

8. Maan, Dick and John van der Ree. 1990. *Typo-foto/Elementaire typografie in Nederland, 1920–1940.* Utrecht/Amsterdam: Veen/Reflex, page 19.

9. Kiljan, Gerard. 1935. Quoted by Paul Hefting. 1985. *Piet Zwart, Het boek van PTT* (facsimile). Den Haag: Staatsuitgeverij.

10. Maan, D. F. 1982. *De Maniakken, Ontstaan en ontwikkeling van de grafische vormgeving aan de Haagse academie in de jaren dertig.* Den Haag: Rijksmuseum Meermanno-Westreenianum, Museum van het boek, page 8.

11. Maan, D. F. 1982. *De Maniakken, Ontstaan en ontwikkeling van de grafische vormgeving aan de Haagse academie in de jaren dertig.* Den Haag: Rijksmuseum Meermanno-Westreenianum, Museum van het boek, page 10.

12. Maan, D. F. 1982. *De Maniakken, Ontstaan en ontwikkeling van de grafische vormgeving aan de Haagse academie in de jaren dertig.* Den Haag: Rijksmuseum Meermanno-Westreenianum, Museum van het boek, page 10.

13. Maan, D. F. 1982. *De Maniakken, Ontstaan en ontwikkeling van de grafische vormgeving aan de Haagse academie in de jaren dertig.* Den Haag: Rijksmuseum Meermanno-Westreenianum, Museum van het boek, page 8.

14. Maan, D. F. 1982. *De Maniakken, Ontstaan en ontwikkeling van de grafische vormgeving aan de Haagse academie in de jaren dertig.* Den Haag: Rijksmuseum Meermanno-Westreenianum, Museum van het boek, page 13.

15. Maan, D. F. 1982. *De Maniakken, Ontstaan en ontwikkeling van de grafische vormgeving aan de Haagse academie in de jaren dertig.* Den Haag: Rijksmuseum Meermanno-Westreenianum, Museum van het boek, page 36.

16. Maan, D. F. 1982. *De Maniakken, Ontstaan en ontwikkeling van de grafische vormgeving aan de Haagse academie in de jaren dertig.* Den Haag: Rijksmuseum Meermanno-Westreenianum, Museum van het boek, page 36.

17. Faassen, Egbert van. 1988. *N. P. De Koo, ontwerper.* 's-Gravenhage: Haags Gemeentemuseum, page 3.

18. Faassen, Egbert van. 1988. *N. P. De Koo, ontwerper.* 's-Gravenhage: Haags Gemeentemuseum, page 3.

19. Kuipers, Reinold. 1990. *Gerezen wit, Notities bij boekvormelijks en zo, 1945.* Amsterdam: Querido, page 13.

20. Kuipers, Reinold. 1990. *Gerezen wit, Notities bij boekvormelijks en zo, 1945.* Amsterdam: Querido, page 22.

21. Bruinsma, Max, Lies Ros, and Rob Schröder. 1989. *Dick Elffers en de Kunsten*. Netherlands: Het Gerrit Jan Thiemefonds, page 6.

22. Bruinsma, Max, Lies Ros, and Rob Schröder. 1989. *Dick Elffers en de Kunsten*. Netherlands: Het Gerrit Jan Thiemefonds, page 6.

23. Bruinsma, Max, Lies Ros, and Rob Schröder. 1989. *Dick Elffers en de Kunsten*. Netherlands: Het Gerrit Jan Thiemefonds, page 12.

24. Bruinsma, Max, Lies Ros, and Rob Schröder. 1989. *Dick Elffers en de Kunsten*. Netherlands: Het Gerrit Jan Thiemefonds, page 14.

25. Bruinsma, Max, Lies Ros, and Rob Schröder. 1989. *Dick Elffers en de Kunsten*. Netherlands: Het Gerrit Jan Thiemefonds, page 14.

26. Bruinsma, Max, Lies Ros, and Rob Schröder. 1989. *Dick Elffers en de Kunsten*. Netherlands: Het Gerrit Jan Thiemefonds, page 16.

27. Bruinsma, Max, Lies Ros, and Rob Schröder. 1989. *Dick Elffers en de Kunsten*. Netherlands: Het Gerrit Jan Thiemefonds, page 17.

28. Bruinsma, Max, Lies Ros, and Rob Schröder. 1989. *Dick Elffers en de Kunsten*. Netherlands: Het Gerrit Jan Thiemefonds, page 17.

29. Maan, Dick and John van der Ree. 1990. *Typo-foto /Elementaire typografie in Nederland, 1920–1940*. Utrecht/Amsterdam: Veen/Reflex, page 35.

30. Bruinsma, Max, Lies Ros, and Rob Schröder. 1989. *Dick Elffers en de Kunsten*. Netherlands: Het Gerrit Jan Thiemefonds, page 17.

31. Maan, Dick and John van der Ree. 1990. *Typo-foto /Elementaire typografie in Nederland, 1920–1940*. Utrecht/Amsterdam: Veen/Reflex, page 35.

32. Bruinsma, Max, Lies Ros, and Rob Schröder. 1989. *Dick Elffers en de Kunsten*. Netherlands: Het Gerrit Jan Thiemefonds, page 18.

33. Elffers, Dick. 1937. Ontwerpers en de fotografie. In *Prisma der Kunsten*. Rotterdam, pages 108–110.

34. Bruinsma, Max, Lies Ros, and Rob Schröder. 1989. *Dick Elffers en de Kunsten*. Netherlands: Het Gerrit Jan Thiemefonds, page 21.

35. Kiljan, Gerard, Paul Schuitema, Henny Cahn, and Piet Zwart. 1939. Nog meer discussie over het Grafies-nummer. In *De 8 & Opbouw*, page 160.

36. Elffers, Dick. 1939. Introduction. In *Grafies-nummer van De 8 & Opbouw*, pages 129–130.

37. Bruinsma, Max, Lies Ros, and Rob Schröder. 1989. *Dick Elffers en de Kunsten*. Netherlands: Het Gerrit Jan Thiemefonds, page 22.

Chapter 8

1. Kroonenburg-de Kousemaeker, Claar van and Annelies Haase. 1984. De rol van Sandberg. In *De Doorbraak van de Moderne Kunst in Nederland*, ed. Willemijn Stokvis. Amsterdam: Meulenhoff/Landshoff, page 70.

2. Jong, Dr. L. de. 1990. *De Bezetting na 50 Jaar, Deel 1*. 's-Gravenhage: SDU Uitgeverij, page 18.

3. Fontaine Verwey, Prof. Mr. H. de la. 1958. Introduction. In *Het Vrije Boek in Onvrije Tijd*, ed. Dirk de Jong. Leiden: A. W. Sijthoff's Uitgeversmaatschappij, page 2.

4. Jong, Dr. L. de. 1990. *De Bezetting na 50 Jaar, Deel 1*. 's-Gravenhage: SDU Uitgeverij, page 34.

5. Jong, Dr. L. de. 1990. *De Bezetting na 50 Jaar, Deel 1.* 's-Gravenhage: SDU Uitgeverij, page 68.

6. Petersen, Ad and Pieter Brattinga. 1975. *Sandberg, A Documentary.* Amsterdam: Kosmos, page 27.

7. Petersen, Ad and Pieter Brattinga. 1975. *Sandberg, A Documentary.* Amsterdam: Kosmos, page 27.

8. Drukker, Ber. 1977. Fré Cohen, een onvolledige karakteristiek. In *Fré Cohen, Rond Paasheuvel en Prinsenhof.* Stadsdrukkerij van Amsterdam.

9. *In Het Verborgen Gedrukt.* 1945. Exhibition Museum, Boymans Rotterdam.

10. Dooijes, Dick. 1976. *Sjoerd H. De Roos, zoals ik mij hem herinner.* 's-Gravenhage: Rijksmuseum, Meermanno-Westreenianum & museum van het boek, page 21.

11. *In Het Verborgen Gedrukt.* 1945. Exhibition Museum, Boymans Rotterdam.

12. Petersen, Ad and Pieter Brattinga. 1975. *Sandberg, A Documentary.* Amsterdam: Kosmos, page 28.

13. Petersen, Ad and Pieter Brattinga. 1975. *Sandberg, A Documentary.* Amsterdam: Kosmos, page 30.

14. Petersen, Ad and Pieter Brattinga. 1975. *Sandberg, A Documentary.* Amsterdam: Kosmos, page 30.

15. Petersen, Ad and Pieter Brattinga. 1975. *Sandberg, A Documentary.* Amsterdam: Kosmos, page 40.

16. Bruinsma, Max, Lies Ros, and Rob Schröder. 1989. *Dick Elffers en de Kunsten.* Netherlands: Het Gerrit Jan Thiemefonds, page 22.

17. Petersen, Ad and Pieter Brattinga. 1975. *Sandberg, A Documentary.* Amsterdam: Kosmos, page 26.

18. Gerdes, Ed. 1943. Introduction. In *Kunstenaars zien de Arbeidsdienst.* Catalogue. Amsterdam: Stedelijk Museum.

19. Straten, Hans van. 1980. *Hendrik Nicolaas Werkman.* Amsterdam: Meulenhoff, page 175.

20. Straten, Hans van. 1980. *Hendrik Nicolaas Werkman.* Amsterdam: Meulenhoff, page 181.

21. Straten, Hans van. 1980. *Hendrik Nicolaas Werkman.* Amsterdam: Meulenhoff, page 184.

22. Kuitenbrouwer, Carel. July 1989. Graphic Holland, A Prominent Place. *Dutch Arts.* Dutch Ministry for Cultural Affairs. The Hague: SDU Publishers, page 27.

23. Crouwel, Wim. 1988. Lower Case in the Dutch Lowlands. In *Octavo,* London.

24. Dooijes, Dick. 1959. *Traditie en vernieuwing, tien jaar Nederlandse drukkunst/1945–1955.* Amsterdam: Nederlandse Vereniging voor Druk-en Boekkunst, page 24.

25. Petersen, Ad and Pieter Brattinga. 1975. *Sandberg, A Documentary.* Amsterdam: Kosmos, page 44.

26. Brattinga, Pieter. 1987. *Influences on Dutch Graphic Design, 1900–1945.*

27. Bruinsma, Max, Lies Ros, and Rob Schröder. 1989. *Dick Elffers en de Kunsten.* Netherlands: Het Gerrit Jan Thiemefonds, page 24.

28. Petersen, Ad and Pieter Brattinga. 1975. *Sandberg, A Documentary.* Amsterdam: Kosmos, pages 49–50.

29. Kuipers, Reinold. 1990. *Gerezen wit, Notities bij boekvormelijks en zo, 1945.* Amsterdam: Querido, page 43.

30. Ovink, G. W. 1965. 100 Years of Book Typography in The Netherlands. In *Book Typography, 1815–1965 in Europe and The United States of America,* ed. Kenneth Day. Chicago: University of Chicago Press, page 272.

31. Dooijes, Dick. 1966. *Over typografie en grafische kunst.* Amsterdam: Lettergieterij en Machinehandel voorheen N. Tetterode, page 66.

Bibliography

Ades, Dawn. 1978. *Dada and Surrealism Reviewed*. London: Arts Council of Great Britain.

Ades, Dawn. 1984. *Posters: The 20th Century Poster. Design of the Avant Garde*. New York: Abbeville Press.

Aldus. 1989. *"Allemaal Flauwekul" en Andere Typografische Notities*. Amsterdam: De Buitenkant.

Art and Writing (Schrift und Bild). Stedelijk Museum Amsterdam, 3 May–10 June 1963. Staatliche Kunsthalle Baden-Baden, 14 June–4 August 1963.

Baena, Duke De. 1975. *The Dutch Puzzle*. The Hague: L. J. C. Boucher.

Baljeu, Joost. 1974. *Theo van Doesburg*. London: Studio Vista, Cassell & Collier Macmillan.

Barnicoat, John. 1985. *Posters: A Concise History*. London: Thames and Hudson.

Bart van der Leck, 1876–1958. 1976. Otterlo: Rijksmuseum Kröller-Müller. Amsterdam: Stedelijk Museum.

Beckett, Jane. 1980. The Netherlands. In *Abstraction: Towards a New Art, Painting 1910–20*. London: The Tate Gallery.

Beeren, W. A. L. 1978. *The Next Call van H. N. Werkman*. Groningen: Instituut voor Kunstgeschiedenis.

Berlage, Dr. H. P., W. M. Dudok, Ir. Jan Gratama, Ir. A. R. Hulshoff, Herm. van der Kloot Meijburg, J. F. Staal, editors. J. Luthmann, secretary. *Gemeenschaps-'en Vereenigingsgebouwen, Moderne Bouwkunst in Nederland No. 17*.

Berman, Merrill C. 1987. *Captured Glance: The Avant-Garde and Advertising in the Twenties*. New York: Helen Serger/La Boetie.

Blankenstein, B. Januari–Februari 1946. *Werkman, H. N*. In *TéTé (Technisch Tijdschrift voor de Grafische Industrie)*, Nummer 6 en 7, eerste Jaargang.

Blokker, Jan. 1989. *De Wond'ren Werden Woord en Dreven Verder, Honderd Jaar Informatie in Nederland 1889–1989*. Amsterdam: J. A. Blokker.

Blotkamp, Carel, and others. Trans. Charlotte I. Loeb and Arthur L. Loeb. 1982. *De Stijl: The Formative Years*. Cambridge, MA: MIT Press.

Bolliger, Hans. 1978. *Kurt Schwitters*. Köln: Gallerie Gmurzynska.

Bool, Flip. 1989. De nieuwe typo- en fotografie. In *Voor Arthur Lehning*, Toke van Helmond and J. J. Overstegen, editors. Maastricht: Gerards en Schreurs.

Bibliography

Bool, Flip, and Ingeborg Leijerzapf. 1982. Fotografie. In *Berlin–Amsterdam, 1020–1940, Wisselwerkingen,* pages 237–245. Amsterdam: E. M. Querido's Uitgeverij.

Bool, Flip, and Kees Broos. 1989. *De Nieuwe Fotografie in Nederland.* Amsterdam.

Bool, Flip, and Kees Broos. 1980. *Domela.* Den Haas: Haags Gemeentemuseum.

Bosters, Cassandra. 1991. *Ontwerpen voor de Jaarbeurs.* Utrecht: Centraal Museum.

Boterman, Jan P. 1989. *Sjoerd H. De Roos, typografische geschriften 1907–1920,* 's-Gravenhage: SDU Uitgeverij.

Braches, Ernst. 1973. *Het boek als Nieuwe Kunst, 1892–1903. Een studie in Art Nouveau.* Utrecht: Oosthoek's Uitgeversmaatschappij BV.

Brattinga, Pieter. 1987. *Influences on Dutch Graphic Design, 1900–1945.* Amsterdam.

Bromberg, Paul, editor. *Werkman.* Arnhem: Netherlands Informative Art Editions. S. Gouda Quint-D. Brouwer and Son.

Broos, Kees. 1981. *Piet Zwart, Retrospektive Fotografie.* Düsseldorf: Edition Marzona.

Broos, Kees. 1982. From De Stijl to a New Typography. In *De Stijl, 1917–1931, Visions of Utopia,* Mildred Friedman, editor. New York: Abbeville Press.

Broos, Kees. 1982. *Piet Zwart, 1985–1977.* Amsterdam: Van Gennep.

Broos, Kees, and Konrad Matschke. 1990. *Ring "neue werbegestalter" 1928–1933, Amsterdamer Ausstellung 1931.* Wiesbaden: Museum Wiesbaden.

Bruinsma, Max, Lies Ros, and Rob Schröder. 1989. *Dick Elffers en de Kunsten.* Netherlands: Het Gerrit Jan Thiemefonds.

Budliger, Hansjörg, Jost Hochuli, Kurt Weidemann, Berthold Wolpe, Hans Peter Willberg, and Rudolf Hostettler. *Jan Tschichold, Typographer and Type Designer, 1902–1974.* 1982. Edinburgh: National Library of Scotland.

Buitkamp, Dr. J. 1990. *Geschiedenis van Het Verzet, 1940–1945.* Houten: Fibula/Unieboek.

Caflisch, Max. 1989. *Hoogtepunten van het letterontwerpen in Nederland.* Utrecht: Van Boekhoven-Bosch.

Carter, Sebastian. 1987. *Twentieth Century Type Designers.* London: Trefoil Publications.

Chappell, Warren. 1986. *A Short History of the Printed Word.* Boston: Nonpareil Books.

Cohen, Arthur A. 1980. *Zwart, Piet, Typotekt*. New York: Ex Libris.

Colpaart, Adri. 1986. *Sandberg, Bij voorkeur een ruwe contour.* Zwolle: Librije Hedendaagse Kunst.

Craig, James, and Bruce Barton. 1987. *Thirty Centuries of Graphic Design*. New York: Watson-Guptill.

Crouwel, Wim. 1988. Lower Case in the Dutch Lowlands. In *Octavo*. London.

Dam, P. R., and Joh. Schaafsma. 1990. *Verzameling De Roos, affiches uit de jaren 1937–1948.* Leeuwarden: Gemeentearchief.

Dam, Peter van, and Pim Reinders. 1990. *Johann George van Caspel, Affichekunstenaar (1870–1928)*. Amsterdam: Stadsuitgeverij.

Damase, Jacques. 1984. *Le Mouvement de L'Espace*. Paris: Jacques Damase.

Damase, Jacques. 1966. *La Révolution Typographique*. Genève: Motte.

De Stijl, 1932. Dernier Numéro

De Stijl. 1951. Amsterdam: Stedelijk Museum.

Divendal, Joost. March 4, 1985. *Werkman en de druksels van het paradijs.* 's-Gravenhage: De Waarheid.

Divendal, Joost. Thursday, January 25, 1990. *Hendrik Nicolaas Werkman, Het Verlangen naar Paradijs.* Amsterdam: De Trouw.

Doesburg, Theo van (I. K. Bonset). July 2, 1924. Letter to H. N. Werkman.

Doesburg, Theo van, Kurt Schwitters, and Kate Steinitz. 1925. *Die Scheuche Märchen.* Hannover: Apossverlag.

Doesburg, Theo van. 1921. Letter to Antonie Kok.

Doesburg, Theo van. 1920. *Klassiek, barok, modern.* Antwerp: De Sikkel.

Doesburg, Theo van. 1917/18–1928. *De Stijl*, Vol. I–VIII.

Dooijes, Dick. 1991. *Mijn leven met letters*. Amsterdam: De Buitenkant.

Dooijes, Dick. 1988. *Wegbereiders van de Moderne Boektypografie in Nederland*. Amsterdam: De Buitenkant.

Dooijes, Dick. 1987. *Over de drukletterontwerpen van Sjoerd H. de Roos*. Zutphen: Bührmann-Ubbens Papier.

Dooijes, Dick. 1986. *Boektypografische Verkenningen*. Amsterdam: De Buitenkant.

Dooijes, Dick. 1977. Over Fré Cohen, de AJC en het Kunstgebeuren in de jaren '20. In *Fré Cohen, Rond Paasheuvel en Prinsenhof.* Amsterdam: Stadsdrukkerij.

Dooijes, Dick. 1976. *Sjoerd H. de Roos, zoals ik mij hem herinner.* 's-Gravenhage: Rijksmuseum, Meermanno-Westreenianum & Museum van Het Boek.

Dooijes, Dick. 1970. *Hendrik Werkman.* Amsterdam: J. M. Meulenhoff.

Dooijes, Dick. 1966. *Over typografie en grafische kunst.* Amsterdam: Lettergieterij en Machinehandel voorheen N. Tetterode.

Dooijes, Dick. 1959. *Traditie en vernieuwing, tien jaar Nederlandse drukkunst/1945–1955.* Amsterdam: Nederlandse Vereniging voor Druk-en Boekkunst.

Dooijes, Dick, and Pieter Brattinga. 1968. *A History of the Dutch Poster. 1890–1960.* Amsterdam: Scheltema & Holkema.

Dooijes, Dick, Ber Drukker, Dolf Stork, and others. 1977. *Fré Cohen, Rond Paasheuvel en Prinsenhof.* Amsterdam: Stadsdrukkerij.

Douwes Dekker, N. A. 1967. *Typography en Affiches, Dick Elffers.* 's-Gravenhage: Museum van het boek, Rijksmuseum Meermanno-Westreenianum.

Droste, Magdalena. 1990. *Bauhaus, 1919–1933.* Köln: Benedikt Taschen Verlag.

Duister, Frans. October 5, 1977. *Druksels uit het paradijs.* Amsterdam: Het Parool.

Duncan, Alastair. 1988. *Art Deco.* London: Thames and Hudson.

Elffers, Dick. 1939. Introduction. In *Grafies-nummer van De 8 & Opbouw.*

Elffers, Dick. 1937. Ontwerpers en de fotografie. In *Prisma der Kunsten,* Rotterdam

Ex, Sjarel, and Els Hoek. 1985. *Vilmos Huszár, Schilder en Ontwerper 1884–1960.* Utrecht: Reflex.

Faassen, Egbert van. 1988. *N. P., de Koo, ontwerper.* 's-Gravenhage: Haags Gemeentemuseum.

Faassen, Egbert van. 1988. *Drukwerk voor PTT, Typografie en Vormgeving voor een Staatsbedrijf in de Jaren Twintig en Dertig.* Den Haag: SDU-Uitgeverij.

Fern, Alan M. 1968. *Word and Image: Posters from the Collection of the Museum of Modern Art.* New York: New York Graphic Society.

Fitzgerald, F. Scott. 1945. *The Crack-Up.* New York: New Directions.

Fontaine Verwey, Prof. Mr. H. de la. 1958. Introduction. In *Het Vrije Boek in Onvrije Tijd,* Dirk de Jong, editor. Leiden: A. W. Sijthoff's Uitgeversmaatschappij.

Forde, Gerard. 1991. *The Dutch PTT, 1920–1990, Design in the Public Service.* London: Design Museum.

Friedi, Friedrich. 1990. *The ring "neue werbegestalter" 1928–1933.*
London: Octavo, synthesis 90.7.

Gerdes, Ed. 1943. Introduction. In *Kunstenaars zien de Arbeidsdienst.*
Catalog. Amsterdam: Stedelijk Museum.

Gescheurd door Sandberg. 1982. Gemeente Amersfoort/Sud
Amsterdam.

Graatsma, William, Jo van Rosmalen, Dick Dooijes, Ernst Braches,
and Albert Helman. 1986. *Nypels, Charles: Meester Drukker.*
Maastricht: Charles Nypels Stichting.

Graatsma, William. n.d. *Piet Zwart, Normalieënboekje.* Nuth:
Drukkerij Rosbeek.

Grieshaber, H. A. P. 1957/58. *Hommage À Werkman.* Stuttgart:
Fritz Eggert; New York: George Wittenborn.

Haaren, Hein van. 1991. *Tegen de lust, Toespraak bij de uitreiking van
de Piet Zwart Prijs 1991 aan Wim Crouwel.* Beroepsvereniging
Nederlandse Ontwerpers.

Halsbeke, Charles-Léon van. 1929 (pseudonym of A. A. M. Stols)
L'art Typographique dans les Pays-Bas Depuis 1892. Maestricht &
Bruxelles: Éditions A. A. M. Stols.

Hammacher, A. M. 1947. *Jean François Van Royen.* 's-Gravenhage:
D. A. Daamen's Uitgeversmaatschappij N. V. en A. A. M. Stols.

Hartz, S. L. 1960. *Van Krimpen.* London: The Penrose Annual.

Havelaar, Just. Dr. H. P. Berlage. Circa 1926. In *Nederlandse
Bouwmeesters.* Amsterdam: Van Munster's Uitgevers Maatschappij.

Hefting, Paul. 1988. *Nederlandse Postzegels, 1987.* 's-Gravenhage:
Staatsbedrijf der PTT en de SDU Uitgeverij.

Hefting, Paul. 1985. *Piet Zwart, Het boek van PTT.* Facsimile.
Den Haag: Staatsuitgeverij.

Heller, Steven, editor. 1989. *De Stijl, Design and Styles.* New York:
The Pushpin Group.

Heller, Steven, and Seymour Chwast. 1988. *Graphic Style.*
New York: Harry N. Abrams.

Henkels, Ds. F. R. A. 1960. H. N. Werkman en de schilderkunst.
In *Groningen.*

Henkels, F. R. A. 1946. *Logboek van de Blauwe Schuit.* Amsterdam:
A. A. Balkema.

Henkels, F. R. A. 1945? *Werkman, Over de nagedachtenis van onzen
vriend.* Heerenveen.

Henkels, F. R. A., and Jan Martinet. 1982. *H. N. Werkman,
Chassidische Legenden.* Groningen: Wolters-Noordhoff, Bouma's
Boekhuis.

Heuvel, Hans van den, and Gerard Mulder. 1990. *Het vrije woord, De illegale pers in Nederland 1940–1945.* 's-Gravenhage: SdU Uitgeverij.

Imanse, Geurt. 1984. *De Nederlandse Identiteit in de Kunst na 1945.* Amsterdam: Meulenhoff/Landshoff.

Imanse, Geurt, Tilman Osterwold, John Steen, and Andreas Vowinckel. 1982. *Van Gogh tot Cobra, Nederlandse Schilderkunst 1880–1950.* Amsterdam: Meulenhoff/Landshoff.

In Het Verborgen Gedrukt. 1945. Exhibition Museum Boymans, Rotterdam.

Jaffé, H. L. C. 1986. *Over utopie en werkelijkheid in de beeldende kunst. Verzamelde opstellen van (1915–1984).* Amsterdam: Meulenhoff/Landshoff.

Jaffé, H. L. C. 1983. *Theo van Doesburg.* Amsterdam: Meulenhoff/Landshoff.

Jaffé, H. L. C. 20 November 1964. *Uitreiking van de David Röellprijs aan Piet Zwart. Een pictorale biografie van Piet Zwart door Pieter Brattinga.* Amsterdam: Prins Bernhard Fonds.

Jaffé, H. L. C. 1962. Holland. In *Art Since 1945. New York: Washington Square Press.*

Jaffé, H. L. C. 1956. *De Stijl/1917–1931.* Amsterdam: Meulenhoff/Landshoff.

Jong, Dirk de. 1958. *Het Vrije Boek in Onvrije Tijd.* Leiden: A. W. Sijthoff's Uitgeversmaatschappij.

Jong, Dr. L. de. 1990. *De Bezetting na 50 Jaar, Deel 1.* 's-Gravenhage: SDU Uitgeverij.

Jong, Dr. L. de. 1988. *De Geschiedenis van Het Koninkrijk der Nederlanden in de Tweede Wereld Oorlog.* Amsterdam: Budgetboeken.

Kempers, Bram. 1988. *Socialisme, kunst en reclame.* Amsterdam: Uitgeverij De Arbeiderspers.

Kepes, Gyorgy. 1944. *Language of Vision.* Chicago: Paul Theobald.

Kiljan, Gerard, Paul Schuitema, Henny Cahn, and Piet Zwart. 1939. Nog meer discussie over het Grafies-nummer. In *De 8 & Opbouw.*

Koch, André. 1988. *W. H. Gispen, 1890–1981.* Rotterdam: Uitgeverij de Hef.

Koolwijk, Tom van, and Chris Schriks. 1986. *Kleine Prentkunst in Nederland in de 20e eeuw.* Zutphen: De Walburg Pers.

Krimpen, Huib van. October 1989. Type Design in The Netherlands and the Influence of the Enschedé Foundry. In *Fine Print,* San Francisco, Vol. 15, No. 4.

Krimpen, Huib van. 1986. *Boek over het maken van boeken.* Veenendaal: Gaade Uitgevers.

Krimpen, Jan van. 1990. *Over het ontwerpen en bedenken van drukletters.* Amsterdam: De Buitenkant.

Krimpen, Jan van. 1930. Typography in Holland. In *The Fleuron,* No. VII.

Krimpen, Jan van. 1922. Palladium Prospectus.

Krimpen, Jan van. 1922. S. H. de Roos, Boekkunstenaar en Letterontwerper. In *Nieuwe Arnhemsche Courant.*

Kroonenburg-de Kousemaeker, Claar van, and Annelies Haase. 1984. De rol van Sandberg. In *De Doorbraak van de Moderne Kunst in Nederland,* Willemijn Stokvis, editor. Amsterdam: Meulenhoff/Landshoff.

Kuipers, Abe. 1987. *A van der Veen Oomkens, een Groninger lettergieterij in de negentiende eeuw.* Groningen: J. Niemeijer.

Kuipers, Reinold. 1990. *Gerezen wit, Notities bij boekvormelijks en zo.* Amsterdam: Querido.

Kuitenbrouwer, Carel. July 1989. Graphic Holland, A Prominent Place. In *Dutch Arts.* The Hague: SDU Publishers.

Lawson, Alexander. 1990. *Anatomy of a Typeface.* Boston: David R. Godine.

Ledoux, Tanja. 1988. *Berlage als boekbandontwerper, illustrator en typograaf.* Wageningen: Fine and Rare Books.

Lehning, Arthur M. 1979. *International Revue i 10, 1927–1929.* Facsimile edition. Amsterdam: Van Gennep.

Lemoine, Serge. 1987. *Dada.* New York: Universe Books.

Lewis, John. 1978. *Typography: Design and Practice.* New York: Taplinger.

Lissitsky, El. 1890–1941. 1990. Eindhoven: Stedelijk Van Abbemuseum.

Lommen, Mathieu. 1991. *De grote vijf.* Amsterdam: M. M. Lommen.

Lommen, Mathieu. 1987. *Letter ontwerpers.* Haarlem: Joh. Enschedé en Zonen.

Lopes Cardozo, A., and A. Stroeve. 1987. Graphic Design Since 1945. In *Holland in Form. Dutch Design 1945–1987,* Gert Staal and Hester Wolters, editors. 's-Gravenhage: Stichting Holland in Vorm.

Lottner, Perdita, and Alexander Cizinsky. 1990. *Ring "neue werbegestalter" 1928–1933, Ein Überblick.* Hannover: Sprengel Museum.

Maan, D. F. 1982. *De Maniakken, Ontstaan en ontwikkeling van de grafische vormgeving aan de Haagse academie in de jaren dertig,* Den Haag: Rijksmuseum Meermanno-Westreenianum, Museum van het boek.

Maan, Dick, and John van der Ree. 1990. *Typo-foto/Elementaire typografie in Nederland, 1920–1940.* Utrecht/Amsterdam: Veen/Reflex.

Maan, Dick, and John van der Ree. 1986. *Paul Schuitema.* Rotterdam: Museum Boymans-van Beuningen.

Martinet, Jan. 1985. *Chassidische Legenden, Een Suite van II. N. Werkman.* Groningen: Wolters-Noordhoff, Bouma's Boekhuis.

Martinet, Jan. Editor. 1982. *Brieven van H. N. Werkman, 1940–1945.* Amsterdam: Uitgeverij, De Arbeiderspers.

Martinet, Jan. 1982. *De Schilder Hendrik Werkman.* Groningen: Martinipers.

Martinet, Jan. 1977. *The Next Call.* Facsimile. Utrecht: Reflex.

Martinet, Jan. 1977. *Hendrik Nicolaas Werkman, 1882–1945.* Amsterdam: Stedelijk Museum.

Martinet, Jan. 1967. *H. N. Werkman, en de Chassidische Legenden.* Algemene Adviezen, F. R. A. Henkels, Inleiding, Hans van Straten. Haarlem: J. H. Henkes Grafische Bedrijven.

Martinet, Jan. März 1965. *H. N. Werkman.* Typographische Monatsblätter.

Martinet, Jan. 1963. *Hot Printing.* Amsterdam: Stedelijk Museum.

Martinet, Jan. 1958. De Blauwe Schuit. In *Museumjournaal: serie 3, nr. 9–10.*

McMurtrie, Douglas C. 1967. *The Book: The Story of Printing and Bookmaking.* New York: Oxford University Press.

Meggs, Philip B. 1983. *A History of Graphic Design.* New York: Van Nostrand Reinhold.

Monguzzi, Bruno. 1987. *Piet Zwart: The Typographical Work 1923–1933.* Milano: Rivista trimestrale, Anno IX, 30/2 guigno.

Monguzzi, Bruno. November–December 1988. *Piet Zwart.* Graphis Magazine, No. 258.

Moor, Christiaan de. 1960. *Postzegelkunst, de vormgeving van de Nederlandse postzegel.* Staatsbedrijf der PTT–Nederland.

Muller, Ellen, and Magda Kyrova. 1983. *Antoon Molkenboer, Ontwerpen voor muziek en toneel, 1895–1917.* Den Haag: Haags Gemeentemuseum.

Müller, Fridolin, Pieter F. Althaus, and Jan Martinet. 1967. *H. N. Werkman.* London: Alec Tiranti.

Müller-Brockmann, Josef and Shizuko 1971. *History of the Poster.* Zurich: ABC Verlag.

Müller-Brockmann, Josef. 1971. *A History of Visual Communication.* Niederteufen: Verlag Arthur Niggli AG.

Neumann, Eckhard. 1967. *Functional Graphic Design in the 20's.* New York: Reinhold.

Nijhoff, Peter, and Marinus van Uden. 1991. *De kunst van het verleiden: Geëmailleerde reclame in Nederland.* Zwolle: Waanders Uitgevers.

Nypels, Charles. 1953. *Over Typografie.* Amsterdam: Amsterdamse Grafische School.

Oldewarris, Hans. 1975. Wijdeveld Typografie. Amsterdam: *Forum,* no. 1, vol. XXV.

One Hundred Years on View, 1883–1983. 1983. Amsterdam: Het Stedelijk Museum.

Os, Henk van. 1989. *Job Hansen.* Groningen: Wolters-Noordhoff/ Forsten.

Os, H. W. van. 1978. *Wobbe Alkema en de Groninger Schilderkunst.* Groningen: Wolters–Noordhoff en Bouma's Boekhuis.

Os, drs. H. W. van. 1965. *H. N. Werkman.* Groningen: Uitgeverij J. Niemeijer.

Ostayen, Paul van. 1921. *Bezette Stad.* Antwerpen: Het Sienjaal.

Overy, Paul. 1991. *De Stijl.* London: Thames and Hudson Ltd.

Ovink, G. W. 1965. 100 Years of Book Typography in The Netherlands. In *Book Typography, 1815–1965 in Europe and The United States of America,* Kenneth Day, editor. Chicago: University of Chicago Press.

Pannekoek, G. H. Jr. 1923. De Verluchting van Het Boek in *De Toegepaste Kunsten in Nederland.* Rotterdam: W. L. & J. Brusse's Uitgeversmaatschappij.

Pannekoek, G. H., Jr. 1925. *De Herleving van de Nederlandsche Boekdrukkunst Sedert 1910.* Maastricht: Boosten & Stols.

Paul Schuitema. Ein Pionier der Holländischen Avantgarde. 1967. Zürich: Kunstgewerbemuseum.

Paul Schuitema. November 1928. Reclame. In *International Revue i 10, No. 16, Volume I,* Arthur Müller Lehning, editor. Amsterdam, Van Gennep, 1979.

Petersen, Ad. 1982. *De Ploeg.* 's-Gravenhage: Uitgeverij Bzztôh.

Piet Zwart, Typotekt. Exhibition Catalogue no. 257. Amsterdam: Stedelijk Museum.

Pleij, Herman. 1979. *Het gilde van de Blauwe Schuit.* Amsterdam: Meulenhoff/Landshoff.

Praag, Ph. van. 1983. Sociale symboliek op Nederlandse exlibris. Amsterdam: Wereldbibliotheek.

Program en vrijheid. Dick Elffers en het vormgeving in Nederland Kunstkroniek. 27–29 januari 1990. Amsterdam: Het Financieele Dagblad.

Prokopoff, Stephen S., and Marcel Franciscono. 1987. *The Modern Dutch Poster.* University of Illinois at Urbana-Champaign, Krannert Art Museum. Cambridge, MA: MIT Press.

Raassen-Kruimel, Emkc. 1991. *Nederlandse affiches vóór 1940.* Amsterdam: Stadsuitgeverij.

Radermacher Schorer, M. R. 1951. *Bijdrage tot de Geschiedenis van de Renaissance der Nederlandse Boekdrukkunst.* Utrecht.

Railing, Patricia. 1990. *More About Two Squares.* Forest Row, East Sussex: Artists Bookworks.

Rand, Paul. 1964. Een "type director." Interview in *"Allemaal Flauwekul" en Andere Typografische Notities.* Amsterdam: De Buitenkant, 1989, page 60.

Redeker, Hans. December 20, 1985. *Chassidische Legenden van Hendrik Werkman Herdrukt.* Amsterdam: De Telegraaf.

Reichardt, Jasia. 1964. *Werkman, painter, printer, poet.* London: The Penrose Annual.

Reinders, Pim, Rudy Kousbroek, Jeroen Stumpel, and others. 1987. *Schip en Affiche, Honderd Jaar Rederijreclame in Nederland.* Rotterdam: Uitgeverij Veen en Reflex en Het Maritiem Museum Prins Hendrik.

Roh, Franz, and Jan Tschichold. 1973. *Photo-eye.* Tübingen: Unveränderter nachdruk, Verlag Ernst Wasmuth.

Roodnat, Bas. April 10, 1984. *Willem Sandberg.* Rotterdam: NRC Handelsblad.

Roos, S. H. de. 1955. Interview in *Haarlems Dagblad.*

Roos, S. H. de. 1933. Holland. In *The Dolphin,* I.

Roos, S. H. de. 1933. Holland. In *The Dolphin,* I.

Roos, S. H. de. 1913. *Toelichting tot de Tentoonstelling van Goed en Slecht Drukwerk, Stedelijk Museum.* Vereeniging "Kunst aan het Volk" te Amsterdam.

Rosmalen, Jo van. 1986. Uit een oud Maastrichts Drukkersgeslacht. In *Charles Nypels, Meester Drukker.* Maastricht: Charles Nypels Stichting.

Royen, J. F. van. 1913. De Hollandsche Mediaeval van S. H. de Roos. In *Onze Kunst 12.*

Royen, J. F. van. 1912. De typographie van 's Rijks drukwerk. In *De Witte Mier.*

Rubin, William S. 1968. *Dada, Surrealism, and Their Heritage.* New York: Museum of Modern Art.

Sandberg, Willem. Typografisch Ontwerper. 1981. In *Willem Sandberg, Portret van een Kunstenaar,* Ank Leeuw-Marcar, editor. Amsterdam: Meulenhoff Nederland.

Sandberg, Willem. October 1970. *Hendrik Nicolaas Werkman. 1882–1945.* Harvard Library Bulletin, Vol. XVIII, No. 4.

Sandberg, Willem. *Experimenta Typographica.* Facsimilies.

Sandberg als Ontwerper. 1986. Amsterdam: Stedelijk Museum.

Sandberg 'Désigne' le Stedelijk. 1973. Paris: Musée des Arts Décoratifs.

Sandberg, Willem, and Erika Billeter. 1966. *H. N. Werkman.* Zürich: Kunstgewerbemuseum.

Schama, Simon. 1988. Foreword. In *The Netherlands and Nazi Germany* by Louis de Jong. The Erasmus Lectures. 1988. Cambridge, MA: Harvard University Press.

Schippers, K. 1974. *Holland Dada.* Amsterdam: Em. Querido's Uitgeverij.

Schmalenbach, Werner. 1956. *Hendrik Nicolaas Werkman.* Hanover: Kestner-Gesellschaft.

Schuhmacher, Wilma. 1984. *Catalogue 210: Boutens en Leopold.* Amsterdam: Antiquariaat Schuhmacher.

Schuhmacher, Wilma. 1989. *Catalogue 220: In den Zoeten Inval: Nederlandse Literatuur en Drukkunst, 246 Collector's Items.* Amsterdam: Antiquariaat Schuhmacher.

Schuitema, Paul. 1961. Neue Typografie um 1930. In *Neue Grafik.*

Schuitema, Paul (under the pseudonym S. Palsma). 1933. Foto als wapen in de klassestrijd. In *Links Richten.*

Schuitema, Paul, and Gerard Kiljan. 1933. Foto als beeldende element in de reclame. In *Reclame.*

Schuitema, Paul. 1929. Gisteren en Vandaag. In *Schoonheid en Opvoeding.*

Schuitema, Paul. 1928. Talk for Arti et Industriae.

Schattuck, Roger, 1968. *The Banquet Years.* New York: Vintage Books.

Sierman, Koosje. January 19, 1990. *Vleesch en been, S. H. De Roos: Een Nuchtere Idealist.* Rotterdam: Cultureel Supplement, NRC Handelsblad.

Smid, Gioia, and Carolien van der School. 1989. *Dames in Dada.* Amsterdam: Stichting Amazone.

Spencer, Herbert. 1987. *The Liberated Page.* San Francisco: Bedford Press.

Spencer, Herbert. 1983. *Pioneers of Modern Typography.* Cambridge, MA: The MIT Press.

Stokvis, Willemijn, editor. 1984. *De Doorbraak van de Moderne Kunst in Nederland.* Amsterdam: Meulenhoff/Landshoff.

Stols, A. A. M. 1935. Het schoone boek in *De toegepaste kunsten in Nederland.* Rotterdam: W. L. & J. Brusse's Uitgeversmaatschappij N.V.

Straten, Hans van. 1980. *Hendrik Nicolaas Werkman.* Amsterdam: Meulenhoff.

Straus, Monica. October 1989. Dutch Book Design: The Avant-Garde Tradition. In *Printing Arts in The Netherlands.* Fine Print, Vol. 15, No. 4.

Tracy, Walter. 1986. *Letters of Credit.* Boston: David R. Godine.

Tracy, Walter. 1988. *The typographic scene.* London: Gordon Fraser.

Tummers, Nic. H. M. 1968. *J. L. Mathieu Lauweriks, zijn werk en zijn invloed op architectuur en vormgeving rond 1910: "De Hagener Impuls."* Hilversum: Uitgeverij G. van Saane "Lectura Architectonica."

Unger, Gerard, and Marjan Unger. 1989. *Dutch Landscape with Letters.* Utrecht: Van Boekhoven-Bosch.

Venema, Adriaan. 1980. *Nederlandse Schilders in Parijs 1900–1940.* Baarn: Het Wereldvenster.

Venema, Adriaan. 1978. *De Ploeg, 1918–1930.* Baarn: Het Wereldvenster.

Venema, Adriaan. April 15, 1977. *Vier vergeten kunstenaars.* Rotterdam: NRC Handelsblad.

Vries, Hendrik de, and Dr. A. J. Zuithoff. 1945. *Werkman, Drukker-Schilder.* Amsterdam: Stedelijk Museum.

Warncke, Carsten-Peter. 1990. *De Stijl/1917–1931.* Köln: Bebedikt Taschen Verlag.

Weber, G. 1974. *Vordemberge-Gildewart Remembered.* London: Annely Juda Fine Art.

Wendingen. 1982. Documenti dell'arte olandese de Novecento. Firenze: Palazzo Medici-Ricardi.

Wendingen. 1918–1931. Series 1–12.

Werkman's druksels vol mystiek. October 1, 1977. Amsterdam: De Volkskrant.

Werkman, Fie. 1987. *Herinneringen aan mijn vader Hendrik Nicolaas Werkman.* Groningen: Wolters-Noordhoff/Forsten.

Werkman, H. N., 1882–1945. 1962. Amsterdam: Stedelijk Museum, catalog 292.

Werkman, H. N. September 25, 1942. Letter to Paul Guermonprez.

Werkman, H. N. 1938. *Preludium.* Groningen: H. N. Werkman.

Werkman, H. N. October, 1932. *Proclamatie.* Groningen: H. N. Werkman.

Werkman, H. N. November, 1932. *Proclamatie.* Groningen: H. N. Werkman.

Werkman, H. N. 1923–1926. *The Next Call 1–9. Groningen.*

Werkman, H. N. 1924. Letter to Michel Seuphor.

Werkman, H. N. 1923. Announcement for *The Next Call.*

Werkman, M. H. 1910. *Museum van Plastische Verzen.* Groningen: H. N. Werkman.

Wescher, Herta. Trans. Robert E. Wolf. 1966. *Collage.* New York: Harry N. Abrams.

Wiegers, Jan. ca. 1945. *De Buitenlandse Reis.* Unpublished manuscript.

Wiegers, Jan, editor. 1921–22. Blad voor Kunst. Groningen: H. N. Werkman.

Wissing, Benno. December 8, 1963. *Paul Schuitema.* London: Typographica New Series.

Wright, Edward. 1967. Paul van Ostaijen. In *The Liberated Page,* Herbert Spencer, editor San Francisco: Bedford Press, 1987.

Zwart, Piet. 1939. Timbres au profit des vitraux de Gouda et timbres-poste ordinaires. In *Les timbres-poste des Pays-Bas de 1929 à 1939.* Den Haag.

Zwart, Piet. *Normalieënboekje.* reprint. Drukkerij Rosbeek BV, Nuth.

Zwart, Piet. 1929. In *Het Vaderland.*

Zweden, Johan van. December 1945. *H. N. Werkman, De Groningse Drukker-Schilder.* In *Apollo, I.* Den Haag: Uitgevers.

Index